Adaptability Screening for the Armed Forces

Edited by
Thomas Trent
Janice H. Laurence

Washington, DC

Office of Assistant Secretary of Defense
(Force Management and Personnel)

1993

Contents

Preface

Adaptability screening for the Armed Forces remains a priority for personnel analysts within the Department of Defense (DoD) and the Military Services. Among the driving forces for this attention are the high monetary costs, decrease in readiness, and general turbulence created when many of the forces fail to adapt and are separated from service prior to completing an obligated term of enlistment. New means of controlling personnel attrition have been investigated with the hopes of quelling both adaptability problems and controversy over current adaptability screening practices. The Principal Director for Military Manpower and Personnel Policy, Office of the Assistant Secretary of Defense for Force Management and Personnel requested this monograph. His goal was to determine the applicability of highly promising, yet frequently disparaged, biographical inventories for selecting men and women into the enlisted ranks of the Armed Services. Fulfilling this request required pressing into service the following authors--all of whom have long-standing experience in the development of non-cognitive as well as cognitive instruments for military personnel screening.

Chapter 1 sets the historical context by describing the evolution of education standards for military selection. To this end, Janice Laurence from the Human Resources Research Organization (HumRRO) includes an analysis of the political confluence of the Congress, the Department of Defense, and associations of educators.

Laurence is joined by Brian Waters (HumRRO) in Chapter 2; they review the civilian and military literature that covers applications of biodata for pre-employment screening. In doing so, the authors delineate biodata's strengths and weaknesses and highlight related issues that military manpower managers must consider as they adapt traditional personnel screening to post-Cold War opportunities and constraints.

The first two chapters set the stage for the description of two biodata instruments that comprise the Adaptability Screening Profile (ASP). The ASP reached the penultimate step toward implementation as a DoD enlistment screen. At the 11th hour, however, the Pentagon's Manpower Accession Policy (MAP) Steering Committee suspended further work on the ASP, primarily on the grounds that it was vulnerable to applicant response distortion, military recruiter coaching, and test misnorming.

In Chapter 3, Tom Trent from the Navy Personnel Research and Development Center (NPRDC) discusses the development of and validity evidence for Part 1 of the ASP, which was originally titled the Armed Services Applicant Profile (ASAP). The ASAP represented a consolidation of many years of work on biographical inventories that was pursued separately at the military personnel research laboratories. Ironically, this attempt at fielding a Joint-Service instrument resulted in years of inter-Service bickering that doomed this particular instrument to obsolescence.

Concurrent to the development of the ASAP, the Army composed the Assessment of Background and Life Experiences (ABLE). The ABLE, which constituted Part 2 of the ASP, utilizes a construct-driven approach to measure temperament that provides a counterpoint to the empirically-keyed biodata that comprise the ASAP. The ABLE is described and evaluated in Chapter 4 by Len White, Roy Nord, Fred Mael, and Mark Young from the U.S. Army Research Institute for the Behavioral and Social Sciences.

The MAP Steering Committee's indefinite suspension of the ASP led to the development of the Compensatory Screening Model (CSM) as an alternative approach to augmenting the Services' reliance on the education credential tier system. In Chapter 5, Jim McBride of HumRRO describes and analyzes preliminary efforts to develop an actuarial model of adaptability screening that relies on objective personal background and aptitude items.

The plethora of issues concerning the practicality of incorporating biodata and temperament assessments into Armed Services personnel screening is summarized in Chapter 6 by Jack Edwards (NPRDC), Jim McBride, Brian Waters, and Janice Laurence. In addition to a thorough discussion of technical and logistics issues, this chapter concludes with a description of some of the political considerations that have plagued adaptability screening research in DoD.

Finally, a glossary of technical and bureaucratic idioms is provided to lessen the reader's task.

The contents of the monograph were compiled and reviewed by HumRRO under contract to NPRDC (Contract No: N66001-90-D-9507). The NPRDC contract monitor was Tom Trent and the HumRRO project director was Janice Laurence.

In addition to their fellow authors, the editors had many strong supporters. As the lead Service for Joint-Service adaptability screening research, the Navy, through Captain James C. Kinney, Director, Recruiting and Retention Programs, Division of the Bureau of Naval Personnel (BUPERS-23), offered outstanding leadership and vision for the projects leading to this monograph. As the Head, DoD Coordination Branch of BUPERS-23, Dr. Clessen J. Martin facilitated the production of all phases of this volume.

We appreciate the high-level interest, support, and encouragement provided by Mr. Nicolai Timenes Jr., Principal Director, Military Manpower and Personnel Policy, Office of the Assistant Secretary of Defense for Force Management and Personnel (OASD/FM&P). Dr. W.S. Sellman, Director for Accession Policy within OASD/FM&P, served as a driving force for this monograph. He offered wise counsel, encouraged a variety of technical and creative ideas, and contributed a critical yet fair review. Further, discussions with and materials provided by Dr. Janc Arabian, Assistant Director for Accession Policy (OASD/FM&P), and her predecessor, Dr. Anita Lancaster, now Assistant Director for Programs at the Defense Manpower Data Center (DMDC), proved invaluable.

The editors and authors are indebted to the past and present members of the Manpower Accession Policy Working Group (MAPWG) for their technical and policy input to adaptability screening research over the years. In particular, we thank the Chair of this working group, Dr. Linda Curran (DMDC) and the Chairs of its Technical and Policy Committees, Dr. Bruce Bloxom (DMDC) and Mr. Ron Patsey (HQ Department of the Army), respectively.

Last, but not least, we appreciate the able assistance of our colleagues who helped to ready this document for DoD publication. Marjorie Lee worked magic with the word processor as text and tables were added and modified. Lola Zook edited the first draft of the chapters, Pam Croom designed the cover, Jennifer Naughton compiled the glossary, and she and Sue Cuddy gathered the references for Chapter 2. And of course, there were many, including Jeff Barnes from HumRRO and Jerry Laabs and Drew Sands from NPRDC, who were involved in the adaptability screening research chronicled who graciously provided information, encouragement, and a review of the contents of this document.

Thomas Trent
Janice H. Laurence
January 1993

Chapter 1_____

Education Standards and Military Selection: From the Beginning

Janice H. Laurence[1]

Long ago, in the days of the Colonial Militia, a man took up his own musket, provided his own ammunition, clothing, and food to join his fellow militiamen for a short campaign. Manpower costs were negligible, staying power wasn't a big issue, and quality was measured mostly by youth and vitality (see Matloff, 1973). A lot has changed over the centuries. It's been a long time since the troops brought the arms they bear.

In today's U.S. military, it costs Uncle Sam plenty to recruit, outfit, train, and maintain personnel for the large and sophisticated standing "army." The Armed Services enlist, equip, and educate recruits for full-time duty not just in the modern infantry but in hundreds of diverse, technologically sophisticated military occupations. To adequately defend the nation today takes a lot more than the brawn of a few hundred reluctant soldiers for a few weeks. It takes the brains and motivation of over one and a half million soldiers, sailors, marines, and airmen-- some for a career and each, it is expected, for an initial enlistment term, of, on average, about four years.

---

[1]Human Resources Research Organization, Alexandria, Virginia. The opinions expressed are those of the author, not necessarily those of the Department of Defense or the Military Services.

1

Military selection has become a formidable enterprise, to say the least. Even in the leaner post-Cold War era, hundreds of thousands apply and some 200,000 men and women are chosen each year for the active duty enlisted force. They are evaluated in terms of a host of criteria including citizenship, age, physical fitness, and moral character. In addition, there are two, more salient screens. Cognitive aptitude is assessed via the Armed Services Vocational Aptitude Battery (ASVAB). And finally, the schooling which a prospective recruit has acquired is considered in the enlistment decision--not for the content but for the credential.

Though in the past a draft registrant's or enlistment applicant's level of education was used as a proxy for literacy, it now serves as an indicator of adjustment to life in the military. In the early 1940s, a fourth grade education was taken as evidence that a soldier could read and write well enough to be inducted into the rank and file. Less than a decade later, standardized tests replaced this education hurdle. Education screens were resurrected in the 1960s, not to assess aptitude levels but to predict who was likely to finish an obligated term of service.

Readiness is a must to defend our nation in these fast-paced times, and readiness has its base in selecting, training, and managing manpower. Further, maintaining an end-strength of over a million Service members is an expensive endeavor, thus, the Department of Defense strives to achieve a return on its manpower investments. Considering a recruit's education credential during the selection process contributes to this objective.

Predicting Adjustment to Military Life

Once admitted into the enlisted ranks, recruits are expected to progress through training, to perform their duties competently wherever assigned, and to observe military order and discipline. Unfortunately, not all incoming personnel "shape up" and get through basic and technical training. And even for those who do, not all manage to "keep their noses clean" and avoid disciplinary infractions. Still others may play by the rules but may perform well below par on the job for reasons related not just to inaptitude but to lack of motivation. The consequences for substandard performance include reassignment, various forms of punishment from reprimands to time in the stockade, slow promotion progress and, in many instances, an early exit from service.

First-Term Attrition

The most analyzed indicator of maladjustment to the military is first-term attrition--the failure to complete an initial obligated period of service. Among the reasons for its high visibility are its ease of measurement and, more importantly, its excessive costs. A recent report conservatively estimated the cost of first-term adverse attrition at $200 million per year using a 1989 dollar metric (Klein, Hawes-Dawson, & Martin, 1991). The costs mount up because of lost investments in training, higher recruiting and salary costs, veterans' benefits expenditures, and payment of unemployment compensation to separated Service members. There are also non-pecuniary or indirect costs which include force instability, lowered morale, and lack of readiness. Individuals may also pay a price. Recruits who leave before their contracts have expired may be "marked." Failure in military service may significantly affect their future employment opportunities and earning potential.

The departure rates and specific documented reasons may vary across Services, but the general pattern is the same: Most attrition happens early and for adverse reasons (Laurence, 1984; Klein, et al., 1991). While some are lost because of medical disabilities and other nonpejorative causes, most are dismissed on more grievous grounds including, inaptitude, behavior disorders, alcoholism, motivational problems, acquired civil court convictions, drug use, financial irresponsibility, and other signs of misconduct.

Attrition has grown with the volunteer military, perhaps because of longer active duty enlistment terms and policies that rapidly separate marginal recruits.[2] These days, in light of the volunteer status of the military, a recruit may be discharged simply because he or she has had a change of heart about serving (General Accounting Office, 1980). Today, in fact, almost one-third of an entering cohort leaves service before the end of the contracted enlistment term (Buddin, 1984; Laurence, 1987). Whatever the cause, the consequences of such turnover to the military establishment and, in many cases, to the individuals are serious.

---

[2]The philosophy of attrition can be viewed differently depending upon the volunteer status of the military. When people are being forced to serve under the draft, "easy" separation policies might result in a surge of recalcitrant recruits. Discharge under draft conditions might very well be welcome--a reward rather than a punishment. Volunteers, on the other hand, enter willingly and separation may be viewed as a punishment.

Instituting Education Differentials

A substantial breakthrough in predicting and thus potentially controlling attrition happened in 1959, with the publication of an Air Force Personnel Laboratory technical report entitled *Factors Relating to Discharge for Unsuitability Among 1956 Airman Accessions to the Air Force* (Flyer, 1959). After studying the contribution of a number of variables including general and specific aptitudes and age, level of education stood out as the single best predictor of military adjustment. Thus the author, Eli S. Flyer, concluded that "The most dramatic way to reduce unsuitability discharge would be to require a high-school diploma from all Air Force recruits" (p. 15). The relationship between high school graduation status and first-term attrition was corroborated by the other Services and has stood the test of time.

Enlightened by such findings, the Services soon incorporated this personal characteristic into the screening process. Beginning with the Air Force in 1961 and culminating with the Navy and Marine Corps in 1965, so-called "education differentials" were established. Education criteria were used in conjunction with aptitude test scores to screen individuals for entry into the military. That is, more restrictive selection policies were instituted regarding non-high school graduates.

While it was not prudent, given numerical accession requirements, to heed Flyer's suggestion and to actually ban high school dropouts from enlisting or from being drafted, they were required to score higher than graduates on the aptitude screening test to gain entry. For example, in June of 1962, the Army set the minimum aptitude standard for non-high school graduates at the 31st percentile on the Armed Forces Qualification Test (AFQT).[3] High school graduates, on the other hand, could score 10 percentile points lower and still be considered for enlistment. Graduates scoring between the 21st and 30th percentiles were permitted to compensate for their lower AFQT standings by demonstrating at least average performance in more specific aptitude areas (e.g., electronics, clerical, combat). Such lower scoring high school graduates were required to achieve a standard score of 90 or better (on a scale with a mean of 100 and a standard deviation of 20) in three of nine classification subtest

---

[3]Since 1950 but prior to 1976, the AFQT, a combination of verbal, math and spatial subtests, served as a separate enlistment and induction screening test. Since 1976, the AFQT--minus the spatial component--was incorporated into the ASVAB, which is used for both selection and classification purposes.

composites. Induction standards were lower, but still were more selective among non-graduates (see Eitelberg, Laurence, & Waters, 1984). Similarly, while each of the Services has set unique standards which have been adjusted over the years, since the early to mid-1960s non-graduates have been required to possess "a little extra" to compensate for being higher attrition risks as well as for their proclivity to experience more disciplinary, administrative, and retraining actions (Department of Defense, 1974; General Accounting Office, 1976).

Setting more stringent aptitude standards for those who do not hold a diploma does not solve the adaptability problem or, more specifically, does not put their chances of completing an enlistment term on par with diploma holders. High school graduates have almost an 80 percent chance of completing the first three years of service while the corresponding figure for the more "select" nongraduates is between 50 and 60 percent (Department of Defense, 1981; Laurence, 1987). To put it another way; about 20 to 25 percent of graduates leave service by the end of the first three years and over 40 percent of dropouts drop out or are otherwise dismissed from the military within this timeframe. While aptitude does not compensate for the lack of a diploma, education differentials do result in selecting the "best," or most trainable, among the higher risk and thus less preferred candidates. Yes, they are still doubly likely to leave prematurely but those that are selected are likely to get through training and meet the cognitive requirements of various military jobs while they last.

Simplicity Gone Awry

Flyer's seminal study was only the first in a very long line of research to conclude that high school graduates have lower attrition rates. Despite Service variability in overall attrition rates, similar findings have been echoed in countless reports over the past 30 plus years. Sure, there have been new twists including the discovery of higher attrition for women and younger recruits and differences by race and marital status, but if you've heard it once, you've heard it ten million times: The personal characteristic most related to service completion is the education credential. This consistent relationship has served as the basis for an efficient and effective selection screen. Asking a prospective recruit whether he or she held a high school diploma was elegant in its simplicity. This one-item screen was seemingly reliable, and oh so practical.

Singling Out GED High School Equivalency Credentials

Unfortunately, complicating factors were discovered down the road. Defense learned that a simple diploma dichotomy--between the "have diplomas" and the "have not diplomas"--would not hold. There were other credentials out there that had to be reckoned with. The first wrinkle in the system was provided by the General Educational Development (GED) high school equivalency credential. The GED credential is earned as a result of passing a battery of tests designed to measure achievement in subject areas that make up the basic high school curriculum. This venerable program actually began under the auspices of the United States Armed Forces Institute in 1943 (Means & Laurence, 1984). Today the program is directed by the American Council on Education and it benefits soldiers and civilians alike by conferring diploma equivalency status on persons who have not finished high school but nonetheless demonstrate equivalent academic skills and achievements.

Initially no distinction was made between GED holders and traditional high school diploma graduates in the enlistment process. Such persons were classified as high school graduates (HSGs) and, thus, they were a subset of the preferred group of applicants. No doubt, since academic equivalence to a diploma had been bestowed on those who passed the GED tests, equivalence in the military environment was assumed. However, research began to accumulate, and the findings indicated that GED credential recipients did not remain in service as long as holders of regular high school diplomas. Empirical evidence showing their attrition rates to be very similar to non-graduates flew in the face of earlier reasoning. As a result of that research, the enlistment classification of GED credential holders was changed by the Services in the mid-1970s. In 1975, DoD formally modified the high school graduate definition for enlistment purposes, excluding this equivalency certificate. A new acronym--HSDG (high school diploma graduate)--was coined for applicants with the real McCoy, while equivalency certificates were designated as either GED or HSG (minus the D). Those without a diploma or a GED continued to be labelled as "NHSG" (non-high school graduates).

The Evolution of a Three-Tier System

More important than the specific letters of the alphabet used to label these secondary school credentials was that no longer were GED holders among the most preferred group of applicants, enlisted under the lower aptitude standards

6

reserved for high school graduates. GEDs were to be considered as a separate credential category with aptitude standards for them set above the minimums for bona fide diploma graduates and either the same as or below those for NHSGs. In terms of minimum entry requirements, subsequent to the discovery of their contribution to higher attrition rates, such equivalency holders went from de facto HSGs to de jure GEDs. For example, in March of 1975, the Air Force formally recognized the nonequivalence of "regular" diploma graduates and GED holders and simply switched the AFQT minimum for GED holders from the 21st percentile (the high school diploma graduate standard) to the 65th percentile, which was then in effect for nongraduates. All were still required to meet the same additional subtest composite percentile requirements of a combined score of 170 across the Air Force's Mechanical, Administrative, General, and Electronics measures as well as a separate General composite minimum of 45.

By fiscal year 1981, the Services had overhauled their cognitive ability screens and had pretty much settled how they would deal with GEDs relative to grads and nongrads. While official standards are elsewhere documented (Eitelberg, Laurence, & Waters, 1984), the gist went like this: Army, Navy, and Air Force minimum aptitude requirements for GEDs were less restrictive than for nongraduates but more restrictive than for diploma graduates; Marine Corps enlistment standards for GEDs were identical to those set for nongraduates. In sum, the degree to which GEDs were treated distinctly in terms of standards varied by Service, with the Marine Corps maintaining the least distinction between GEDs and NHSGs (followed closely by the Army) and the Air Force maintaining the largest distinction.

Contending With Even More Credentials

So, about a decade after education differentials were established, a third credential category was added to accommodate the errant GED high school equivalents. Unfortunately there were further and further complications to this seemingly simple system used to curb attrition.

The GED wasn't the only "unusual" secondary school level credential out there. There were far more aberrant diplomas, certificates, credentials, and other "school" or at least program vouchers. In the past few decades, this country has witnessed an explosion of secondary school experiences and credentials. There are many alternative paths to the traditional diploma as well as variations in the types of sheepskins issued. Youth can earn different forms of the high school diploma, a variety of "substitute" credentials in lieu of a diploma, and high school equivalency certificates following a premature departure from high school.

If a person doesn't have a traditional diploma as a result of graduating from a 12-year accredited group day school program, he or she is not necessarily sans a piece of paper attesting to some secondary school level experience. Rather than being credentialless nongraduates, military applicants may have other alternative experiences and/or credentials (see Laurence, 1983).

For persons who sit through 12 years of public school but fail to achieve a passing score on a minimum competency requirement, certificates of attendance or completion can serve as the consolation prize. On the other hand, for students who pass the competency test but fail to fulfill all attendance or course requirements, certificates of competency may be granted.

Other certificates of completion or attendance, earned as a result of a short-term vocational school program, add to the confusing array of papers with fancy seals, loops, and curls. Some get a diploma by mail from correspondence schools which boast of giving credit for past experience, a fast pace, and accreditation by the National Home Study Council. Another variant of home study is referred to as home schooling or tutoring wherein parents teach their children at home, with a growing number of states recognizing the legitimacy of this pedagogical practice. Various non-public schools which do not carry and may not even seek state endorsement (e.g., fundamentalist Christian Academies) issue non-state-accredited diplomas for the successful completion of an in-school day program of either self-paced or group instruction. Still others may attend expedited night school classes, take correspondence courses, or cash in credit for life experiences in exchange for adult high school, or so-called "external" diplomas. There are also test-based equivalency credentials including, but not limited to, the familiar GED. College transcripts are not out of the question for those without a traditional diploma. And the list goes on.

This plethora of credentials was forced into just three broad categories for enlistment purposes, with the familiar labels inappropriate if not misleading misnomers for many of the constituent certificates. Although there were empirical data on traditional diploma graduates, GED holders, and non-high school graduates, attrition statistics had never been computed for persons with alternative school experiences and credentials. Further, there wasn't even a comprehensive theory to go on. The Services based their categorization of the myriad of secondary school testimonials on not much more than hunches. As a result, a lot of square pegs were fit into a few round holes.

The Diploma Works, But Why?

The Services knew that the high school diploma was a good predictor of adaptation to the military but they did not know why. What is it about high school graduates that makes them persevere in the military? Deductive reasoning suggests that general cognitive factors may not be a powerful contributor to the better staying power of traditional diploma holders over others. This is surmised from the fact that aptitude has shown only a weak relationship with overall attrition. In fact, graduates scoring in the lowest acceptable AFQT range (10th through 30th percentiles) have lower attrition rates than nongraduates scoring toward the top of the distribution. Further, though there are plans in the offing to crystallize the meaning of high school graduation in this country, at this writing holding a diploma does not signify the attainment of any particular academic standard of achievement. The quality of education--not to mention the requirements for graduation--varies widely from school to school. The final blow to the cognitive factor is that the attrition gap persists in the face of minimum aptitude standards for enlistment in general and even higher minimums set for non-diploma holders.

If it's not academic ability that separates the credential holders, what are the attributes that account for whether a recruit is likely to be a stayer or a leaver? No one knows for sure, but there are several non-cognitive accompaniments to the traditional high school experience that might be proffered as explanatory mechanisms. Receipt of a traditional diploma could signify perseverance, maturity, participation in and accommodation to group learning situations, team spirit, conformity, tolerance of and adaptability to rules and regulations, determination, self-control, and other similar attributes. Finishing high school may socialize one appropriately for aspects of the military environment. After all, sitting in a classroom is part of the training process and rules and regulations are a fact of service life from the "get go." Teamwork is of the essence in the military, and conformity and self-control are drilled. Whether and which of these qualities are involved in the diploma's predictiveness is but speculation. Such characteristics are difficult to measure, let alone affirm their relationship to attrition. And so, the credential category surrogate has remained despite its overly broad and ill-defined nature.

Sorting the Certificates: The Criteria

Because the Services were short on theory, there was "more rhyme than reason" in sorting out newfangled credentials. One criterion for categorization involved accreditation status. Generally, diplomas that were accredited by the state or other accrediting agency were accepted as HSDGs. The rationale offered by Defense for this practice was that the Services were not in the business of judging the merits of educational programs, this being the purview of state departments of education. If the state blessed the secondary school experience as worthy of an endorsed diploma, then DoD called the holder of this piece of paper a high school diploma graduate. For military enlistment purposes, a diploma by any other name was not as sweet.

There were other creative hypotheses that guided the categorization of alternative credentials. The Marine Corps, for example, decided that "seat time" was the key. They were looking for credentials that represented a person's "stick-to-it-ive-ness." Under this logic, certificates of attendance were among the preferred credentials. After all, though the recipient of this badge did not officially graduate, he or she did not opt to leave but instead sat through school to the bitter end.

DoD formally agreed with the Marines on how to categorize certificates of attendance and completion. In a 1978 memorandum to the Service Assistant Secretaries (for Manpower), the Deputy Assistant Secretary of Defense (Military Personnel Policy) noted the increasing tendency for schools to issue attendance and completion credentials in lieu of a diploma (Umstead, 1978). The somewhat convoluted argument for a "graduate" classification was essentially that such persons would have been awarded regular diplomas in the past so why not still count them as such? After all, changing the name of the credential could not be expected to alter their attrition rates. This rationale lacks a solid underpinning because attrition was not tracked separately for subsets of the HSDG category. Higher attrition rates for attendance and completion certificate holders (who were formerly diploma recipients) could easily be masked by lower attrition rates of the more populous "real" graduates.

That same 1978 memo reaffirmed DoD's position vis-a-vis GEDs. This is noteworthy, given the above explanation for the preferred treatment of attendance and completion credentials. Perhaps the GEDs lost out simply because they were tracked in service. Had a rise in GEDs come to DoD's attention without attrition data, policymakers might have reasoned along the same lines as they did for the "sit throughs" and kept only two categories (HSG and NHSG).

Still other criteria were more elusive and capricious. Without empirical data, the Services made up rules as they went along. Consistency within, let alone between, Services regarding the treatment of secondary level credentials was notably absent. Take a look at Table 1.1, for example. In fiscal year 1983, both the Army and the Navy considered applicants with high school equivalencies earned by passing the GED tests somewhere between grads and nongrads. Inexplicably, persons with equivalencies earned on the basis of a California testing program (the California High School Proficiency Exam or CHSPE) were deemed nongrads by these same Services. The Air Force's twist was to consider CHSPE applicants as grads but not extend the same enlistment rule to GEDs. Further, although the Army did not consider a high school's accreditation status in the enlistment decision, it did require "proper" endorsement of correspondence and adult high schools. The Marine Corps, which did not recognize GEDs, threw in a puzzler by counting correspondence school certificate holders as grads; with seat time as the guiding principle, a case can be made for attendance and completion certificates but the logic of then counting correspondence credentials as preferred is not easy to follow. On the other hand, equally puzzling was the Air Force's preferred treatment of correspondence diplomas but no similar preference for attendance certificates.

The footnotes to Table 1.1 reveal even more nuances. Adding to the cross-hatching of Service enlistment philosophies is the knowledge that these policies were not exactly static. For example, just a year earlier the Air Force considered high school attendance and completion certificates on a par with state-accredited high school diplomas (see Laurence, 1983). And it was just a few years earlier (between 1979 and 1981) that the Army, Navy, and Marine Corps abandoned their state accreditation criterion for considering a diploma as a diploma (Lancaster, 1988).

Another entry in Table 1.1 that has an intriguing history is "High School Diploma Based on GED." Some states issued a high school diploma on the basis of passing the GED tests. Though the diploma did not come from a local school, it was endorsed by the state and thus was genuine. Until Service recruiting headquarters got wise, such diplomas often passed as HSDGs. Some local recruiters even encouraged enlistment prospects to take the GED tests in states granting such diplomas.   By doing so, the candidate was more likely to qualify and the recruiter had one less quality person to "sell."

Table 1.1 Service Treatment of Secondary School Education Credentials for Enlistment Purposes During FY 1983				
Secondary School Credential	Treatment for Enlistment Purposes[*]			
	Army	Navy	Marine Corps	Air Force
High School Diploma (State Accredited)	Grad	Grad	Grad	Grad
High School Diploma (Non-State Accredited)	Grad	Grad[1]	Grad	Non
High School Attendance Certificate	Grad	Grad	Grad	Non
High School Completion Certificate	Grad	Grad	Grad	Non
GED Certificate	GED[2]	GED[2]	Non	GED[2]
High School Diploma Based on GED	GED[2]	GED[2]	Non	GED[2]
Adult High School Diploma	Grad[3]	Grad[4]	Grad[5]	Grad[6]
California High School Proficiency Examination (CHSPE) Certificate	Non	Non	Non	Grad
Correspondence School	Grad[7]	GED	Grad[7]	Grad[8]

This information was compiled from official memoranda as described in Laurence, J.H. (1984, February). *Education standards for military enlistment and the search for successful recruits* (FR-PRD-84-4). Alexandria, VA: Human Resources Research Organization.

[*]Grad is high school diploma graduate. GED is high school equivalency. Non is non high school graduate.
[1]Enlisted as high school diploma graduates on a case-by-case waiver basis.
[2]Enlisted under standards separate from both high school diploma graduates and nongraduates but reported as non-high school graduates.
[3]Enlisted as high school graduates provided that the diploma was awarded or authorized by the state.
[4]Enlisted as high school diploma graduates provided that the program is recognized by the state.
[5]Only individuals accessed as part of test programs (to determine success rates of adult high school programs) are enlisted as high school diploma graduates; all others are enlisted as non-high school graduates.
[6]Enlisted as high school graduates provided that the diploma was not issued as a result of the GED test only.
[7]Enlisted as high school diploma graduates provided that the course/program is accredited by the National Home Study Council.
[8]Enlisted as high school diploma graduates provided that the school is accredited by the state or jurisdiction.

The Politics of Categorizing Education Credentials

Fitting in new credentials became more than a minor irritant for the Services as they soon learned that "misclassification" could cost them more than a slight increase in attrition. Mounting public criticism of education enlistment policies became a major problem. Word that applicants from nontraditional schools or those holding diploma alternatives were welcome by some Services but not others spread to concerned parents, educational institutions issuing the credentials in question, and ultimately to Congress' ears (Sellman, 1988).

Imagine the following scenario. A graduate from a non-accredited fundamentalist Christian Academy was welcomed by the Army but more or less shunned by the Air Force. Why? Apparently the applicant was suspect not because of religious affiliation but because he held a diploma from a school that generally did not seek state recognition and thus was not accredited by the state. But why did the Air Force care and not the Army? Good question! Though attrition was the rationale for setting education enlistment policies, first-term survivability data were lacking for this and other non-traditional credentials.

Interested parties wanted to know why it was harder for holders of certain credentials to enlist in their Service of choice. It was relatively easy to account for the differences in aptitude standards across Services. Given the unique missions of the Army, Navy, Marine Corps, and Air Force and the concomitant variance in job types, divergent minimum requirements and aptitude mixes across Services appear tenable (Waters, Laurence, & Camara, 1987).[4] What was perplexing was that different Services preferred different credentials.

The Effects of Quality Goals

There was more at stake for nonpreferred groups than having to score higher than bona fide high school graduates on the enlistment screening test. The Military Services go after quality recruits--those who score in the upper half of the AFQT distribution *and* are high school graduates. Recruiters are goaled (and rewarded) accordingly. Congress itself monitors the quality of incoming personnel and in FY 1982 enacted limits on the proportion of lower aptitude recruits who could be brought into the military each year via 10 United States

---

[4]It is relevant to point out, of course, that there are jobs that are common across Services. Differences in minimum requirements may then be justified on the basis of relative recruiting ease.

Code, Section 520(a). This same statute rules that nongraduates may not be accepted for enlistment with AFQT scores below the 31st percentile. Furthermore, in response to previous quality problems, the mandate stipulates that at least 65 percent of Army non-prior service male accessions must be high school diploma graduates.

Service members who pull recruiting duty are, for the most part, very pressured people. Not only must they sign up a certain number of recruits but they must find enough recruits with the right characteristics. And, as luck would have it, higher quality youth tend to be less inclined to enlist (Nieva, Wilson, Kolmstetter, Madigan, & Greenlees, 1991). The recruiting market is continually assessed by headquarters and enlistment prerequisites are modified. As a result, depending upon applicant supply and demand, at times the Services turn away alternative credential holders regardless of their AFQT scores.

This entry denial did not sit well with the affected groups. What's more, certain credentials and educational programs were being denigrated inadvertently in the application process. The coupling of aptitude requirements with education credentials has been confusing from the start. As alluded to earlier in this chapter, in the military of the early to mid-1900s, educational *attainment* was used as a cognitive aptitude screen. In the early to mid-1960s education *credentials* were introduced as a selection criterion. Credentials were then, and continue to be, used to predict attrition. Again, the setting of higher aptitude minimums for nongraduates is meant to limit those without a "real" diploma, if and when they are enlisted, to individuals who can be expected to perform relatively well in training and on the job. That is, those alternative credential holders and nongraduates actually enlisted should be less likely to be booted out for inaptitude alone; their poorer adjustment to military life should not be attributed to greater cognitive deficiencies than high school diploma graduates. Despite this explanation of Service education policies, it is difficult for most people to disassociate the meaning of education credentials from cognitive ability or achievement level.

The military now uses the ASVAB to gauge ability to absorb training quickly and perform adequately on the job. The education credential is used to easily screen out many who are not likely to adjust to military life and complete an enlistment term. Nevertheless, the military's selection policies regarding education are often misinterpreted as meaning that regular diploma holders are preferred because they are more skilled and able or just plain smarter. In other words, it is difficult to disentangle the credential's schooling signal from its perseverance predictiveness. Even recruiters have contributed to the confusion because they haven't been able to explain, appropriately, the reasons for turning away those not considered diploma graduates.

Reactions: Some Specifics

Clearly agencies that issue alternative credentials were upset that the reputations of their programs were suffering as a result of the Services' actions. Regardless of the military's intent, enlistment policies acted to denigrate the "excluded" credentials and hurt those holding them. Further, it was feared the viability of certain programs would be negatively affected if word got out that *even* the military wouldn't accept their credentials.

Initially, alternative credentialing program executives lobbied the Services directly. They wrote to military officials attesting to the academic rigor of their curricula and extolling the virtues of their graduates. For example, correspondence schools accredited by the National Home Study Council were successful early on in getting most of the Services to accept their graduates. The final hold-out was the Marine Corps and even the Corps came around after the American School gave its pitch in 1978. One consultant for the California Department of Education wrote to the Chairman of the Joint Chiefs of Staff, General David C. Jones, (with a "cc" to Secretary of Defense Weinberger) in April 1982 on behalf of California's adult education graduates. The salutation to this letter read "Dear Dave" with the penman capitalizing on his past Air Force acquaintance with the Chairman, to make heard his complaint that the Navy and Marine Corps had downgraded such graduates when making assignments. A spokesman for California adult education wrote to the Marine Corps, also in April of 1982, to raise a fuss about adult diplomas not being recognized. In closing, the messenger indicated that if "appropriate" action was not taken soon, Congress would be apprised of the situation.

Spokespersons for alternative education credentials did not remain limited to program Pooh Bahs but increasingly included members of Congress. One of the first to write DoD was the Honorable Bill Nichols (D-AL). In a letter dated October 26, 1981 to Lawrence J. Korb, Assistant Secretary of Defense (ASD) for Manpower, Reserve Affairs, and Logistics (MRA&L), Congressman Nichols asserted that he voiced the concerns of "several members of Congress" (Nichols, 1981) as he pushed for HSDG status for graduates of nonaccredited schools. Six months later, this same House member went up the chain of command and sent a dispatch to then Secretary of Defense Caspar W. Weinberger (Nichols, 1982). Only this time, Nichols, the Chairman of the Military Personnel and Compensation Subcommittee of the House Committee on Armed Services, championed the GED cause. He recognized that attrition rates were higher for GED equivalency holders but his bone of contention was that the Services' overly broad education policies disqualified many would-be-successful recruits. He encouraged DoD to adopt new screening criteria based on individual attributes as a replacement for the three broad credential categories. Weinberger's reply attested to the validity of the enlistment policies but acknowledged that there was room for improvement (Weinberger, 1982).

The Congressman continued his correspondence with the Secretary of Defense. His next letter, in December of 1982, addressed the plight of the unaccredited Christian schools, and the individuals who were being adversely affected, a second time. He related the story of a young man from New Mexico who was denied enlistment into the Air Force and asked why the accreditation issue had not yet been resolved. Though the Secretary was inclined to revise enlistment policy right then and there, his advisors and their staffers urged him not to direct such a change at that time. Their arguments did in fact dissuade Mr. Weinberger from making a precipitous policy shift. Instead Chairman Nichols was informed that DoD would base its decision on the results of newly initiated research which promised to shed light on the ever-growing credential controversy.

Toward a Unified Solution

DoD was indeed planning to answer the mail. Rather than just continuing to explain to Congress and concerned groups the rationale for education policies, including Service inconsistencies, a unified empirical answer was in the offing. The Office of the Assistant Secretary of Defense for Manpower, Installations and Logistics convened a Joint-Service Education Credentials Working Group and sponsored pertinent research.

The Educational and Biographical Information Survey (EBIS)

In March of 1982, DoD contracted with the Human Resources Research Organization (HumRRO) to evaluate existing education enlistment policies as well as to collect further data on such things as secondary school credentials and experiences. To help inform accession policy, HumRRO developed, administered, and analyzed data from the Educational and Biographical Information Survey (EBIS). EBIS items covered not just type of education credential and type of school but additional biographical items that had proven predictive in earlier research (Means & Perelman, 1984). More specifically, the EBIS items pertain to educational achievement, school behavior and attitudes, family relations, work history, status variables, arrest record, and alcohol/drug use.[5]

The EBIS was administered to more than 34,000 applicants for enlistment and 40,000 new recruits between February and June of 1983. A great deal of biographical data were available through the EBIS, but most pertinent to solving the credential conundrum were items that elicited information regarding respondents' education credentials and types of schools attended. Such items were used to categorize EBIS sample members into the following credential groups and subgroups:

Education Credential

- Public High School Graduates
- Private High School Graduates
  -- Catholic
  -- Other Church-Related
  -- Non-Church-Related
- High School Graduates, High School Type Unknown
- Some College, No Regular Diploma
  -- Having Alternative Credential(s)
  -- Having No Alternative Credential
- GED Credential
- Other Equivalence Certificate
- Adult Education Diploma
- Correspondence School Diploma
- No Credential

---

[5] These latter two types of items were included primarily to evaluate the Services' moral character standards for military entry. For more details on the development of the EBIS, see Means & Perelman (1984). In addition, there are numerous reports on the results of the EBIS and related research bearing on education enlistment policies, moral character standards, and biographical inventories. For further information, those interested should contact the author at the Human Resources Research Organization.

Linking EBIS data with Defense's automated personnel files made it possible to track attrition status for these specific credential types. The adaptability of recruits with non-regular diplomas could be ascertained from actual data. Furthermore, EBIS data merged with Service loss records could supply an up-to-date assessment of the contribution of credential category relative to other recruit background characteristics such as work history. The only hitch was that the data had to be prepared for analyses and the EBIS analyses, in turn, required a longitudinal look. It would take a few years for the data to mature and yield stable estimates of attrition. EBIS applicants had to be given time to enter service and, along with the recruit sample, needed time to demonstrate adaptability or the lack thereof. Remember, the traditional criterion measure was 36-month attrition. Yes, it was going to take time to answer the mail.

Meanwhile, Back on the Hill

As DoD and the Services awaited an empirical basis for categorizing alternative credentials into enlistment priority groups, loyalists kept those cards and letters coming. Oregon Senator Bob Packwood took up where Congressman Nichols left off. In May of 1982, Packwood wrote to DoD Legislative Affairs about a letter he received from the principal of Faith Bible Christian School. He was deeply concerned that a diploma from such a non-accredited school proved to be an obstacle to enlistment. He moved on to the preservation of individual freedoms and the guarantees of the First Amendment.

One key aspect of the dialogue between Congress and Defense is the difference in perspectives. Congressional arguments were, to a great extent, on behalf of the individual while DoD's logic was tied to group statistics. Another way of viewing this difference of opinion is that the contrast was between the individual (Congress' view) and the institutional perspective (DoD's view). Congress was voicing concern that individuals who wanted to serve in the military and who might be successful were denied entry because they were part of a "group." DoD was trying to accept quality recruits and in so doing reduce attrition and its associated costs, efficiently. Both stands are valid but often they are not completely reconcilable.

The most persistent battle over the status of the Christian Schools was waged by Congressman Thomas Kindness (R-Ohio). The Congressman began with a missive to Secretary of the Air Force, Verne Orr, on February 17, 1983. He urged the Air Force to resolve the matter as had the Army and Navy by allowing graduates of schools such as the Heritage Christian School in Cleveland to be enlisted as diploma graduates regardless of accreditation status. The Air Force's response was that the jury was still out; there were as yet no data on which to base a decision.

Kindness was not discouraged. He wrote back to Orr on March 25, 1983, somewhat piqued that the Air Force had not promptly acceded. If the Air Force wasn't going to be "practical and sensible," then he threatened to go directly to the Secretary of Defense and the White House!

The correspondence continued and escalated. The Air Force position was "not now, no way." As promised, Representative Kindness sent a letter directly to Weinberger on April 25, 1983 wherein he accused the Air Force of "footdragging" on the issue of non-certified religious high school graduates. The Air Force would rather have fallen on its sword than make a premature policy turnaround. After a series of internal Defense coordination memoranda, the Honorable Caspar Weinberger sent a reply to the Honorable Thomas Kindness on May 16, 1983. Over Weinberger's signature, Defense explained education enlistment policies yet again. Kindness was told that the Air Force chose to be more cautious than its fellow Services in amending its position on the accreditation issue while awaiting the EBIS results. The Secretary stated that he would not direct the Air Force to alter its enlistment policies at that time. The Air Force had won the battle, but the war went on.

Preliminary EBIS Results

Despite the promise of upcoming empirical data, letters continued to be posted regarding the plight of Christian Academy graduates. What finally stopped the mail from this constituency was favorable preliminary EBIS results.

The original study plan was to wait until the sample members could be judged on the basis of attrition status after 36 months in service before recommending any policy action. However, respondents were tracked periodically as they moved through their first terms. Early snapshots (e.g., after 3 months in service) indicated that private school graduates were doing as well as public school graduates; graduates from non-accredited schools were roughly on par with those from accredited schools; and graduates of church-related schools had rates similar to non-church school graduates. These early data coupled with the barrage of "congressionals" led to an ahead-of-schedule policy change. By FY 1985, the

Joint-Service Group members (including the Air Force spokesperson) agreed to formally drop the accreditation requirement.

The GED lobbyists also kept the heat on during the course of the EBIS study but the initial results were not so promising in their case. Nonetheless, the American Council on Education's GED Testing Service and DoD had a running dialogue going. By September of 1983, the GED Testing Service had compiled a package pertinent to the GED/military recruiting problem. Among the contents were 15 issues raised in opposition to then-existing policies. For example, GED Testing Service representatives charged that DoD was misusing the GED test since it was not designed for the purpose of predicting attrition. They claimed that recipients of their credential had education skills equivalent to high school graduates. They argued that recruiters had found loopholes that enabled some GEDs to be counted as HSDGs--so why not just stop discriminating against the rest of GED holders? They pushed for DoD to measure the individual attributes associated with attrition directly rather than using group data. And they expressed outrage that recruiters were discrediting the credential and in many cases not allowing those with a GED to try to qualify for service entry.

DoD formally addressed these and other concerns with what was fast becoming a standard response set. The Services were alerted to the above-mentioned recruiting injustices by the Deputy Assistant Secretary of Defense for Military Personnel and Force Management through a memo to the Service Assistant Secretaries for Manpower. Recruiters were told to allow a GED holder to take the ASVAB and were instructed how to explain the reason for rejecting such an applicant without denigrating the credential. But in the interim, as well as in the end, there was no triumph for the GED cause.

Establishing Common Credential Definitions

The Working Group members weren't just sitting back reading the mail while the data matured. Aside from convening for the Christian school brouhaha, they met periodically to establish precise, Service-common definitions of education credentials. DoD and the Services were no longer amateurs in the matter of secondary school credentials. The new definitions were far less ambiguous and reflected the proliferation of alternative certificates. For example, the definition of a high school diploma graduate included that the applicant had attended and completed a 12-year/day program of classroom instruction and possessed a locally issued diploma. A diploma issued as a result of GED testing would no longer fly.

A new coding system was devised to account for the numerous credentials and allow future tracking of the attrition rates of their holders. Today, the following codes are in place:

1	Less than High School Diploma
7	Correspondence School Diploma
8	Completed One Semester of College
9	Currently in High School
B	Adult Education Diploma
C	Occupational Program Certificate
D	Associate Degree
E	Test-Based Equivalency Diploma
G	Professional Nursing Diploma
H	Home Study Diploma
J	High School Certificate of Attendance
K	Baccalaureate Degree
L	High School Diploma
M	Credential Near Completion
N	Master's Degree
R	Post Master's Degree
S	High School Senior
U	Doctorate Degree
W	First Professional Degree

This rather strange, non-continuous alphanumeric system came about to avoid confusion with old codes and their corresponding less precise definitions. That is, under the old system, the nebulously defined high school diploma held a code of 2 and a high school equivalency certificate held a code of 3.

The Joint-Service Education Credentials Working Group was also busy analyzing preliminary EBIS data to appropriately categorize the codes and determine the impact of proposed credential reclassification on the Services. Given that early results suggested that alternative credentials should not be placed in a category with regular diploma graduates, the Services were anxious to determine how this would affect the proportions of high school diploma graduates reported to Congress. Would the policy changes stemming from the results of EBIS make it appear as if recruit quality had gone down? The answer to this was, "Not much." Simulations on the FY 1983, 1984, and 1985 cohorts showed the Army to be most affected by removing certificates of completion and attendance, adult high school diplomas, and correspondence school diplomas from the high school diploma graduate category. Around 5 percent fewer appeared as HSDGs. The Navy was affected by less than half a percent and no effect was shown for the Air Force. The Army swallowed hard but reasoned that some real live recruiting could compensate for the simulated reduction in HSDGs as a result of credential reclassification; recruiters would simply focus their efforts on signing up "true" graduates. Ultimately the attitude within all the Services was "bring on the EBIS data."

The Unified Solution

Final EBIS Tabulations

Because of the relentless politicking over the fate of many of the alternative credentials, DoD was pressured to release the EBIS data. As a result, Defense settled on a 30-month attrition criterion rather than the customary 36 months. Table 1.2 shows the long-awaited results.

EBIS analyses indicated that alternative credential holders and those with no credential did not, on average, adapt to military life as well as those with regular or traditional diplomas. That is, their attrition rates were shown to be higher--in most cases more than 50 percent higher--than those found for traditional diploma graduates.

Attrition rates for the alternative credential groups were over 10 percentage points higher than for regular diploma holders. Across DoD, the attrition rate for high school graduates was about 23 percent. For GED certificate holders, the rate was around 39 percent. The rates for the other alternative credential groups were close behind (with 36 percent, 37 percent, and 30 percent for other equivalency holders, adult education diploma holders, and correspondence school diploma holders, respectively).

With the exception of the category, "Some College, No Regular Diploma," the attrition rates for all high school graduate subgroups were lower than each of the alternative credential subcategories. These data lent credence to the earlier decision regarding non-accredited Christian schools.

22

Table 1.2

Thirty-Month Attrition Rates for EBIS Respondents By Service and Education Credential

Education Credential	Service				
	Army	Navy	Marine Corps	Air Force	Total DoD
High School Graduate	26.9	20.7	27.4	16.4	22.9
Public High School	26.3	20.8	27.8	16.2	22.6
Private High School	29.6	18.2	23.3	17.1	22.8
Catholic	28.8	19.3	23.8	14.4	21.7
Other Church-Related	25.0	15.9	19.4*	13.4	19.3
Non-Church-Related	32.8	15.7	26.9*	29.0	27.3
High School Type Unknown	27.8	21.3	22.1	18.0	23.6
Some College, No Regular Diploma	41.2	22.2	47.1*	25.3	34.9
Alternative Credential(s)	46.0	26.0	57.1*	27.0	38.8
No Alternative Credential	30.2	10.0*	30.8*	20.8*	25.2
Alternative Credential^a	39.6	33.2	43.0	33.3	37.4
GED Credential	42.9	35.2	40.9	33.5	39.3
Other Equivalency Certificate	33.8	31.7	55.0*	34.3	35.6
Adult Education Diploma	36.3	33.7	48.7	33.3	36.6
Correspondence School Diploma	29.7	20.0*	54.6*	33.3*	29.9
No Credential^b	46.9	38.1	43.6	28.3	44.5

Source: Self-report education credential data are taken from the Educational and Biographical Information Survey (EBIS). The Defense Manpower Data Center is the source of Service and attrition data.

Note: Small sample size may be associated with unstable results. Therefore, caution should be used when interpreting data in cells having fewer than 50 observations. These cells are indicated by an asterisk.

[a] Of these respondents, 197 reported holding two or more alternative credentials. These respondents were counted in each category of alternative education that applied; therefore, the sum of these categories will not equal the number of alternative credential holders.

[b] These individuals indicated that they held neither a high school diploma nor an alternative credential.

23

The "college" findings were at odds with historical data (cf. Eitelberg, 1983) showing this group to be relatively good risks, with attrition rates lower than those with a regular diploma. The discrepancy was attributed, at the time, to the ambiguity in the EBIS item. That is, individuals who completed their equivalency or adult diploma requirements at a college were assumed to be the culprits. This hypothesis was supported when the "Some College" category was divided into those with and without alternative credentials and the latter subgroup's attrition rate was in line with the overall high school graduate category.

Not only were the attrition rates for equivalency credential holders and adult education diploma holders much higher than for regular diploma graduates, but their rates were closer to the no credential group than to the high school graduate group. And, although there were Service differences in overall attrition rates, the relationships among the credential groups held across Services.

Other EBIS items were used to try to shed more light on the standings of the education credential groups. Neither aptitude scores, nor occupational assignment, nor pre-service employment, nor pre-service arrest record appreciably diminished the differences in attrition among education credential holders. Furthermore, regardless of gender, race, age, geographic region, and socioeconomic status, each subcategory of alternative credential holders, as well as the "No Credential" group, showed higher attrition rates than their graduate counterparts, and higher rates than the high school graduate groups with different demographic characteristics. DoD had done its homework. An examination of behavioral and demographic variables was shown not to mitigate the attrition differences. Attrition was not simply spuriously related to credential.

A New Three-Tier System is Born

Armed with actual data on the adaptability of recruits with non-regular diplomas, the Services now had an empirical basis for categorizing the myriad of credentials into enlistment priority groups. A March 24, 1987 memorandum from Chapman B. Cox, Assistant Secretary of Defense (Force Management and Personnel), to the Service Manpower Assistant Secretaries established "new policy for determining the educational enlistment status of individuals applying for military enlistment" (Cox, 1987, p.1).

Based on the EBIS study, the Services sorted the carefully defined education credentials into three tiers as follows:

Tier 1: High School Graduate

High School Diploma
Completed One Semester of College

Tier 2: Alternative Credential Holder

Test-Based Equivalency Diploma
High School Certificate of Attendance
Adult Education Diploma
Correspondence School Diploma
Occupational Program Certificate
Home Study Diploma

Tier 3: Non-High School Graduate

There remained three tiers but the composition had changed. Furthermore, for the first time, all Services were categorizing credentials in the same way. They were still free to determine their own enlistment standards and enlistment priority for each tier but a correspondence school diploma was committed to Tier 2 regardless of Service. And, a new acronym was coined--ACH (for alternative credential holder)--to replace HSG.

While DoD had hoped to enact the policy on April 1, 1987, the Services' recommendation of delaying full implementation until the beginning of the next fiscal year (October 1, 1987) prevailed. A mid-year policy change would have been an administrative nightmare for the Services, given that some recruits had signed a contract to enter service sometime within the next year through the Delayed Entry Program (DEP).[6] The rub was that when they swore in they had done so under the old system, and the Services did not want to renege on the enlistment priority status that had been given to some alternative credential

_____

[6]The DEP is a common enlistment management tool. Recruits enter the DEP for up to one year but with a predetermined entry date generally according to when a training seat is available. In addition, in some cases high school seniors contract to enter service subsequent to graduation with the DEP acting as a holding tank of sorts.

holders. At the same time they wished to avoid the confusion that would stem from co-mingling old and new codes within a given cohort. Thus, the resolution was to put the new system into effect on April 1, 1987 for those entering the DEP and planning to "ship" in FY 1988. On October 1, 1987, the new policy would be binding for all.

Though the Services now had an empirical leg to stand on, they planned to monitor the attrition rates of the various education groups and further evaluate their placement within tiers. This precaution was taken to bolster the self-report EBIS results with verified credential status obtained from enlistment records. But again, as with the EBIS data, results would take time. Enough people holding each credential had to be enlisted under the new and improved coding system and then their perseverance had to be evaluated as they progressed through a term of service. The Services were also researching other means to lessen attrition--namely, biographical inventories. The hope was that questionnaires pertaining to prospective recruits' background characteristics and experiences might add to the prediction of satisfactory adjustment, at least within credential groups. But, there was no need to be frantic; after all, the new policy was backed by solid evidence making it beyond reproach. Or so they thought.

The Problem With the Solution

It would be an understatement to say that the transition to the new education enlistment policies did not proceed smoothly. This time, the war was declared by the Adult Education constituency, with Ohio and California on the front lines. Adult education graduates had enjoyed top "high school diploma graduate" status by the Army and Navy--the largest Services--until the credential categories were revised.

Actually, this battle began even before the new attrition screening system was implemented. In January of 1987, the Office of Vocational and Adult Education of the U.S. Department of Education warned state directors of adult education of the impending policies. Shortly thereafter, letters were directed to the Secretary of Defense and his assistants. In one two-page letter from the Principal of Akron Evening High School, addressed to the Principal Director of Military Manpower and Personnel Policy within the Office of the Assistant Secretary of Defense for Force Management and Personnel, the policy decision was described as unfounded, appalling, based on flawed expertise, whimsical assumptions and questionable data, blatantly skewed, a perilously prejudicial position which was nearly clandestinely disseminated, and had not one redeeming feature (Moore, 1987). There was no need to read between the lines here; this fellow hated the prospective policy.

Adult education lobbyists were relentless. They had a strategy that included sending letters to Pentagon officials, soliciting the help of federal and state legislators, getting news coverage, trying to discredit DoD's data, and if possible taking a case or two to the courts through the American Civil Liberties Union. As the president of the California Council for Adult Education put it: "The more "hell" ...we can raise, the better" (Powers, 1987). Fortunately for Defense, this advocate for adult education admitted that the attrition statistics could not be repudiated.

The fact that the policy was indeed implemented did not deter lobbying efforts on behalf of adult diploma holders. The adult education agents followed through on their threats. Much to DoD's surprise and dismay, the assault on education credential standards was coming on strong from this newly disenfranchised group. No longer was this just a continual GED problem.

Just two days after the policy went into effect for those in the DEP, 20 members of Congress signed, sealed, and delivered a letter to the Assistant Secretary of Defense for Legislative Affairs (Sawyer, Hawkins, Clay, Dellums, Fauntroy, Ford, Jeffords, Lewis, Martinez, Owens, Regula, Schroeder, Hall, Penny, Eckart, Stokes, Towns, Feighan, Eppy, & Skelton, 1987). This wasn't a "congratulations on your new policy" call. Rather, these members of the House of Representatives questioned the accuracy of the DoD study and attacked the "ill-advised and shortsighted" tiers while extolling the virtues of people who return to high school to get a diploma. DoD sent a prompt standard reply to the members of Congress and then put out the word that Tier 2 applicants should not be called nongraduates and should be told that they are *eligible* to enlist (slots permitting, of course).

DoD's course of action did not quell the concerns of adult educators. Letters with "cc"s to members of Congress and high level Pentagon officials kept coming. Representative Thomas Sawyer (D-OH) went so far as to introduce a bill on June 17, 1987 before the House Armed Services Committee (HASC) to halt the implementation. The HASC wanted a delay at least until October 1, 1988 so that the General Accounting Office could evaluate the study on which the new policy was based. DoD's reply was that the policy had already been implemented by the Army in January 1987 and across the Services for those in the DEP in April. Furthermore, DoD argued that the new screening system would save big bucks. They presented figures to show that in FY 1986, $24 million would have been saved if those nontraditional credential holders enlisted as graduates had instead been considered as Tier 2. Though Congress agreed that adaptability screening and saving money were noble and wise, the message came through that adult education (and in particular the Ohio contingent) was not the group to cross.

The GAO investigation proceeded, with Senator John Glenn (D-OH) now taking the lead. GAO researchers met briefly with the EBIS study sponsors and contractors. With an agenda set by Congress, they hurriedly dissected the study's final policy report. Among the criticisms levied by the Congressional agency were: a) the correlation between education credential tiers and attrition was rather inconsequential (i.e., r = .14); b) the EBIS was not detailed enough and not all variants of education credentials could be identified such as night school graduates; c) the number of adult education credential holders from Ohio wasn't large enough to evaluate reliably; d) the criterion of attrition included adverse and nonadverse reasons lumped together; e) the sample was one of convenience obtained in the Spring of 1983 and might yield different results if convened at another time; f) a couple of EBIS items pertaining to school grades did not contain all possible response options; g) sensitive items (i.e., dealing with drug use and arrest record) were included which might be associated with underreporting by respondents.

Those who conducted and analyzed the EBIS were poised and ready to respond to the GAO. Counterpoints were relatively easy to present, as it appeared that the criticisms were not serious. For example, the "low correlation" was not only statistically significant but was of great practical importance since it represented huge cost savings. Such a value should have been interpreted in light of the range of possible values (three for education credential tiers and two for attrition). That is, technically speaking, if not much variation is possible, as is the case with this predictor and this criterion, a correlation coefficient is attenuated and may not even be the best way to evaluate the relationship. Furthermore, restriction of range within military recruit characteristics masks the true relationship between credentials and attrition. Alternative credential holders and lower aptitude applicants are less likely to be enlisted and thus those on whom the relationship is assessed represent a select group. More recent corrections for such restriction, for example, show a boost in the correlation from about .16 to about .22 (Trent

& Quenette, 1992). The other criticisms were far easier to deal with but supporting arguments fell on deaf ears.

A Solution to the Solution?

A bold letter from HASC Representatives Les Aspin (D-WI, Chairman) and Sawyer in February of 1988 asked not for a temporary reprieve for adult diploma holders but for their assignment to the preferred tier. In their letter, these Congressmen went so far as to say, if you do this "there will be no reason to continue the GAO report on this matter" (Aspin & Sawyer, 1988, p. 1). Aspin and Sawyer also called for the Services to accelerate their alternative approach to adaptability screening so that individual rather than group characteristics would drive selection decisions.

The proverbial straw that broke the camel's back was a similar letter by Senator Glenn, Chairman of the Subcommittee on Manpower and Personnel of the Senate Committee on Armed Services (Glenn, 1988). Shortly thereafter, on February 29, 1988 a memo went out to the Service Assistant Secretaries for Manpower from the Honorable Grant S. Green, Jr., Assistant Secretary of Defense (Force Management and Personnel) stating that it was "best to honor the congressional request" (Green, 1988). Given the strong pressure applied and the fact that only a handful of adult education diploma holders would be expected to seek enlistment, DoD weighed the potential costs and benefits and decided to yield. Effective starting April 1, 1988 for FY 1989 accessions-to-be waiting in the DEP, adult diploma graduates would be part of Tier 1 at least until data from the new credential coding system might indicate otherwise.

Education Credential Tiers Today

Except for the recategorization of adult diploma holders, the policies devised by the Joint-Service Education Credentials Working Group are in force today. Though such policies are alive, they are not necessarily well.

Attrition by Education Credential: The Latest Data

As promised, DoD continued to examine the attrition rates of the various credential holders now that a common and precise coding system was in place. Defense began by looking at the FY 1988 cohort after six months in service; such data were available for perusal in the early summer of 1989. This did not provide much of a test because the sample sizes within some of the credential categories (e.g., home study students) were quite low. And so, DoD waited to bolster the numbers by adding a fiscal year.

Actually, the FY 1988 cohort was evaluated at 6 months and again at 12 months. The FY 1989 cohort was added to the FY 1988 and 6- and 12-month attrition was restudied. Three years (FYs 1988 through 1990) worth of data were also combined and attrition at the one-year point calculated.

Each time the conclusions were the same. Adult diploma holders didn't seem to belong in Tier 1 and neither did those without a traditional diploma who completed just one semester of college. In contrast, home schoolers looked as if they should have been "upped" a tier.

The latest attrition data compiled were for the combined FY 1988 - FY 1989 cohorts after 24 months of service. Table 1.3 presents these data. This table shows a pattern typical of DoD's previous glimpses of attrition for the various credential groups.

With the attrition rate of high school graduates across all Services (at 20 percent at the 24-month mark) as the benchmark, Tier 1 seems out of alignment. Those without a high school diploma but with just one semester of college under their belts have rather high rates in comparison. The rate for adult education diploma holders is even higher at 34 percent. These latter figures seem more in line with the rates shown for Tier 2 members such as equivalency holders (around 37 percent) and correspondence school diploma graduates (around 34 percent).

Other anomalies which this table reveals are the relatively low attrition rates for occupational program certificate holders and home study diploma graduates. At around 21 percent each, the rates for these groups are more akin to those for regular high school graduates. Though the rates for some of the alternative credentials within specific Services do not seem to conform to the total DoD patterns, the numbers are often too small to make reliable comparisons. For example, there are only 15 home study diploma holders in the Army to judge. One "attriter" out of 15 appears to make a lot more of a difference than one out of 98. Where the numbers are ample, the patterns are the same despite the differences in the magnitude of attrition by Service.

30

Table 1.3
Twenty-Four-Month Attrition Rates for FY 1988-1989 NPS Accessions by Education Credential and Service

Tier/Education Credential[a]	Army		Navy		Marine Corps		Air Force		Total DoD	
	N	% Attrition	N	% Attrition	N	% Attrition	N	% Attrition	N	% Attrition
Tier 1										
High School Graduate[b]	182,230	20.1	147,577	21.9	61,939	20.3	79,134	16.2	470,880	20.0
College										
One Semester	1,734	33.5	1,884	33.7	331	33.5	563	12.8	4,512	31.0
2 years or more	5,821	17.2	2,839	19.3	619	19.5	1,942	11.3	11,221	16.8
Adult Education	1,477	30.5	3,027	36.4	311	33.8	66	27.3	4,881	34.4
Tier 2										
H.S. Equivalency	12,293	36.7	6,610	37.2	701	39.7	471	29.7	20,075	36.8
Occ. Program Cert.	20	35.0	87	17.3	12	41.7	28	14.3	147	21.1
H.S. Cert. of Attendance or Completion	98	30.6	205	29.3	1,683	28.4	28	21.4	2,014	28.5
Correspondence School Diploma	16	31.3	3	.0	93	36.6	3	.0	115	33.9
Home Study Diploma	15	40.0	11	27.3	21	28.6	51	11.8	98	21.4
Tier 3										
Less than H.S. Diploma	5,008	38.8	8,563	38.9	468	34.2	124	25.8	14,163	38.6

[a] Codes A, M, S, 2, 3, 5, 6, 9 excluded (N=5,711)
[b] Excludes old Code 2 for diploma graduate (N=3,799) and Code 5 for high school seniors (N=1)

More Grumbling About Credential Categorization

Not only did the data speak for themselves, but disaffected groups continued to vie for Tier 1 status. Though adult education lobbyists were silenced, old and new voices were raised.

Somewhat shocked and amazed by the adult education decision, the GED contingent renewed its protest. Earlier the GED Testing Service of the American Council on Education (ACE) had tried to enlist the help of adult education groups in their fight against DoD's credential policies. Such groups declined, viewing the matter as strictly a GED problem. When adult diploma holders were adversely affected, they changed their tune and their campaign against DoD was welcomed by ACE. In fact, GED administrators, believing they had reinforcements, let their guard down and focused their attention elsewhere. Later they discovered that adult education efforts were successful but GED equivalency holders were left by the wayside.

The GED Testing Service set forth its position in a memorandum to the ACE Commission on Educational Credit and Credentials late in 1990 (Staff, 1990). They claimed, as they had before, that DoD was misusing GED status and, was inadvertently denigrating the credential, and that the tier system had no basis because not all groups in Tier 1 had lower attrition (namely, the adult diploma holders). Rather than calling for an adjustment to the policy, they called for its abolishment and replacement with an alternative adaptability screening system based upon biographical information that DoD had promised earlier.

Congress has been making inquiries of late as well, not only on behalf of GED constituents (e.g., an April 7, 1992 letter from Senator Lloyd Bentsen, D-TX) but to address the concerns of correspondence school graduates and, more forcefully, the home school lobby. In the case of the former, it seems that correspondence school is the way to go in remote sites such as Alaska and public servants such as Senator Ted Stevens (R-AK) are concerned about not closing the military career path to such youth.

Even more noise has been made recently about those who are legally educated at home. Senator Jesse Helms (R-NC) together with House members Joel Hefley (R-CO), William Dannemeyer (R-CA), William Dickinson (R-AL), and James Sensenbrenner (R-WI) wrote a low-key letter to Assistant Secretary of Defense (Force Management and Personnel) Christopher Jehn on October 11, 1991.

Subsequent letters from Congressman Frank R. Wolfe (R-VA) and Senator Bob Dole (R-KS) sent in April of 1992 urged a Tier 1 status for home schoolers.

In response to recent queries, DoD asked for patience. Rather than moving education credentials around and so adjusting tiers, the whole system may be replaced. Again, that's maybe.

A Replacement for Education Credential Tiers?

Fearing that external political pressure would serve to put the kibosh on the three-tier system, DoD had continued to investigate alternative means of adaptability screening. With the Navy in charge, the Services pooled their knowledge and resources and developed a biographical questionnaire called the Armed Services Applicant Profile (ASAP). This instrument comprised items in a multiple-choice format pertaining to background characteristics and behaviors such as high school academics and work history. ASAP was administered from December 1984 through February 1985 to military applicants across all four Services, yielding "biodata" for over 120,000 people. The ability of this instrument to predict attrition was estimated along the way, with the latest data showing a (simple but corrected) correlation of about .3. This value looks pretty good next to the analogous coefficient of .22 for credential tiers (see Trent & Quenette, 1992).

Regardless of the *apparent* power of the ASAP over the existing system, many technical, practical, and political concerns impeded progress toward operational implementation. Though a detailed discussion of these concerns is beyond the scope of this chapter, they are discussed in Chapter 6. Suffice it to say, internal politics were just as intractable as external. And, after more than a decade of researching some other means of screening for term completion, the "solutions" have yet to be adopted.

Among the issues raised by Service researchers and policymakers was the potential for recruiter coaching and applicant faking of this self-reported inventory of items. In response to this concern over possible compromise, portions of the Army's Assessment of Background and Life Experiences (ABLE) which were devised to detect faking were recommended to supplement the ASAP. The ABLE was a temperament inventory developed by the Army just subsequent to the ASAP and designed to predict more than just attrition (e.g., leadership potential).

With the Army's push toward ABLE and the ASAP progress to date, a combined instrument (with a shortened ASAP and portions of ABLE) known as the Adaptability Screening Profile (ASP) was pilot tested toward the end of 1988 (Barnes, Gaskins, Hansen, Laurence, Waters, Quenette, & Trent, 1989).

Worried that the power of such a self-report biodata inventory to predict attrition would not stand up over time, DoD came up with an alternative to the alternative. Instead of supplanting education credential tiers with ASAP or ASP alone, the idea was to develop a compensatory screening model (CSM). The CSM approach would consider an applicant's credential (actually the specific credential rather than grouped into tiers) along with other characteristics routinely gathered in the enlistment process (e.g., age, marital status, aptitudes) and maybe even ASAP (or ASP) score (or maybe not, given technical and practical concerns). A person would be evaluated on the basis of all such information and, as the name implies, the *compensatory* screening model would enable one attribute to compensate for another. That is, for example, a GED credential holder would suffer because of the low weight given to the credential but could boost his or her "score" by having other characteristics indicative of term completion (Dempsey, Laurence, Waters, & McBride, 1991).

Though preliminary research has been done, the fate of the CSM is uncertain. Credential tiers are efficient and with revamping could be made a bit more effective. The CSM, on the other hand, would involve more extended applicant processing time not to mention being a bigger burden on other resources. Though the payoff in terms of attrition reduction looks good in theory, there is less certainty about its value in practice, particularly in light of concerns over biodata, which is the CSM's strongest element (at least in a research setting).

The Choices

The future of adaptability screening awaits decision. Under consideration now are three options: 1) revise the current three-tier system; 2) adopt a compensatory screening model (but hold the biographical inventory) in its stead; or 3) adopt the CSM with the ASP included. The Services have rendered their opinions in favor of option number 1. The CSM approach seems popular only within the Navy and even for this Service the scope is limited. The Services seem to be saying, "Why bother?" After all, recruiting is pretty good right now and to replace the tiers with CSM might make quality look less rosy than it is.

The Navy at least, perhaps owing to its more stubborn attrition and recruiting problems, is willing to accept a change in the status quo, at least a little. In July 1992, the Navy initiated an operational test of its own version of a CSM for those who do not hold a regular high school diploma. Though high school graduates are exempt, the adaptability of a small percentage of alternative credential holders and those without any secondary school documentation is being evaluated on the basis of variables like specific credential, years of schooling, age, employment status, AFQT scores, moral waiver status, and military youth program participation. After two years the Navy will decide whether the CSM is worth it. And who knows, the other Services just might come on board. Of course, it is possible that the Navy could throw the CSM overboard before its trial period is scheduled to end. Regardless of attrition rates, if quality *appears* to suffer (i.e., the Navy's percentage of HSDGs dwindles), someone down the road may abandon the CSM for appearance's sake.

Education Standards: In the End

Although the course of education standards has been charted in this chapter from the beginning, the near future--let alone the end--is uncertain. The options, together with the Services' predilections, are being weighed by the Assistant Secretary of Defense for Force Management and Personnel--Honorable Christopher Jehn. Will the tier system, first established in the 1960s, survive in one form or another? It seems safe to assume that the tiers will remain, but just as the tiers evolved with additional data over the years, changes will be made to the current system. From the data alone, a logical solution would be to move adult education credentials and transcripts attesting to the completion of one semester of college to Tier 2 while moving home study diplomas to Tier 1. One need only to reread this chapter to ponder the potential reactions to such a decision. Certainly the evidence from the past suggests that adjusting tiers will not pass unnoticed. Opposition is likely to be loud and indefatigable.

Which will it be? What will the future hold for adaptability screening? To partially answer this, an odd twist to an old adage seems apropos: "The less things change, the more they remain the same."

References

Aspin, L., & Sawyer, T. C. (1988, February 5). Letter to Dr. David J. Armor, Principal Deputy Assistant Secretary of Defense (Force Management and Personnel) Washington, DC: U.S. House of Representatives, Committee on Armed Services.

Barnes, J. D., Gaskins, R. C, III, Hansen, I A., Laurence, J. II., Waters, B. K., Quenette, M. A., & Trent, T. (1989, March). *The Adaptability Screening Profile (ASP): Background and pilot test results* (IR-PRD-89-06). Alexandria, VA: Human Resources Research Organization.

Buddin, R. (1984, July). *Analysis of early attrition behavior* (R-3069-MIL). Santa Monica, CA: RAND Corporation.

Cox, C.B. (1987, March 24). Memorandum for Assistant Secretary of the Army (M&RA), Assistant Secretary of the Navy (M&RA), Assistant Secretary of the Air Force (MRA&I). Subject: Definitions of Educational Credentials for Enlistment Eligibility Purposes. Washington, DC: Assistant Secretary of Defense (Force Management and Personnel).

Dempsey, J. R., Laurence, J. H., Waters, B. K., & McBride, J. R. (1991, November). *Proposed methodology for the development of a compensatory screening model for attrition* (FR-PRD-91-17). Alexandria, VA: Human Resources Research Organization.

Department of Defense. (1974, January). *Defense manpower quality requirements.* Report to the House Committee on Armed Services. Washington, DC: Office of the Assistant Secretary of Defense (Manpower, Reserve Affairs and Logistics).

Department of Defense. (1981, December). *Implementation of new Armed Services Vocational Aptitude Battery and actions to improve the enlistment standards process.* Report to the House and Senate Committees on Armed Services. Washington, DC: Office of the Assistant Secretary of Defense (Manpower, Reserve Affairs and Logistics).

Eitelberg, M. J. (1983, September). *A preliminary evaluation of education standards for military enlistment.* Monterey, CA: Naval Postgraduate School.

Eitelberg, M. J., Laurence, J. H., & Waters, B. K., with Perelman, L. P. (1984, September). *Screening for service: Aptitude and education criteria for military entry.* Washington, DC: Office of Assistant Secretary of Defense (Manpower, Installations and Logistics).

Flyer. E. S. (1959, December). *Factors relating to discharge for unsuitability among 1956 airmen accessions to the Air Force* (WADC-TN-59-201). Lackland Air Force Base, TX: Personnel Research Laboratory.

General Accounting Office. (1976, January). *Problems resulting from management practices in recruiting, training, and using non-high school graduates and mental category IV personnel* (FPCD-76-24). Report to the Congress of the United States. Washington, DC: Author.

General Accounting Office. (1980, February). *Attrition in the military-An issue needing management attention.* Report to the Congress of the United States. Washington, DC: Author.

Glenn, J. (1988, February 10). Letter to Dr. David J. Armor, Principal Deputy Assistant Secretary of Defense (Force Management and Personnel) Washington, DC: United States Senate, Committee on Armed Services.

Green, G. S., Jr. (1988, February 29). Memorandum for Assistant Secretary of the Army (M&RA); Assistant Secretary of the Navy (M&RA); Assistant Secretary of the Air Force (M&RA). Subject: Educational Enlistment Policy. Washington, DC: Assistant Secretary of Defense (Force Management and Personnel).

Klein, S., Hawes-Dawson, J., & Martin, T. (1991). *Why recruits separate early* (R-3980-FMP). Santa Monica, CA: RAND Corporation.

Lancaster, A. R. (1988, August). *Education standards for enlistment: A need for reform.* Paper presented as part of Symposium "Military personnel selection and public policy: Revising education enlistment standards" at the 96th Annual Convention of the American Psychological Association, Atlanta, GA.

Laurence, J. H. (1983, November). *Secondary education credentials: A military enlistment policy dilemma* (FR-PRD-83-22). Alexandria, VA: Human Resources Research Organization.

Laurence, J. H. (1984, February). *Education standards for military enlistment and the search for successful recruits* (FR-PRD-84-4). Alexandria, VA: Human Resources Research Organization.

Laurence, J. H. (1987, September). *Military enlistment policy and education credentials: Evaluation and improvement* (FR-PRD-87-33). Alexandria VA: Human Resources Research Organization.

Lukeman, A. (1987, April 27). Memorandum for Deputy Chief of Staff for Personnel, HQ, Department of the Army; Deputy Chief of Naval Operations (Manpower, Personnel and Training), Office of Chief of Naval Operations; Deputy Chief of Staff for Personnel, HQ, U.S. Air Force; Deputy Chief of Staff for Manpower, HQ, U.S. Marine Corps. Subject: Educational Enlistment Standards. Washington, DC: Office of the Assistant Secretary of Defense (Force Management and Personnel).

Matloff, M. (1973). *American military history.* Washington, DC: Office of the Chief of Military History, U.S. Army.

Means, B., & Laurence, J. H. (1984, June). *Characteristics and performance of recruits enlisted with General Educational Development (GED) credentials* (FPRD-84). Alexandria, VA: Human Resources Research Organization.

Means, B., & Perelman, L. S. (1984, June). *The development of the Educational and Biographical Information Survey* (FR-PRD-84-3). Alexandria, VA: Human Resources Research Organization.

Moore, S. A. (1987, February 12). Letter to Colonel R. W. Lind, Principal Director, Military Manpower and Personnel Policy, Office of the Assistant Secretary of Defense (Force Management and Personnel). Akron, OH; Akron Evening High School.

Nichols, B. (1981, October 26). Letter to the Honorable Lawrence J. Korb, Assistant Secretary of Defense (Manpower, Reserve Affairs, and Logistics). Washington, DC: U. S. House of Representatives, Committee on Armed Services.

Nichols, B. (1982, April 22). Letter to the Honorable Caspar W. Weinberger, Secretary of Defense. Washington, DC: U.S. House of Representatives, Committee on Armed Services.

Nieva, V. F., Wilson, M. J., Kolmstetter, E. B., Madigan, M. K., & Greenlees, J. B. (1991). *Youth Attitude Tracking Study: Propensity report, Fall 1990.* Arlington, VA: Defense Manpower Data Center.

Powers, L. (1987, March 11). Letter to Mr. Spurgeon A. Moore, Principal, Evening High School, Akron Public Schools. Martinez, CA: California Council for Adult Education.

Sawyer, T. C., Hawkins, A. F., Clay, W., Dellums, R. V., Fauntroy, W. E., Ford, W. D., Jeffords, J. M., Lewis, J., Martinez, M. G., Owens, M., Regula, R., Shroeder, P., Hall, T. P., Penny, T. J., Eckart, D. E., Stokes, L., Towns, E., Feighan, E. F., Epsy, M., Skelton, I. (1987, April 3). Letter to Ms. Margo Carlisle, Assistant Secretary of Defense (Legislative Affairs). Washington, DC: Congress of the United States, House of Representatives.

Sellman, W. S. (1988). *Military adaptability screening: A manpower management perspective.* Paper presented as part of Symposium "Military personnel selection and public policy: Revising education enlistment standards" at the 96th Annual Convention of the American Psychological Association, Atlanta, GA.

Staff. (1990, September). Memorandum to Commission on Educational Credit and Credentials. Subject: Statement on military recruiting policy. Washington, DC: The General Educational Development Testing Service of the American Council on Education.

Trent, T., & Quenette, M. A. (1992, February). *Armed Services Applicant Profile (ASAP): Development and validation of operational forms* (TR-92-9). San Diego, CA: Navy Personnel Research and Development Center.

Umstead, S. M., Jr. (1978, February 9). Memorandum for Assistant Secretary of the Army (M&RA), Assistant Secretary of the Navy (MRA&L), Assistant Secretary of the Air Force (MRA&I). Subject: High School Diploma Graduate Status. Washington, DC: Assistant Secretary of Defense (Manpower, Reserve Affairs and Logistics) (Military Personnel Policy).

Waters, B. K., Laurence, J. H., & Camara, W. J. (1987). *Personnel enlistment and classification procedures in the U.S. Military.* Washington, DC: National Academy Press.

Weinberger, C. W. (1982, May 10). Letter to the Honorable Bill Nichols, Chairman, Military Personnel and Compensation Subcommittee, Committee on Armed Services, House of Representatives. Washington, DC: Secretary of Defense.

Chapter 2_____

Biodata: What's It All About?

Janice H. Laurence and Brian K. Waters[1]

"B" is for the Background and Behavioral elements. "I" is for the Interest measures. "O" is for the "Other" items. "D" is for the Demographics. "A" is for the Attitudes and Accomplishments. "T" is for the Temperaments. And "A" is for Anything else that's suitable. Put them all together and you have BIODATA--a veritable hodgepodge of ingredients. Biographical data inventories or "biodata" are rather amorphous "tests" that have been developed as non-cognitive predictors of performance. Items from these domains have been assembled into questionnaires and employed as predictors of various aspects of human performance. Despite widespread development and use, not to mention encouraging validation results, biodata are surrounded by a cloud of controversy pertaining not only to their utility but to their very essence.

The military, like civilian industry, has been attracted to biodata as a selection device. The civilian sector often looks to this screening tool as a valid and fairer alternative to cognitive ability tests for predicting job proficiency as well as other available criteria. The Military Services have examined biodata not as an alternative selector but as an additional hurdle. Cognitive aptitude testing remains

---

[1]Human Resources Research Organization, Alexandria, Virginia. The opinions expressed are those of the authors, not necessarily those of the Department of Defense nor the Military Services.

the primary enlistment screen because of its proven value in predicting training performance and job proficiency. Biographical data are aimed most often at predicting another aspect of military performance--attrition--the failure to complete the first enlistment term. The purpose of this chapter is to provide "background data" for Chapters 3, 4, and 5. Thus it is not meant to be an exhaustive review but a description and discussion of biographical inventories. Subsequent chapters detail the military's most recent efforts toward developing and implementing such measures to predict adaptability to service. To appreciate the potential value of adaptability screening for the Armed Forces, the basics of the content, characteristics, and issues surrounding biodata must be understood.

The Evolution of Biodata

Some variant of the axiom that past behavior is a good predictor of future behavior launches nearly every discourse on biodata. And using "past" biographical information as part of the personnel selection process has a longstanding history. The antecedents of the biographical inventory genre include pre-employment information gathering techniques such as interviews and application blanks. For these screening mechanisms, job candidates are typically asked to discuss, list, or describe previous employment experiences (including such things as dates of employment, job responsibilities, salary history, and references) as well as other background characteristics such as hobbies and interests. Demographics such as marital status and residence have also been included as pertinent bits of information from which to make a hiring (or some other employment-related) decision.

Improvements over the more or less hit-or-miss compilation of facts about the applicant came about with the weighted application blank (WAB), which involves weighting relevant information according to its contribution to the prediction of performance criteria (England, 1971). Yet another approach is the biographical information blank (BIB). BIBs represent further attempts to capitalize on the predictive power of background items and to standardize the collection and interpretation of a broad range of such information. BIBs are often differentiated from WABs not only by their multiple-choice format, but by the inclusion of a greater number and wider range of items such as "softer" questions covering attitudes, values, and opinions.

The contributions that biodata bring to the selection process include efficiently gathering and standardizing numerous instances of tacit past behavior. As biographical inventories have evolved, their content has gone beyond face valid or transparent questions about relevant background and work experience to cover tangentially related items and those with no intuitive relationship to the criterion as well.

Standardized, self-report, multiple-choice biographical information blanks began moving to the forefront of personnel selection systems in the 1950s (Dunnette, 1966; Reilly & Chao, 1982). They continued to gain momentum because research results indicated that less adverse impact was associated with biodata than with cognitive ability tests (Wigdor & Garner, 1982). Although cognitive measures typically demonstrate higher predictive validity, minority group members are also likely to score lower on them, thus they are more likely to screen out such applicants. With respectable validities, commonly in the .2 to .4 range,[2] and inconsequential--or at least easily correctable--subgroup differences (Cascio, 1976; Owens & Henry, 1966; Reilly & Chao, 1982), biodata came to be seen as a practical alternative to increasingly attacked and legally challenged general ability tests (Hunter & Hunter, 1984).

Scoring Biodata

Conventional ability test items are scored on the basis of being correct. A relationship with the criterion (e.g., job performance) is bolstered by assembling relevant items, but the items are scored independently of the criterion and assessed after the fact via a validity coefficient. For a typical mathematics knowledge item such as $18 \times 2 = ?$, only one response option--a) 36; b) 20; c) 26--is correct. Only by choosing option "a" would the respondent get a point. A distinguishing feature of "traditional" biodata is that items and total scores are directly tied to the criterion. There are no correct answers, per se, for a biographical inventory. For example, a biodata item such as: "Which of the following high school subjects did you like best?" might have the following response options: a) math; b) English; c) science; d) history; e) other. None of these options is "correct" in its own right, thus each option gets scored or weighted. The typical procedure for developing, scaling, and scoring biographical

---

[2]In the personnel selection arena, "raw" or uncorrected validities within this range are considered quite acceptable; in fact they seldom exceed this range (see Ghiselli, 1966; Reilly & Chao, 1982 for a discussion of maximum validities for predicting training and job performance).

inventories is, in essence, to gather items previously found to be related to the criterion of interest and to weight individual response options according to predictive power; that is, their ability to discriminate between persons at the high and low ends of the criterion (Devlin, Abrahams, & Edwards, 1992). There are a number of empirical keying variants including the horizontal percent method, the vertical percent method, unit weighting response alternatives, and regression-based scaling.

The horizontal percent method is the simplest and most commonly applied scaling technique (Cascio, 1982; Devlin et al., 1992; Guion, 1965). First, it entails creating high and low criterion groups (e.g., upper third vs. bottom third of the sample with respect to the particular performance criterion in question; or in the case of a dichotomous criterion such as turnover, the sample is simply split in two). Next, for each item response alternative, the number of respondents in the high criterion group who selected an item alternative is divided by the total number of respondents who selected the alternative yielding the percent of high criterion respondents for each item option (e.g., 82 percent of persons who chose a particular alternative were in the high criterion group). Finally, this value is typically divided by 10 (e.g., 82 percent becomes 8.2) and the whole number portion is retained (e.g., 8.2 becomes 8) as the weight.

The vertical percent method is similar to the horizontal method, but deviates in that percentages choosing each response option are calculated within the high and low criterion groups and then the differences between these percentages serve as the weights (cf. Stead & Shartle, 1940). Regression-based scaling is based upon the "optimum" weights for each item alternative as derived from multiple regression techniques used to predict the criterion from the combination of biodata items (cf. Perry, 1965; Steinhaus & Waters, 1991). Unit weighting is based upon the results of any of the above empirical keying methods but replaces the specific weights derived by calculating percentages, difference scores, or regression coefficients with weights of either 1 or 0 depending upon the relative value of the alternative to differentiate between high and low criterion groups. There are still other empirical keying methods (e.g., pattern of response method and factor analytic methods) that rely upon the contribution of the item as a whole in determining weights rather than weighting each and every response option (cf. Owens, 1976; Telenson, Alexander, & Barrett, 1983).

All of these methods of empirical keying produce rather similar results (Aamodt & Kimbrough, 1985; Devlin, et al., 1992; Guion, 1965; Mitchell &

Klimoski, 1982; Telenson, et al., 1983; Steinhaus & Waters, 1991; Uhlman, Reiter-Palmon, & Connelly, 1991). Initial validities do vary somewhat with the method employed (Devlin et al., 1992) but, with a large sample, there is little practical difference among the methods. Although regression-based weights may produce higher initial validity coefficients (Steinhaus & Waters, 1991), if one considers the potential for coefficients to shrink when the weights are applied to a new "cross-validation" sample or over time, the simpler and efficient horizontal percent method may be the best choice.

Biodata's Predictive Power

Biodata's appeal is attributable, in large part, to demonstrated predictive or criterion-related validity (Childs & Klimoski, 1986; Owens & Henry, 1966). This section contains a sample of the evidence that has accumulated concerning biodata's predictive power. Ghiselli (1955) gave biodata a favorable review several decades ago. He reported that 75 percent of validity coefficients examined were greater than .30. Later studies and reviews have also issued accolades. In a comprehensive review of the validity of alternative job training and job proficiency predictors, Reilly and Chao (1982) concluded on the basis of conservative estimates that the generic biographical inventory was indeed a close runner-up to cognitive ability tests. Biographical inventories had a mean, *cross-validated* (but uncorrected) validity coefficient of .35 across all criteria and occupations examined. Previous and subsequent reviews have also concluded that biodata are almost as useful as cognitive ability as predictors of training and job success (Asher, 1972; Barge & Hough, 1984; Dunnette, 1966; England, 1971; Ghiselli, 1955; Owens, 1976; Rothstein, Schmidt, Erwin, Owens, & Sparks, 1990).

A great many studies, employing varied criteria and diverse samples have attested to the power of biodata. Even higher correlation coefficients are reported before cross-validation and for some criteria. Ghiselli (1955) found that the mean coefficient for trainability was .44 and .41 for job performance. Smith, Albright, Glennon, and Owens (1961) reported a coefficient of .61 between biodata items covering home and family background, previous employment, athletic interests, and school and college activities and supervisory ratings for researchers at the Standard Oil Company. This study's sample also yielded coefficients each of .52 for both creativity and the number of filed patent disclosures. Barge and Hough (1988) reported median biodata validities of .25,

.32, .30, and .26 for training performance, job proficiency, job involvement (e.g., turnover, absenteeism, tenure), and adjustment (e.g., delinquency, substance abuse), respectively.

Though the most popular criteria are turnover, tenure, and absenteeism (Barge, Hough, & Dunnette, 1984; Guion, 1965), empirically-keyed biodata have been found to be valid predictors of not only these but other criteria such as productivity, creativity, earnings, performance appraisal ratings, academic performance, honesty, managerial effectiveness, and accident rates. Whether or not the reported coefficients have been cross-validated or corrected for range restriction, the validities for biodata are sizeable. Given such consistent findings, it is indeed understandable that industry has jumped on the biodata bandwagon. Biodata have been used to screen life insurance and other sales agents, police officers, airline management employees, college students, researchers, engineers and other professionals, supermarket checkers, supervisors and staff alike. In fact, because of expected high validity and low adverse impact, a biographical inventory called the Individual Achievement Record (IAR) was constructed and adopted not long ago for screening entry-level professional and administrative job candidates for Federal civilian employment (Gandy & Sharf, 1988).

Biodata in the Military

The military has certainly contributed to the biodata literature. And from the numerous military studies, biodata have been found to be valid predictors in this environment as well. A conservative estimate (given that the coefficients were cross-validated) of .30 was provided by Reilly and Chao (1982) as the average validity to be expected in the military context. An extensive, though not exhaustive, chronological list of military biodata studies is provided in Table 2.1.

Actually, the use of biodata by the military predates even the earliest listed reference. To aid job assignment, in World War I and World War II, incoming recruits were questioned about their civilian work experience (Palmer, Wiley, & Keast, 1948). Owens (1976) cites many examples from World War II of the ability of more formally organized biodata to predict leadership ratings of officers and the training success of pilots and navigators. Henry (1966) reported that one biodata item alone--"Did you ever build a model airplane that flew?"--predicted flight success in World War II almost as well as the entire battery of measures used to select pilots at the time.

46

Table 2.1 Military Biodata Publications			
Author(s)	Year	Title	Sample
Plag, J. A.	1962	Pre-enlistment Variables Related to the Performance and Adjustment of Navy Recruits	20,000 Navy recruits
Gunderson, E. K. E.	1963	Biographical Indicators of Adaptation to Naval Service	743 Navy Enlisted men
Johnson, C. D. Waters, L. K. Helme, W.H.	1964	Factor Analysis of Experimental Non-cognitive Measures of Combat Potential	925 Army Infantrymen
Dann, J. E. Abrahams, N. M.	1969	Validation of a Biographical Information Blank as a Predictor of Retention among Mechanical and Electrical-Electronics Enlisted Personnel	6,635 School-Qualified Navy Recruits
Bowser, S. E.	1974	Non-Cognitive Factors as Predictors of Individual Suitability for Service in the U. S. Navy	6,412 Navy Recruits
Guinn, N. Johnson, A.L. Kantor, J. E.	1975	Screening for Adaptability to Military Service	15,252 Basic Airmen
Yellen, T. M. I.	1975	Validation of the Delinquent Behavior Inventory as a Predictor of Basic Training Attrition	1,800 Navy Discharged Recruits
Nevo, B.	1976	Using Biographical Information to Predict Success of Men and Women in the Army	390 Male & 524 Female ex-soldiers
Bloom, W.	1977	Air Force Medical Evaluation Test	24,000 AF Enlistees
Erwin, F. W. Herring, J. W.	1977	The Feasibility of the Use of Autobiographical Information as a Predictor of Early Army Attrition	6,608 Army Recruits
Guinn, N. Kantor, J. E. Vitola, B. M.	1977	Effectiveness of Adaptability Screening	12,599 Airmen
Sands, W.A.	1977	Screening Male Applicants for Navy Enlistment	68,616 Navy Recruits

(Continued)

Author(s)	Year	Title	Sample
Table 2.1 Military Biodata Publications (Continued)			
Booth, R. F. McNally, M. S. Berry, N. H.	1978	Predicting Performance Effectiveness in Paramedical Occupations	2,835 HMs & 848 DTs
Frank, B. A. Erwin, F. W.	1978	The Prediction of Early Army Attrition through the Use of Autobiographical Information Questionnaires	7,000 Basic Combat Training Enlistees
Hoiberg, A. Pugh, W. M.	1978	Predicting Navy Effectiveness: Expectations, Motivation, Personality, Aptitude, and Background Variables	7,923 Navy Enlisted
Seeley, L. C. Rosen, T. Stroad, K.	1978	Early Development of the Military Aptitude Predictor (MAP)	278 Army Trainees
Sands, W. A.	1978	Enlisted Personnel Selection for the U. S. Navy	68,616 NPS Navy Recruits
Haymaker, J. C. Erwin, F. W.	1980	Investigation of Applicant Responses and Falsification Detection for MAP	748 Army Recruits
Eaton, N. K. Weltin, M. Wing, H.	1982	Validity of the Military Applicant Profile (MAP) for Predicting Early Attrition in Different Educational, Age, and Racial Groups	4,282 Army Recruits
Atwater, D. C. Abrahams, N. M.	1983	Adaptability Screening: Development and Initial Validation of the Recruit Background Questionnaire (RBQ)	15,434 Navy Recruits
Finstuen, K. Alley, W. E.	1983	Occupational and Personnel Correlates of First-Term Enlisted Tenure in the Air Force	280,039 Air Force Enlistees
Walker, C. B. Teevan, B.	1983	Validation of an Expanded Item Pool for the Army's Military Applicant Profile (MAP)	943 Army Recruits
Barge, B. N. Hough, L. M.	1984	Utility of Biographical Data: A Review and Integration of the Literature	Review of Literature
Erwin, F. W.	1984	Development of New Military Applicant Profile (MAP) Autobiographical Questionnaires for Use in Prediction of Early Army Attrition	9,603 Army Recruits/263 also as Applicants

(Continued)

Table 2.1 Military Biodata Publications (Continued)

Author(s)	Year	Title	Sample
Means, B. Perelman, L. S.	1984	The Development of the Educational and Biographical Information Survey	34,000 Applicants /40,000 Recruits
Means, B. Waters, B. K. Morris, S. M.	1984	Self-Reports of Biographical Information Before and After Military Service	855 Applicants /Recruits
Walker, C. B.	1984	Validation of the Army's Military Applicant Profile (MAP)	7,820 Army Enlisted
Laurence, J. H. Means, B.	1985	A Description and Comparison of Biographical Inventories for Military Service	Review of Biodata Item Validities
Diamond, E. E.	1985	Development of the Military Adaptability Scale (MAS)	540 Navy Recruits
Walker, C. B.	1985	The Fakability of the Army's Military Applicant Profile (MAP)	1,836 Army Recruits
Atwater, D. C. Abrahams, N.M. Wiskoff, M. F. Sands, W. A. Trent, T.	1986	Evaluation and Control of Faking in Biodata Instruments	Review of Faking Studies
Means, B. Heisey, J.	1986	Educational and Biographical Data as Predictors of Early Attrition	40,000 Recruits
Smith, E. P. Walker, C. B.	1986	Short Versus Long-Term Tenure as a Criterion for Validating Biodata	9,416 Army Recruits
Trent, T.	1987	Armed Forces Adaptability Screening: The Utility of the Biographical Inventory	26,000 Applicants/ Recruits
Trent, T.	1987	Armed Forces Adaptability Screening: The Problem of Item Response Distortion	26,000 Applicants/ Recruits
Dolgin, D. L. Gibb, G. D.	1988	A Review of Personality Measurement in Aircrew Selection	Review of Literature
Roomsburg, J. D.	1988	Biographical Data as Predictors of Success in Military Aviation Training	137 ROTC Students/ 145 OTS Students

(Continued)

Table 2.1 Military Biodata Publications (Continued)			
Author(s)	Year	Title	Sample
Steinhaus, S. D.	1988	Predicting Military Attrition from Educational and Biographical Information	34,824 Applicants & 40,387 Accessions
Appel, V. H. Grubb, P. D.	1989	The Anatomy of a Conceptually-based Biographical Survey Instrument	Conceptual Model
Barnes, J.D. Gaskins, R.C. Hansen, L.A. Waters, B.K. Quenette, M.A. Trent, T.	1989	The Adaptability Screening Profile (ASP): Background and Pilot Test Results	311 Navy Recruits
Barrett, L. E.	1989	Cognitive Versus Non-cognitive Predictors of Air Force Officer Training	3,142 OTS Applicants
Hough, L. M.	1989	Implementation Issues for Biodata Measures	Review of Literature
Laabs, G. J. Trent, T. Quenette, M. A.	1989	The Adaptability Screening Program: An Overview	120,175 Military Applicants
Stricker, L. J.	1989	Assessing Leadership Potential at the Naval Academy with a Biographical Measure	642 Naval Academy Students
Trent, T.	1989	The Adaptability Screening Profile: Technical Issues	120,000 Applicants & 56,000 Recruits
Trent, T. Quenette, M. A. Pass, J. J.	1989	An Old-Fashioned Biographical Inventory	120,000 Applicants & 56,000 Recruits
Walker, C. B. White, L. A. Schroyer, C.	1989	Implementing the U. S. Army's Assessment of Background and Life Experiences (ABLE)	2,249 Army Recruits
Waters, B. K. Laurence, J. H.	1989	Issues in the Development of the Educational and Biographical Information Survey (EBIS)	34,824 Applicants & 40,387 Recruits

(Continued)

Table 2.1 Military Biodata Publications (Continued)			
Author(s)	Year	Title	Sample
Hanson, M. A. Paulin, C. Borman, W. C.	1990	Development of an Experimental Biodata/Temperament Inventory for NROTC Selection	175 Board-Eligible NROTC Applicants
Hanson, M. A. Hallam, G. L. Hough, L. M. Carter, G. W. McGuire, D. P.	1990	Controlling Score Distortion on the Adaptability Screening Profile (ASP): Preliminary Research	Review of Literature & ASAP/ABLE Analyses
Hough, L. M. Eaton, N. K. Dunnette, M. D. Kamp, J. D. McCloy, R. A.	1990	Criterion-Related Validities of Personality Constructs and the Effect of Response Distortion on those Validities	9,359, 245 and 125 Army Recruits
Palmer, D. R. White, L. A. Young, M. C.	1990	Response Distortion on the Adaptability Screening Profile (ASP)	502 Male Army Recruits
Trent, T. Quenette, M. A. Laabs, G. J.	1990	An Alternative to High School Diploma for Military Enlistment Qualification	11,525 Navy Applicants/ Recruits
Steinhaus, S. D. Waters, B. K.	1991	Biodata and the Application of a Psychometric Perspective	38,824 Applicants & 40,387 Recruits
Devlin, S. E. Abrahams, N. M. Edwards, J. E.	1992	Empirical Keying of Biographical Data: Cross-Validity as a Function of Scaling Procedure and Sample Size	21,931 Applicants to Naval Academy

Since the 1960s, the military has accumulated evidence of biodata's ability to predict a number of criteria such as drug abuse, career progression, effectiveness ratings, desertion, and delinquency. The number one criterion, however, is attrition during the first term of service among enlisted (as opposed to officer) personnel. This criterion is similar to turnover which is the most popular criterion for biodata in the civilian sector. However, attrition may be considered more serious or at least more negative than turnover given that military personnel are contractually obligated to fulfill an enlistment term and replacement of lost personnel through lateral entry into the military is practically nonexistent.

The seriousness and costs of attrition led the military to search for useful predictors. In the 1960s, military researchers relentlessly examined the relationship between attrition and variables routinely collected as part of the enlistment process (e.g., Flyer, 1963; Plag, Goffman, & Phelan, 1967; Plag, Goffman, & Phelan, 1970). Such studies of attrition identified education, aptitude, and age as a useful combination of predictors with a multiple correlation of .35 (Lockman & Warner, 1977). Ultimately, education credential was found to be the single best predictor of attrition, and, since the mid 1960s, this one piece of background data has served as the operational screen for attrition across all four Services (see Chapter 1 of this volume for a detailed discussion of the relationship between education credential and attrition). In addition, the Navy used the results of Plag's research to set up actuarial tables akin to weighted application blanks. The first, implemented in 1973, was called the Odds for Effectiveness (OFE). The OFE considered a prospective recruit's education level, level of aptitude, number of suspensions or expulsions from high school, and arrests for non-traffic offenses (Sands, 1976). Later, the Navy reduced the number of variables used to predict attrition to three: 1) aptitude category; 2) education; and 3) age, and called the new predictor model Success Chances for Recruits Entering the Navy (SCREEN) (Lockman & Lurie, 1980).

Throughout the 1970s and 1980s, the Military Services experimented with or implemented a variety of standardized biographical questionnaires aimed at predicting attrition (see Laurence & Means, 1985 for a description of the various inventories). The Air Force developed the Military Adaptability Screening Test (MAST) and later transformed it into the 50-item History Opinion Inventory (HOI) (Guinn, Johnson, & Kantor, 1975) that is currently used to identify recruits likely to have problems adapting to the Air Force. Recruits so identified are counseled and if warranted, later dismissed from service. The Navy began experimenting with the 55-item Recruiting Background Questionnaire (RBQ) in

1974 (Atwater & Abrahams, 1983). The Army actually implemented its 60-item Military Applicant Profile (MAP) as a selection device for 17-year old non-high school graduates in 1979 (Walker, 1986). Later, in 1985, the MAP was used to screen all nongraduates. In an attempt to validate and explicate Service education and moral character standards, the Department of Defense funded the development and administration of the Educational and Biographical Information Survey (EBIS) (Laurence, 1987; Laurence & Means, 1985; Means & Perelman, 1984; Steinhaus, 1988). When the General Accounting Office (GAO, 1982) recommended a consolidation across Services of efforts to develop biodata for attrition prediction, the Services responded with the development and 1985 administration of the Armed Services Applicant Profile (ASAP) (see Chapter 3 for detailed discussion of the ASAP).

These and other biographical inventories have covered much the same content areas. In fact, the ASAP drew heavily from the MAP and RBQ. Similar to the content found in civilian biodata, the items assembled by the military have tapped educational achievement; school behavior/attitudes; family relations; work history; status variables; arrests; alcohol/drug use; youthful transgressions; self-perceptions; military attitudes/expectations; and other attitudes and past behaviors (Laurence & Means, 1985). Different inventories have emphasized certain item types more than others. For example, the MAP relied heavily on self-perception items (e.g., How do you usually get along with other people?). In general, though, school behaviors and attitudes are prominent on all these questionnaires. Educational achievement items are also notable. These two item types were also rather consistently effective in predicting attrition. Demographic (status) variables and arrest items have not been shown to be particularly useful attrition predictors. Other item types tend to have modest validities.

Generally, studies of military biodata instruments' ability to predict attrition at various points (e.g., 6, 12, 24, 36 months) during the first term have resulted in uncorrected validities increasing with the length of the criterion from about .10 at the 6 month point to about .30 or so at the 36 month point. Biographical inventories have also demonstrated incremental validity beyond the current education credential screen though the practical value of the increment is debatable.

Biodata Issues and Problems

High validity coefficients and popular appeal aside, strong criticisms of biodata have been levied. The lament, described in Chapter 1, that high school graduation status works as an attrition predictor but no one knows *why*, holds for the majority of items that comprise an empirically-keyed biographical inventory. The construction and scoring of biodata have been referred to as blind, dustbowl, or shotgun empiricism. A common characterization of biodata inventory construction is that a multitude of items are plucked from the sky, without any rhyme or reason, and retained if they adequately contribute to criterion prediction.

Stability

The lack of a strong theoretical foundation for biodata is claimed responsible for the instability of validity. By keying items to the criterion, there is a tendency to capitalize on chance. When weights derived from one sample (particularly a small sample) are applied to a new sample, initial high validities have been noted to diminish (Dunnette, 1966; Guion, 1965; Mumford, Stokes, Owens, & Sparks, 1989). The finding that biodata's relationship with the criterion fades over time and across samples detracts from their major assets--efficiency and high validity. Even favorable biodata reviews caution that keys must be continually monitored and updated when validity wanes (Reilly & Chao, 1982). A pivotal example of dwindling validity is provided by the Army's MAP. The deterioration of this inventory's validity was attributable to sampling deficiencies, compromise, inadequate monitoring, lack of maintenance, and shifts in the characteristics of applicants (Walker, 1989).

Another aspect of a biographical inventory's stability is its reliability. The traditional concept of test reliability asserts that a test should be a consistent measuring device, yielding consistent scores for a given subject. Reliability is typically assessed in one of three ways. There is test-retest reliability which involves presenting the same instrument over two occasions. Another measure is alternate forms reliability, wherein the correspondence of scores across parallel versions of a test is assessed. Third, there is internal consistency reliability which examines the consistency of item responses within the test. Test-retest reliability estimates of biodata, though most appropriate in this case, have generally not been computed (most likely for practical reasons). When feasible to administer the instrument twice, the resulting reliabilities are variable ranging from .30 to .80 or so with a median in the .70s (Campbell & Zook, 1991; Mumford & Owens, 1987;

Wiskoff, Zimmerman, Parker, & Sherman, 1989). The existence of parallel biodata inventories is not a common topic in the extant literature. One attempt to create parallel forms was for the military's ASAP (see Chapter 3 for a description). Cumulative frequency distributions of raw scores across the two forms of the ASAP were nearly identical and therefore suggest high reliability. However, this was but one study, and the *same* group of respondents did not take both forms. Internal consistency evaluations have been reported in the literature. As a result of the heterogeneity of item types and content, internal consistency estimates of biodata reliability have been relatively low (Campbell & Zook, 1991; Mumford & Owens, 1987). So, in a sense, how a person scores may not be stable throughout the biodata "test." Certainly the concept of stable, replicable data is important for biodata but the appropriateness of the most commonly reported internal consistency reliability coefficient is dubious.

Defining Biodata

This chapter asks of biodata, "What's it all about?" Dissatisfaction with the instability of biodata has pushed for a better conceptual understanding. Claiming that biodata inventories work because they sample past behavior and past behavior predicts future behavior is tenuous when one considers the wide array of item types that have been called biodata.

Biodata's success has been attributed to their face validity or the fact that they cover elements in common with the criterion. In some cases this is quite plausible as with Freeberg's (1967) ability to predict college grades from high school grades. A substantial degree of correspondence between predictor and criterion can also be seen between "quitting high school" and "quitting the military." But this one-to-one matching of items to criterion doesn't hold for items about marital status and tatoos as can be found on the ASAP.

Before one can understand *why* biodata work, it is necessary to understand *what* constitutes biodata. Mael (1991) discusses a number of dimensions along which biodata items vary such as: verifiable vs. unverifiable; historical vs. futuristic; actual behavior vs. hypothetical behavior; memory vs. conjecture; factual vs. interpretive; specific vs. general; response vs. response tendency; external vs. internal event; controllable vs. noncontrollable; first-hand vs. second-hand; job relevant vs. non-relevant; non-invasive vs. invasive; equal access vs. non-equal access, and so forth. Items within all of these and other categories, and on both sides of each dichotomy, have been and are considered biodata by some.

Indeed, there has been no consensus as to what is a fitting item for a biographical questionnaire. Legal and ethical considerations may restrict the inclusion of certain blatant or subtle demographic items as well as limiting the inclusion of highly invasive questions or asking about background characteristics that are beyond the respondent's control. For example, an item such as "How old were you when you opened your first bank account," might be removed following a sensitivity review because respondents from different socioeconomic levels don't have equal access to such "behavior." Even the military's World War II "model airplane" question might be objectionable today on similar grounds.

The search for the appropriate content for biographical inventories and the construct or constructs that underlie them is really just beginning. There have been a few attempts at providing a theoretical basis for biodata aside from the simplistic "past predicts future" axiom. Owens, the so-called father of biodata, coined the developmental-integrative theory which his student successors have modified a bit and called the ecology model of biodata (Mumford & Nickels, 1990; Mumford et al., 1989; Owens, 1976; Owens & Schoenfeldt, 1979). This behavioristic model looks not at individual biodata items but at the cohesive pattern that results from choices made to maximize rewards. Essentially, a pattern of items is thought to be predictive because it demonstrates one's history of reinforcement. Further, the model posits that if an experience or situation is reinforcing then the person is likely to repeat such an experience. Such a theory provides a rationale for items dealing with skills, abilities, and knowledge. Mael (1991) invokes another theoretical perspective for biodata--social identity theory. Under this rubric, situations and events are seen to shape behavior such that individuals come to identify themselves with various groups. From this theoretical perspective, biodata items should be historical in nature.

On a less esoteric level, others have suggested that biodata are predictive because such inventories are multidimensional and therefore better cover the criterion space that is also multidimensional (Barge, 1987). Though theorizing is welcomed and may ultimately solve a few of biodata's mysteries, as of yet, even the least abstract notions about biodata's effectiveness (i.e., their heterogeneity or multidimensionality) does not lay a firm blueprint for construction. As Mael (1991) pointed out, studies have not yet unequivocally determined optimal item characteristics (e.g., factual vs. interpretive). Further, such knowledge may solve some methodological problems in construction but not get at the necessary constructs. Are biodata equally effective in predicting all aspects of performance (e.g., skilled technical, motivational)? And if not, what behaviors and item types are best for which criteria? There are a myriad of behaviors that can be covered through biodata. Which ones should be tapped? Questions come faster than answers.

A Rational Approach

Dissatisfaction with the atheoretical nature of "traditional," empirically-keyed biodata paved the way for a rational approach to development and scoring (Hough et al., 1990). Champions of this approach begin, not by assembling items, but with a job analysis to define the criterion domain.   Job and situation analysis results together with information gleaned from the existing literature, and/or life history interviews are used to define the important constructs that biodata should tap. Items, written to cover these constructs, are scored on the basis of their a priori, theoretical or rational relationship to the criterion (Mumford & Fleishman, 1990; Mumford & Owens, 1987; Mumford et al., 1989).   Items have psychological meaning and therefore response options are more or less "correct" and scored accordingly.

The move to rational construction and scoring has served to further blur the distinction between biodata and temperament or personality instruments (Mael, 1991). Though many would not distinguish between biodata and temperament items, those who grapple with the difference might claim that the latter items are individual and dispositional in nature while the former cover input variables (e.g., parent's behavior and demographics) and actual behavior and events which may or may not override one's underlying disposition.   Temperament appears promising because it measures behavioral consistencies across relevant situations. Whether one's temperament is formed on the basis of biodata type inputs and events, or the converse, is left for personality theorists and other psychologists to ponder. Temperament scales and rational scoring of "biodata" bring meaning to the measurement. Items are written to tap dimensions such as achievement, dependability, adjustment, agreeableness, and so on. This rational strategy for construction yields instruments that have construct and content validity.

The Army's MAP had many temperament type items. When the empirically-keyed MAP was pulled from operational use, the Army was in the process of taking a bolder step toward temperament with the rationally developed and scored Assessment of Background and Life Experiences (ABLE). Though personality measures were not known for their validity, an Army-sponsored review (Kamp

& Hough, 1988) indicated that to understand the strengths of temperament measures, neither personality constructs not criteria should be lumped together as was done in previous reviews. This review uncovered promising applications, not for predicting job proficiency but for the more motivational or "will do" aspects of performance. The ABLE was constructed by carefully linking particular constructs to particular criteria (see Chapter 4 of this volume for a thorough discussion of the ABLE). Its many scales have been shown to be fairly good predictors of effort, leadership, discipline, and physical fitness (Hough, Eaton, Dunnette, Kamp, & McCloy, 1990)

Attempts to understand what biodata measure have not unilaterally abandoned empirically derived inventories, but have examined their internal characteristics in addition to noting item validities. Biodata responses have been factor analyzed so as to determine which items cluster together. Results of such analyses have been used to scale biodata on the basis of the relationship of clusters, rather than individual items, to the criterion (Steinhaus, 1988). The types of items identified include: general adjustment, maturity, academic achievement, social effectiveness, independence, self-esteem, achievement motivation, and conformity (Glennon, Albright, & Owens, 1966; Mumford & Fleishman, 1990; Mumford & Owens, 1987). The opinion is that more transportable or generalizable biodata inventories would result from tapping these dimensions (Mumford & Fleishman, 1990). When tapping such dimensions, however, it is important to consider the demographics of the population to which the biodata will be applied. Researchers have often found characteristics such as gender and age to moderate validities (Mumford & Owens, 1987). It would make sense, for example, to use items covering high school activities and achievements among applicants for military enlistment since they typically have just graduated from high school, have little job experience and are about 19 years old. These same items might not work for selecting scientists and engineers.

Another approach to understanding and scoring biodata involves subgrouping (Mumford et al., 1989; Owens, 1976) or constructing profiles of respondents according to their similarity on clusters of biographical items. In this case, the items may be dissimilar, but individuals are similar on a particular set of heterogeneous items. The focus is on the characteristics that discriminate between groups. Owens and colleagues, using their Biographical Questionnaire, have identified subgroups (13 for males and 15 for females) among college students (Owens, 1976).

It is interesting that in the move toward rationally constructed and keyed biodata, the more longstanding results of empirically-keyed inventories have often served as the foundation. For example, construction of a rationally-keyed biodata inventory designed for Navy Reserve Officer Training Corps selection began with a review of empirical items that worked. Furthermore, rational weights were refined according to the construction sample's responses (Hanson, Paullin, & Borman, 1990). Empirically-keyed biodata may not be totally "irrational" either. Not only have factor analyses been performed to gleen a post hoc understanding of biodata content but they have been constructed by researching previous item types that work. The military's EBIS and ASAP were both constructed in such a manner (see Means & Perelman, 1984 and Chapter 3 of this volume for details of EBIS and ASAP construction, respectively). The point is, rational and empirical biodata should not be seen as Yin and Yang measures--they can and do coexist.

How has predictive validity fared with the emphasis placed on construct and content validity? Some findings show the homogenous, rational approach to yield predictive validities comparable to empirically-keyed biodata (Hornick, James, & Jones, 1977; Matteson, 1978). Owens' subgroups have been found to be fairly stable as well (Eberhardt & Muchinsky, 1982; Neiner & Owens, 1982), though the subgrouping approach has not been well researched beyond a rather dated sample of college students and restricted academic criteria. Consideration of the subgrouping approach is usually in the context of classification rather than selection. All-in-all, those who follow the biodata literature conclude that factorial-based, rationally-keyed, and temperament type measures have lower validities than empirically-keyed biodata but are more stable (Mitchell & Klimoski, 1982; Mumford & Owens, 1987). In the spirit of promoting content and construct validity and stability while maintaining predictive validity, rationally-constructed yet empirically-keyed biodata are gaining in popularity. Preliminary results of such efforts are encouraging. Relatively recent studies have demonstrated that empirical keys hold up across cultures (Crosby & McManus, 1989) and across organizations and over time (Rothstein et al., 1990). A mixture of rational and empirical keying was found superior to the former alone for the Leadership Effectiveness Assessment Profile (LEAP)--a conceptually based biodata instrument being developed to predict Air Force officer leadership behaviors (Appel, Quintana, Cole, Shermis, & Grubb, 1991). The LEAP findings are particularly salient since the test of predictive validity was applied to the same items and sample. Other studies pitting empirical and rational keys against each other have suffered from a lack of control of item and sample characteristics.

That is, content differences have coexisted with scoring differences making comparisons questionable.

Response Distortion

While incorporation of a conceptual foundation to biodata shows potential for bringing psychological meaning and stability to biodata, it is also feared to detract from its reliability by leading to response distortion. Self-report temperament measures are known for their susceptibility to socially desirable responding (Becker & Colquitt, 1992) and thus it is feared that contemporary biodata, with their softer items and more transparent rational keys, are more likely to suffer from such distortion (Barge & Hough, 1986; Becker & Colquitt, 1992; Mael & Schwartz, 1992). Not only are there concerns that applicants will respond in a manner portraying themselves in the best light, but that they might deliberately answer falsely or "fake" responses so as increase their chances of being selected.[3] Furthermore, applicants might receive coaching on how to improve their scores from published "study" guides or, particularly in the military's case, from recruiters who have a vested interest in having applicants qualify. Though empirically-keyed biodata are not immune to such distortion, their non-transparent items are thought to reduce the likelihood of faking (Dunnette, 1966).

The literature on faking contains mixed results. Faking *can* occur, but whether it usually *does* take place in applied settings is uncertain (Hansen, Hallam, Hough, Carter, & McGuire, 1990; Haymaker & Erwin, 1980; Hough et al., 1990; Schrader & Osburn, 1977). Also uncertain is whether faking has a deleterious effect on validity. One of the most realistic studies to date suggests that applicants can fake but not much faking occurs in practice. Further, the effects of faking on selection decisions are not large (Becker & Colquitt, 1992). Regardless of such encouraging findings, various assumptions and possible sampling deficiencies have not eased the skepticism regarding the occurrence and effects of faking.

Precautions against response distortion are advocated by biodata experts (Reilly & Chao, 1982; Schrader & Osburn). Strategies for minimizing distortion include: a) deterence through warnings of verification and; b) detection with specifically designed "lie" scales (Hansen et al., 1990; Vezina, 1987). Deterence is also

---

[3]In the military context, compulsory service could induce faking in a manner to reduce the probability of selection.

thought to be enhanced through informed instrument development efforts (Hansen et al., 1990). Regardless of whether empirical-keying is adopted, many authorities advocate certain types of items over others. Historical, objective, discrete, verifiable (in principle), external, and less-transparent items are encouraged (Becker & Colquitt, 1992; Mael & Schwartz, 1992; Schaffer, Saunders, & Owens, 1976). Further, Mumford and colleagues (1989) offer tips for biodata construction that include scattering items covering a particular construct throughout the questionnaire and putting more concrete, verifiable, and specific items up front to retard faking or inducing a socially desirable response set. Mael and Schwartz (1992) created a biodata analog to the ABLE temperament inventory and adminstered it along with the ABLE to cadets at the U.S. Military Academy. The biodata version contained historical, external, objective, first-person, verifiable (in principle) items which were found related to the ABLE temperament constructs. The biodata were found to be comparable to ABLE in terms of validity and less related to social desirability.

Another melding of temperament and biodata designed to maximize predictive validity, promote understanding, and combat faking is represented by the military's Adaptability Screening Profile (ASP). The ASP combines the empirically-keyed ASAP and the rationally scored ABLE--with its response distortion detection scales. Heretofore, the ASP has not been implemented for operational use as an attrition screen, most notably because of concerns over its utility and likelihood of compromise.

Summary

Non-cognitive measures have evolved over the decades, but in the process of efficiently gathering large amounts of life history data in a standardized fashion, problems have surfaced along the way. Clearly, biodata show promise, particularly for hard-to-predict criteria (e.g., criteria other than training or job proficiency), but haphazard measurement and deteriorating validity coefficients have been cause for concern. Attempts to measure the constructs underlying the criteria through a rational approach are both a blessing and a curse. Although rational keys make more psychological sense and are thus less likely to capitalize on chance, they carry greater threats of blatant faking and coaching particularly in the military enlistment selection arena. With the potential for response distortion, instability, invasion of privacy, and the like hanging over biographical inventories, it is no small wonder that the Navy recently reverted to the BIB's ancestor, the WAB, as an attrition screening aid (see Chapters 1 and 5 for more details on the Navy's trial weighted application blank). More conceptual and methodological ground must be covered for biographical inventories before the Services would feel at ease with abandoning their one biodata item predictor of attrition--education credential.

Given that biodata and temperament inventories' strengths are countered by weaknesses or at least numerous uncertainties, it is justifiable to wonder if such instruments will be adopted by the military for the selection of enlisted personnel. Perhaps biodata's central axiom can provide a rhetorical question to consider: If past behavior predicts future behavior, can we expect the military to continue to develop biodata for the selection of enlisted personnel but not to implement such measures operationally?

References

Aamodt, M. G., & Kimbrough, W. W. (1985). Comparison of four methods for weighting multiple predictors. *Educational and Psychological Measurement, 45,* 477-482.

Appel, V. H., Quintana, C. M., Cole, R. W., Shermis, M. D., Grubb, P. D. (1991, December). *The Leadership Effectiveness Assessment Profile (LEAP): Officer instrument field testing and refinement.* San Antonio, TX: UES, Inc., Human Factors & Logistics Division.

Asher, J. J. (1972). The biographical item: Can it be improved? *Personnel Psychology, 25,* 251-269.

Atwater, D. C., & Abrahams, N. M. (1983). *Adaptability screening: Development and initial validation of the Recruiting Background Questionnaire (RBQ)* (NPRDC TR 84-11). San Diego, CA: Navy Personnel Research and Development Center.

Barge, B. N. (1987). *Characteristics of biodata items and their relationship to validity.* Paper presented at the 95th annual meeting of the American Psychological Association, New York, NY.

Barge, B. N., & Hough, L. M. (1988). Utility of biographical data for predicting job performance. In L. M. Hough (Ed.), *Literature review: Utility of temperament, biodata, and interest assessment for predicting job performance* (pp. 91-130). Alexandria, VA: U.S. Army Research Institute for the Behavioral and Social Sciences.

Barge, B. N., & Hough, L. M. (1984). *Utility of biographical data: A review and integration of the literature.* Minneapolis, MN: Personnel Decisions Research Institute.

Barge, B. N., Hough, L. M., & Dunnette, M. D. (1984, December). *Behavioral reliability: A review of academic literature and organizational programs* (Institute Report No. 96). Minneapolis, MN: Personnel Decisions Research Institute.

Becker, T. E., & Colquitt, A. L. (1992). Potential versus actual faking of a biodata form: An analysis along several dimensions of item type. *Personnel Psychology, 45,* 389-406.

Campbell, J. P., & Zook, L. M. (Eds.). (1990). *Improving the selection, classification, and utilization of Army enlisted personnel: Final report on Project A* (ARI Research Report 1597). Alexandria, VA: U.S. Army Research Institute for the Behavioral and Social Sciences.

Cascio, W. F. (1982). *Applied psychology in personnel management* (second edition). Reston, VA: Reston Publishing

Cascio, W. F. (1976). Turnover, biographical data, and fair employment practice. *Journal of Applied Psychology, 61*(5), 576-580.

Childs, A., & Klimoski, R. J. (1986). Successfully predicting career success: An application of the biographical inventory. *Journal of Applied Psychology, 71*(1), 3-8.

Crosby, M. M., & McManus, M. A. (1989). *Can empirically keyed biodata be transported across culture and language?* Farmington, CT: LIMRA International.

Devlin, S. E., Abrahams, N. M., & Edwards, J. E. (1992). Empirical keying of biographical data: Cross-validity as a function of scaling procedure and sample size. *Military Psychology, 4,* 119-136.

Dunnette, M. D. (1966). *Personnel selection and placement.* Belmont, CA: Wadsworth.

Eberhardt, B., & Muchinsky, P. (1982). Biodata determinants of vocational typology: An integration of two paradigms. *Journal of Applied Psychology, 67,* 714-727.

England, G. W. (1971). *Development and use of weighted application blanks* (Rev. Ed.). Minneapolis, MN: University of Minnesota, Industrial Relations Center.

Flyer, E. S. (1963, June). *Prediction of unsuitability among first-term airmen from aptitude indexes, high school reference data, and basic training evaluations* (PRL-TDR-63-17, AD-420 530). Lackland AFB, TX: 6570th Personnel Research Laboratory, Aerospace Medical Division.

Freeberg, N. E. (1967). The biographical information blank as a predictor of student achievement: A review. *Psychological Reports, 20,* 911-925.

Gandy, J. A., & Sharf, J. C. (1988, November). *Biodata instrument for civil service examining: Development and initial validation.* Paper presented at the 30th Annual Conference of the Military Testing Association. Washington, DC: U.S. Office of Personnel Management.

General Accounting Office. (1982, March). *Service programs to reduce costly attrition by developing and using biodata inventories* (FPCD-82-27). Washington, DC: Author.

Ghiselli, E. E. (1966). *The validity of occupational aptitude tests.* New York: Wiley.

Ghiselli, E. E. (1955). *The measurement of occupational aptitude.* Berkeley, CA: University of California Press.

Glennon, J. R., Albright, L. E., & Owens, W. A. (1966). *A catalog of life history items.* Greensboro, NC: The Creativity Research Institute of The Richardson Foundation.

Guinn, N., Johnson, A. L., & Kantor, J. E. (1975). *Screening for adaptability to military service* (Report No. AFHRL-TR-75-30). Lackland Air Force Base, TX: Air Force Human Resources Laboratory.

Guion, R. M. (1965). *Personnel testing.* New York, NY: McGraw-Hill.

Hanson, M. A., Hallam, G. L., Hough, L. M., Carter, G. W., & McGuire, D. P. (1990, August). *Controlling score distortion on the Adaptability Screening Profile (ASP): Preliminary research* (Institute Report No. 197). Minneapolis, MN: Personnel Decisions Research Institutes, Inc.

Hanson, M. A., Paullin, C., & Borman, W. C. (1990). *Development of an experimental biodata/temperament inventory for NROTC selection.* Minneapolis, MN: Personnel Decisions Research Institutes.

Haymaker, J. C., & Erwin, F. W. (1980). *Investigation of applicant responses and falsification detection procedures for MAP* (RBH AR 1-80). Washington, DC: Richardson, Bellows, and Henry, Inc.

Henry, E. R. (1966). *Research conference on the use of autobiographical data as psychological predictors.* Greensboro, NC: The Richardson Foundation, The Creativity Research Institute.

Hough, L. M., Eaton, N. K., Dunnette, M. D., Kamp, J. D., & McCloy, R. A. (1990). Criterion-related validities of personality constructs and the effect of response distortion on those validities. *Journal of Applied Psychology, 75,* 581-595.

Hunter, J. E., & Hunter, R. F. (1984). Validity and utility of alternative predictors of job performance. *Psychological Bulletin, 96,* 72-98.

Kamp, J. D., & Hough, L. M. (1988). Utility of temperament for predicting job performance. In L. M. Hough (Ed.), *Literature review: Utility of temperament, biodata, and interest assessment for predicting job performance.* (ARI Research Note 88-02, pp. 1-90). Alexandria, VA: U.S. Army Research Institute for the Behavioral and Social Sciences.

Laurence, J. H. (1987). *Military enlistment policy and education credentials: Evaluation and improvement* (FR-PRD-87-33). Alexandria, VA: Human Resources Research Organization.

Laurence, J. H., & Gribben, M. A. (1990, July). *Military selection strategies* (FR-PRD-90-15). Alexandria, VA: Human Resources Research Organization.

Laurence, J. H., & Means, B. (1985). *A description and comparison of biographical inventories for military selection* (FR-PRD-85-5). Alexandria, VA: Human Resources Research Organization.

Lockman, R. F., & Lurie, P. M. (1980, February). *A new look at success chances of recruits entering the NAVY (SCREEN)* (CNA CRC 425). Alexandria, VA: Center for Naval Analyses.

Lockman, R. F., & Warner, J. T. (1977, March). *Predicting attrition: A test of alternative approaches* (CNA Professional Paper-177). Alexandria, VA: Center for Naval Analyses.

Mael, F. A. (1991). A conceptual rationale for the domain and attributes of biodata items. *Personnel Psychology, 44*, 763-792.

Mael, F. A., & Schwartz, A. C. (1992). *Capturing temperament constructs with objective biodata.* Paper presented at the 7th Annual Conference of the Society for Industrial and Organizational Psychology, Montreal, Quebec.

Matteson, M. T. (1978). An alternative approach to using biographical data for predicting job success. *Journal of Occupational Psychology, 51*, 155-162.

Means, B., & Perelman, L. S. (1984, June). *The development of the Educational and Biographical Information Survey* (FR-PRD-84-3). Alexandria, VA: Human Resources Research Organization.

Mitchell, T. W., & Klimoski, R. J. (1982). Is it rational to be empirical? A test of methods for scoring biographical data. *Journal of Applied Psychology, 46*, 281-284.

Mumford, M. D., & Fleishman, E. A. (1990, June). *Attributes condtioning the capacity for effective development: Background data measures for predicting performance in variable situations.* Fairfax, VA: Center for Behavioral and Cognitive Studies, George Mason University.

Mumford, M. D., & Nickels, B. J. (1990). Making sense of people's lives: Applying principles of content and construct validity to background data. *Forensic Reports, 3*, 143-167.

Mumford, M. D., & Owens, W. A. (1987). Methodology review: Principles, procedures, and findings in the application of background data measures. *Applied Psychological Measurement, 11*, 1-31.

Mumford, M. D., Stokes, G. S., Owens, W. A., & Sparks, C. P. (1989). Developmental determinants of individual action: Theory and practice in the application of background data measures. In M. D. Dunnette (Ed.), *Handbook of Industrial and Organizational Psychology II*. Palo Alto, CA: Consulting Psychologists Press.

Neiner, A. G., & Owens, W. A. (1982). Relationships between two sets of biodata with 7 years separation. *Journal of Applied Psychology, 67,* 146-150.

Owens, W. A. (1976). Background Data. In M. D. Dunnette (Ed.), *Handbook of Industrial and Organizational Psychology* (Chap. 14, pp 609-644). Chicago, IL: Rand McNally.

Owens, W. A., & Henry, E. R. (1966). *Biographical data in industrial psychology: A review and evaluation.* Greensboro, NC: The Creativity Research Institute of The Richardson Foundation.

Owens, W. A., & Schoenfeldt, L. F. (1979). Toward a classification of persons. *Journal of Applied Psychology, 64,* 569-607.

Palmer, R. R., Wiley, B. I., & Keast, W. R. (1948). *U.S. Army in World War II: The Army ground forces. The procurement and training of ground combat troops.* Washington, D.C.: Historical Division, Department of the Army.

Perry, D. K. (1965, July). *Percentage difference vs. regression in construction application-blank keys* (SP-1963). Santa Monica, CA: System Development Corporation.

Plag, J. A., Goffman, J. M., & Phelan, J. D. (1970). *Predicting the effectiveness of new mental standards enlistees in the U.S. Marine Corps.* San Diego, CA: Navy Medical Neuropsychiatric Research Unit.

Plag, J. A., Goffman, J. M., & Phelan, J. D. (1967). *The adaption of naval enlistees scoring in mental group IV on the AFQT* (Report No. 68-23). San Diego, CA: Navy Medical Neuropsychiatric Research Unit.

Reilly, R. R., & Chao, G. T. (1982). Validity and fairness of some alternative employee selection procedures. *Personnel Psychology, 35,* 1-62.

Rothstein, H. R., Schmidt, F. L., Erwin, F. W., Owens, W. A., & Sparks, C. P. (1990). Biographical data in employment selection: Can validities be made generalizable? *Journal of Applied Psychology, 75*(2), 175-184.

Sands, W. A. (1976, April). *Development of a revised Odds for Effectiveness (OFE) table for screening male applicants for Navy enlistment* (NPRDC TN 76-5). San Diego, CA: Navy Personnel Research and Development Center.

Schrader, A. D., & Osburn, H. G. (1977). Biodata faking: Effects of induced subtlety and position specificity. *Personnel Psychology, 30,* 395-404.

Smith, W. J., Albright, L. E., Glennon, J. R., & Owens, W. A. (1961). The prediction of research competence and creativity from personal history. *Journal of Applied Psychology, 45*(1), 59-62.

Stead, N. H., & Shartle, C. L. (1940). *Occupational counseling techniques.* New York, NY: American Book Company.

Steinhaus, S. D. (1988, March). *Predicting military attrition from educational and biographical information* (FR-PRD-88-06). Alexandria, VA: Human Resources Research Organization.

Steinhaus, S. D., & Waters, B. K. (1991). Biodata and the application of a psychometric perspective. *Military Psychology, 3*(1), 1-23.

Telenson, P. A., Alexander, R. A., & Barrett, G. V. (1983). Scoring the biographical information blank: A comparison of three weighting techniques. *Applied Psychological Measurement, 7,* 73-80.

Uhlman, C. E., Reiter-Palmon, R., & Connelly, M. S. (1991). *A comparison and integration of empirical keying and rational scaling of biographical data items.* Fairfax, VA: George Mason University.

Vezina, P. (1987, September). *Multivariate routines to estimate probable falsification on a pre-existing set of biodata items.* Paper presented at the 95th Annual Convention of the American Psychological Association, New York.

Walker, C. B. (1989, January). *The U.S. Army's Military Applicant Profile (MAP).* Briefing presented to the Joint-Service Selection and Classification Working Group.

Walker, C. B. (1986, June). The Army's Military Applicant Profile: Its background and progress. In *Recent Developments in Military Suitability Research.* Symposium proceedings of the 28th Annual Conference of the Military Testing Association, Munich, Federal Republic of General.

Wigdor, A. K., & Garner, W. R. (Eds.). (1982). *Ability testing: Use, consequences, and controversies* (Parts I & II). Washington, DC: National Academy Press.

Wiskoff, M. F., Parker, J. P., Zimmerman, R. A., & Sherman, F. (1989). *Predicting school and job performance of Marine Security Guards* (PERSEREC TR-90-003). Monterey, CA: Defense Personnel Security Research and Education Center.

Chapter 3_____

The Armed Services Applicant Profile (ASAP)

Thomas Trent[1]

This chapter describes the development of the ASAP and evaluates the validity of biographical data to predict completion of first-term military enlistment. As discussed in Chapters 1 and 2, the objective of the ASAP was to offer a solution to reliance on an increasingly compromised classification of education credentials to control personnel attrition.

First described are a series of item pool constructions, fairness analyses, and pilot tests that led to two biodata forms that were proposed for operational use as part of the Adaptability Screening Profile (ASP). These alternate forms of the ASAP constituted Part-1 of the ASP. Part-2 of the ASP, the Assessment of Background and Life Experiences (ABLE), is subsequently described in Chapter 4. The second part of Chapter 3 presents analyses concerning the ASAP's predictive validity and fairness for subgroups of applicants. The chapter concludes with a discussion of the efficacy of the ASAP in the context of academic standards and operational constraints.

----

[1]Navy Personnel Research and Development Center, San Diego, CA 92152-6800. The opinions expressed in this chapter are those of the author, are not official, and do not necessarily represent those of the Navy Department. The author thanks Steven Devlin and Jack Edwards for their assistance.

Development of a Biodata Inventory

Item Pool Origins

The General Accounting Office report (GAO, 1982) to Congress on employing biodata inventories to reduce personnel attrition resulted in Defense Secretary Caspar Weinberger empaneling the Adaptability Screening Group (ASG), an *ad hoc* committee that represented the Army, Navy, Air Force, and Marine Corps. In responding to the GAO's call for a Joint-Service effort, the role of the ASG was to nominate biodata items for inclusion in the new Department of Defense (DoD) biodata questionnaire. In December 1982, the ASG began reviewing three biodata inventories that were in development or operational use at that time. The instruments are described below.

History Opinion Inventory (HOI). Starting in 1975, the Air Force has used a biodata inventory, the HOI, to screen all recruits during basic training for military adaptability.[2] Based on analyses by Guinn, Johnson, and Kantor (1975), the ASG concluded that (a) the HOI was only marginally predictive of unsuitability discharge and (b) the validation results could not be extrapolated to applicant selection. As a result, none of the 50 HOI true-false items were included in the ASAP item pool.

Recruiting Background Questionnaire (RBQ). The RBQ item pool consisted of 370 items derived primarily from the work of Glennon, Albright, and Owens (1966). Using these items, seven preliminary RBQ forms were developed and administered to Navy recruits starting in the Fall of 1974 (Atwater, Skrobiszewski, & Alf, 1976). Attrition during recruit training was found to be related to 82 of the RBQ items; 70 of the 82 items were also predictive of two-year survival in the Navy. These 70 items were combined with 10 items from Air Force and Army biodata questionnaires to construct two new RBQ forms. From December 1979 through June 1980, the new RBQ forms were administered to 29,464 applicants for Navy enlistment (Atwater & Abrahams, 1983).

Military Applicant Profile (MAP). The primary source of ASAP items was the MAP, a screening instrument for Army applicants who were non-high school

---

[2]The HOI is the first phase of the Air Force Medical Evaluation Test (AFMET). Approximately 6% to 8% of HOI examinees are referred for additional psychological assessment (Fiedler, 1990). The AFMET was also implemented at Navy Recruit Training Centers in October 1991.

diploma graduates. The MAP item pool consisted of 240 items, 85 of which were used operationally (Erwin, 1984). Used from 1979 to 1984, the MAP was developed from military delinquency research during the Korean War (Carleton, Burke, Klieger, & Drucker, 1957) and the Early Experience Questionnaire (Bell, Kristiansen, & Seeley, 1974; Eaton, Weltin, & Wing, 1982).

Construction and Trial Administration of Form-1 and Form-2

The ASG selected 360 items from the RBQ and MAP pools for inclusion in the preliminary ASAP item pool. An additional 21 items were included from undocumented sources. Predictive validity (for attrition) was the primary criterion during item selection. Secondary consideration was given to item content validity with respect to military job relatedness or, more generally, to constructs representing social and institutional adaptability.

Item sensitivity and bias reviews by the Educational Testing Service (Boldt, 1984), the Joint-Service Selection and Classification Working Group, and a biodata expert (W.A. Owens) reduced the pool to 206 items. ASAP Form-1 and Form-2 each included 40 unique and 90 common items; 60 of the common items were from the Army's operational MAP Form-4B. The 80 form-specific items were balanced across the forms according to rational content clusters that were derived from prior MAP research (Eaton et al., 1982).

From December 1984 through February 1985, Form-1 and Form-2 were administered to all individuals ($N = 120,175$) from the continental United States who applied for active duty. While the administration directions instructed the applicants to respond authentically and implied that selected item responses could be verified, only the ASAP's MAP-4B items were used operationally (to screen non-high school graduate applicants to the Army).

Operational Forms Development

Item Scaling. Fully 55,675 of the individuals from the applicant sample subsequently enlisted and were initially tracked through the first 21 months of their enlistment. This accession sample's responses to the ASAP items were keyed to the service completion criterion. A random sample of 26,857 personnel was drawn (model-development sample)[3] with the service completion rates for those personnel endorsing the item response options for the 90 items common to Form-1 and Form-2 resulting in an array of "horizontal" percentages (Guion, 1965). Since items would under some circumstances need to be hand-scored, percentage weights were converted to simple unit weights, using a 3-point (1-2-3) scale (Trent & Quenette, 1992)--the same scale metric used to operationally score the MAP 4-B items. A comparison of this unit weighting procedure to "vertical" percentage difference weighting (see Devlin, Abrahams, & Edwards, 1992) and a regression weighting procedure (Perry, 1965) yielded a conclusion in common with other comparisons (e.g., Aamodt & Kimbrough, 1985) of empirical keying procedures; namely, little practical difference was detected in the validity of the various composite scales.

Item Fairness Analysis. The 90 common and 80 unique items of Form-1 and Form-2 were examined by Wise, Hough, Szenas, Trent, and Keyes (1989) for race- and gender-based fairness and differential validity. Relative to white males, the focal groups (black males, Hispanic males, white females, and black females) showed slight item-mean scoring advantages. Furthermore, none of the items demonstrated adverse impact. To reduce the potential that composite scores would show subgroup differential validity, all items showing negative linear regression slopes for a subgroup were excluded. In all, 28 items were excluded because they violated five item-selection criteria: circumstances not under control of applicant (7 items); racial/ethnic or gender bias (6 items); bias against the economically disadvantaged (8 items); intrusiveness (4 items); and irrational scoring as related to content (3 items).

The ASAP items were matched to a set of constructs shown to be related to military work performance (Peterson et al., 1990). Using these constructs, the keying of item options was reviewed for rational consistency. Minor changes were made in the empirical weights of several item options to reduce irrational scoring.

Pilot Test. Two preliminary 60-item forms of the ASAP (derived from Form-1 and Form-2) were administered in December 1988 to 314 male Navy recruits during boot camp (Barnes et al., 1989). The objectives of this pilot test were to

---

[3]This accession sample was a subset of the applicant model-development sample ($N = 60,235$). In subsequent analyses, the remainder of the accessions were used as a model-evaluation (cross-validation) sample.

(a) determine the appropriate number of operational items in the short forms that would allow equal opportunity for test completion across all levels of aptitude (Armed Forces Qualification Test (AFQT)), and (b) determine the clarity of test booklets, answer sheets, and test administration procedures. Respondents included 32 percent nonwhites; 44 percent of the sample scored below the 50th percentile of the AFQT, including 12 percent in the lowest (IV) aptitude category.

Logistical considerations for subsequent operational testing that would be conducted at Military Entrance Processing Stations (MEPS) and Mobile Examining Team Sites (METS) constrained the ASAP pilot testing period to 20 minutes. Respondents were individually timed, with a mean completion time of 14.8 minutes and a standard deviation of 3.0 minutes. Only 3.2 percent of the recruits, primarily from lower AFQT categories, could not complete all 60 items within the testing session.

Alternate Form Equating. Following the pilot test, Form-A and Form-B were each reduced to 50 items, with item predictive validity (21-month service completion) being the primary inclusion criterion. Each proposed operational form consisted of 21 common items and 29 unique items. The 58 unique items were balanced across forms according to content areas and gender/racial subgroup means and validities. To control context effects, the common items were reordered in the same sequential position on each form, and the unique items were reordered to correspond by content area across forms. Utilizing the Army's "Project A" domain of biodata constructs (Wise et al., 1989), Table 3.1 lists the item content for each form.

Given the emphasis on criterion-related validity, estimates of internal consistency (Cronbach's alpha) resulted in only moderate within-form coefficients--.76 for Form-A and .74 for Form-B. Additional test administration to gather data for test-retest estimates of reliability was not logistically feasible.

The criterion-referenced scale scores were summed across the 50 items to produce a composite ASAP score on each form. The mean scores for Form-A (114.86) and Form-B (114.74) were not significantly different ($t_{120,173}$ = 1.74, p = .082). The standard deviation of Form-B scores (11.02) was slightly higher than the standard deviation for Form-A scores (10.87). Nonetheless, a linear equipercentile equating procedure (Lindsay & Prichard, 1971) demonstrated that the standard error of equating was larger than the error resulting from treating the raw score distributions as equivalent (Waters, 1989). As a result, no conversion of scores was needed for Form-A and Form-B. The similarity of the cumulative percentage distributions for the two forms is portrayed in Figure 3.1.

	Table 3.1	
	Item Content for ASAP Form-A and Form-B	
	Form-A	Form-B
Academic Involvement	9	10
Nondelinquency	8	7
Work Orientation	11	9
Physical Condition	4	5
Interests	2	6
Conscientiousness	2	2
Energy Level	1	1
Military/Independence	1	1
Self-Esteem	1	1
Traditional Values	2	1
Sociability	2	0
Demographics	1	1
Military Career Intentions	1	0
Dominance	2	0
Cooperativeness	1	0
Emotional Stability	0	1
Miscellaneous	2	5
Number of Items	50	50

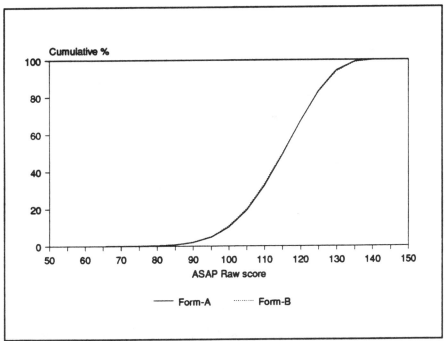

Cumulative %

Figure 3.1 Cumulative percentages of ASAP scores by form

Item Reliability and Validity. Item reliabilities were estimated from corrected item-total score correlations. Mean item-total score correlation coefficients of .21 (*SD* = .11) and .21 (*SD* = .10) were found in Form-A and Form-B, respectively. In the model-development sample, item validities averaged .07 (*SD* = .03) for both forms. (The service-completion criterion is described in the next section of this chapter.) In the model-evaluation sample, the criterion-weighted scoring keys proved to be stable; the mean item validities (r_{pbis} = .07) for the forms were nearly identical to those found with the model-development sample.

Component Structure.   The contemporary school of construct-oriented biodata/temperament inventory construction (e.g., Peterson et al., 1990) is replete with disparaging views about the "shotgun-empiricist" legacy. Like many other instruments, the ASAP is vulnerable to this criticism as its development was largely atheoretical.   That is, ASAP development lacked either a manifest-construct or factor-analytic strategy. The development of the Army's Assessment of Background and Life Experiences (ABLE), the biodata component of Project A (Campbell, 1990), is a counterpoint to the approach on ASAP (see Chapter 4).

For explanatory purposes, the responses of the original applicants (N = 120,175) to the 50 Form-A items and 50 Form-B items were factor analyzed separately using the principal components method (Harman, 1967) with varimax rotation (Kaiser, 1958). Thirteen Form-A components and 14 Form-B components exceeded eigenvalues of 1.00, accounting for 43 percent and 44 percent of the variance, respectively. Examinations of scree plots and iterative interpretations of alternative factor solutions resulted in the extraction of six components that explained 27 percent of the variance in each form.

Intercorrelations of the six factors and other statistics are provided in Table 3.2. The factors within each form were internally heterogeneous (coefficient α for within-component items averaged .51 for Form-A and .47 for Form-B) and moderately intercorrelated. The School Achievement ($F1_A$ and $F1_B$) and Delinquency ($F2_A$ and $F2_B$) factors were the most highly intercorrelated components for both the Form-A and Form-B samples.

Table 3.2
Component Intercorrelations for ASAP Form-A and Form-B Items

	$F1_B$	$F2_B$	$F3_B$	$F4_B$	$F5_B$	$F6_B$
$F1_A$ School Achievement		.41	.26	.22	.32	.19
$F2_A$ Delinquency	.52		.23	.21	.21	.12
$F3_A$ Work Ethic	.25	.18		.14	.18	.17
$F4_A$ Independence	.29	.31	.33		.18	.08
$F5_A$ Social Adaptation	.17	.16	.13	.17		.14
$F6_A$ Physical Involvement	.28	.22	.23	.15	.09	
Eigenvalues						
Form-A	4.90	2.06	1.96	1.72	1.48	1.45
Form-B	4.71	2.10	1.52	1.45	1.52	1.90
N of items						
Form-A	10	9	6	7	11	7
Form-B	14	7	5	8	6	10
Coefficient α						
Form-A	.72	.61	.48	.33	.48	.43
Form-B	.74	.49	.57	.17	.46	.39

Note. Form-A and Form-B component intercorrelations are in bottom-left and upper-right quadrants, respectively. The intercorrelations are between composites of sums of unit-weighted item responses. Form-A applicants, $\underline{N}$ = 61,215; Form-B applicants, $\underline{N}$ = 58,960.

78

The School Achievement component was primarily composed of items previously identified in the rational-construct classification procedure (Table 3.1) as academic involvement and nondelinquency. The academic involvement items included school grades, college aspirations, school course subjects, skipping or failing grades, attitudes toward school and teachers, school club participation, and failing courses. The nondelinquency items concerned school misbehaviors such as disciplinary actions, suspensions, expulsions, and authorized or unauthorized absence.

The Delinquency component ($F2_A$ and $F2_B$) consisted of items concerning drinking, smoking, troublemaking, police/arrest involvement, and running away from home. Work Ethic ($F3_A$ and $F3_B$) involved employment status, quality and duration of employment, and job preference. Independence ($F4_A$ and $F4_B$) items included age, number of full-time jobs, fired from a job, tattoos, independent friends, economic self-suffiency, social independence, self-esteem, and motivation level. Social Adaptation ($F5_A$ and $F5_B$) encompassed items reflecting social alienation, self-esteem, dominance, traditional values, sociability, risk-taking, autonomy from parents, problem solving, flexibility, and sickness. Physical Involvement ($F6_A$ and $F6_B$) tapped items concerning membership on school athletic teams, quality of athletic performance, extent of athletic activities, preference for white-collar or blue-collar work, physical demands of military training, and childhood happiness.

Although the ASAP's components are similar to those reported in the biodata literature (e.g., Mumford & Owens, 1987), a comparison of the ASAP's dimensionality to the dimensions in the Owens[4] Biographical Questionnaire (Owens & Schoenfeldt, 1979) also revealed some differences. Specifically, factor correspondence was evident for School Achievement, Independence, Social Adaptation, and Physical Involvement. However, the ASAP's Delinquency and Work Ethic dimensions did not correspond to any of the Owens factors. Likewise, no ASAP factors corresponded to five of the Owens factors: Socioeconomic Status, Religious Activity, Scientific Interest, Intellectualism, and Sibling Friction. Some of these differences may be explained by socioeconomic differences between the Armed Services applicant sample and Owens' sample of university students.

---

[4]Owens is often referred to as "the father of biodata."

Testing Materials. The proposed implementation of the ASAP/ASP required the following testing materials: test booklets, answer sheets, directions for scoring, test administration manuals, and recruiter brochures.

The 50-item ASAP forms served as the operational portions (Part-1) of the Adaptability Screening Profile's (ASP) Form-01A and Form-01B test booklets. Part-2 of the ASP contained 70-item forms of the ABLE. Part-3 of the ASP contained 28 experimental items that were common to both forms: 14 new ASAP items and 14 ABLE items. Thus, ASP Form-01A and Form 01B each included 148 items.

The answer sheet for the Armed Services Vocational Aptitude Battery (ASVAB) was revised to include a fourth page so that the ASP could be optically scanned. A directions-for-scoring manual with hand-scoring templates was developed in the event of an optical reader failure. An additional manual for test administration documented test-administration protocol at MEPS and METS. A brochure was also written to introduce military recruiters to the ASP. All testing materials were printed by the U.S. Air Force Printing Committee and distributed by the U.S. Military Entrance Processing Command (USMEPCOM) and the Office of Personnel Management (OPM) to support nationwide and overseas administration to enlisted applicants.

By July 1989, the ASP was ready and primed for operational use. In an August 1989 meeting of the Manpower Accession Policy Steering Committee (MAP), however, this implementation was postponed in favor of formulating new alternatives to the use of the biodata instrument. As a result, the Adaptability Screening Project turned in a somewhat new direction that was titled Compensatory Screening Models (CSM). Preliminary development of CSM is described in Chapter 5. The present chapter now turns to an empirical evaluation of the ASAP.

Validity of the ASAP as an Enlistment Screen

Criterion Development

The accession cohort ($N = 55,675$) from the ASAP trial administration was tracked for five years from the time of enlistment application (December through February 1985). As described in Table 3.3, personnel who completed their

80

enlistments, reenlisted, or were continuing their initial enlistments were deemed successful (N = 36,763). Members of this group were scored as "1" on the criterion measure. The median active duty time for this high criterion group was 50 months.

Table 3.3			
Military Service Status by ASAP Score			
		ASAP Score	
	N	Mean	SD
Successful (Code = 1)			
Active Duty/Reenlisted	18,984	119.0	9.5
Completed Term of Service	17,779	118.1	9.6
TOTAL	36,763	118.6	9.5
Not Successful (Code = 0)			
Desertion	176	112.8	9.8
Sexual Perversion	247	115.8	9.1
Drug Use	2,080	111.0	10.1
Criminal/Civil Offense	1,305	112.1	10.6
Fraudulent/Erroneous Enlistment	1,203	112.0	10.5
Behavioral Misconduct/Unsuitability	5,417	112.3	10.2
Training Performance	2,588	112.2	10.3
TOTAL	13,016	112.1	10.3
Excluded from Analysis			
Pregnancy/Parenthood	1,076	117.5	9.0
Dependency	437	117.4	9.9
Medical Condition	3,763	115.0	10.2
Death	159	115.7	9.2
Breach of Contract by Military	97	115.1	11.2
Other Separations	364	121.6	9.1
TOTAL	5,896	116.0	10.0

Individuals (N = 13,016) who failed to complete their enlistment contracts for relatively pejorative reasons (e.g., criminal offenses) were classified as unsuccessful and scored as "0". Attrition occurred most frequently during the initial stages of enlistment--30 percent during the first six months of military service and 50 percent during the first 16 months. This low criterion group scored .64 of a standard deviation (pooled variances) lower on the ASAP, as compared to personnel completing first-term enlistment (M = 118.6; SD = 9.5). Subgroup means ranged from a low of 111.0 for those mustered out of the military for drug-related offenses to a high of 115.8 for sexual offenders.

Members (N = 5,896) who were discharged for nonpejorative reasons (e.g., pregnancy) were not included in the low criterion group and were excluded from further analysis. As belied by relatively low mean ASAP scores, many medical separations are administrative actions of convenience for unsuitability discharges. Nonetheless, medical attrites were excluded to preserve this study's emphasis on predicting opprobrious behavior.

Predictive Validity

Figure 3.2 portrays the association between raw ASAP scores and mean success rates on the criterion in the model-evaluation (cross-validation) sample (N = 24,760). Criterion success rates were considerably lower and more variable at lower ASAP score levels than were success rates at higher ASAP score levels. With respect to disaggregated data, the point-biserial validity coefficient between ASAP scores and the enlistment completion criterion was .29, or .32 when corrected for indirect range restriction.

Incremental Validity. Biodata are generally considered to be non-cognitive assessments; yet in the applicant sample (model-development group, N = 60,235), the correlations of ASAP scores with AFQT scores and high school diploma attainment were .33 and .38, respectively. Table 3.4 shows the incremental validity of the ASAP in relation to these institutional enlistment screens. To account for preselection of the accession sample, subsequent analyses were corrected for curtailment using Lawley's (1943-4) multivariate equations (Sympson & Candell, 1988). Attainment of a high school diploma was correlated (r_{pbis} = .24) with successful service completion, while AFQT scores were only modestly correlated (r_{pbis} = .13) with the criterion.

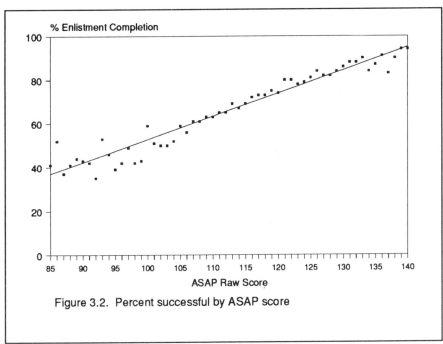

Figure 3.2. Percent successful by ASAP score

Figure 3.2 Percent successful by ASAP score

Variable(s) in Equation	Validity Coefficients		Incremental Change	
	Uncorrected (r_{pbis})	Corrected (r_{pbis})	R^2	F
Table 3.4				
Incremental Validity of ASAP and Institutional Screens				
Stepwise Entry				
1. ASAP	.29	.32	.101	6,776.2
2. H.S. Diploma	.20	.24	.118	1,131.6
3. Alt. Credential	-.12	-.11	.119	67.6
4. AFQT	.07	.13	.120	59.5
Forced Blockwise Entry				
1. H.S. Diploma Alt. Credential AFQT	---	---	.071	1,530.0
2. ASAP	.29	.32	.120	3,334.9

Note. All validity coefficients (point-biserials) and F ratios (R^2 change) were significant at $p < .001$ level.

The ASAP demonstrated somewhat greater predictive validity compared to the AFQT and high school diploma or alternative credential attainment. The AFQT and Alternative Credential variables did not afford a practical increment in R^2 beyond the ASAP score and high school diploma attainment. The biodata measure did exhibit practical incremental validity when the criterion was regressed on the ASAP in addition to AFQT and the education variables. The increment in R^2 of .05 was significant, $(F(1,60230) = 33,349, p < .001)$.

Utility. Employing a linear approximation approach to logistic regression (Aldrich & Nelson, 1984) and data from the model-development sample, parameters were estimated for two comparative models:

(1) $\hat{Y} = \log(P/(1-P)) = .341 + (.317 \text{ x Diploma}) + (.083 \text{ x Alt. Cred.}) + (.002 \text{ x AFQT})$
(2) $\hat{Y} = \log(P/(1-P)) = -.660 + (.010 \text{ x ASAP}) + (.201 \text{ x Diploma}) + (.069 \text{ x Alt. Cred.})$
     $+ (.001 \text{ x AFQT})$

where P is the probability of completing first-term enlistment.

Model (1) represents institutional screening (educational attainment and AFQT), and Model (2) includes the biodata component (ASAP). Using the accession sample (model-development group, $N = 25,019$), the odds ratio $(P/(1-P))$ for each model was initially estimated from a linear probability model $(P = \hat{Y})$ that was adjusted for curtailment (Lawley, 1943-4). That is, the dichotomous criterion was regressed separately on the two sets of explanatory variables to estimate P. The parameters for the logit models were subsequently estimated using the applicant sample (model-development group, $N = 60,235$) and the transformed criterion-- $\log(P/(1-P))$.

The two models were tested for "hit rate" efficiency (proportions of correct decisions) in the accession sample of the model-evaluation group ($N = 24,760$). Employing hypothetical cutting scores, Table 3.5 compares true positive and false negative rates between the institutional screening model and the ASAP-included model. The addition of the ASAP to the institutional model improved the efficiency of prediction. Relative to the rates for the non-ASAP model, success rates of the groups scoring above each of the eligibility cutting scores (correct acceptances) were higher and the success rates for the ineligible groups (erroneous rejections) were lower.

Table 3.5

Cutting Score (% Ineligible)	Correct Acceptances (% True Positives)			Erroneous Rejections (% False Negatives)		
	Model			Model		
	Instit.	+ASAP	delta	Instit.	+ASAP	delta
0	73.3	73.3	0.0	---	---	---
10	75.9	76.3	0.4	50.1	46.7	3.4
20	76.8	78.4	1.6	58.6	52.1	6.5
30	77.6	80.5	2.9	62.7	56.7	6.0
40	78.5	82.1	3.6	65.5	60.1	5.4
50	79.3	83.9	4.6	66.8	62.7	4.1
60	80.2	85.1	4.9	68.3	65.3	3.0
70	81.3	86.1	4.8	69.6	67.7	1.9
80	83.1	87.9	4.8	70.5	69.7	0.8
90	85.6	90.3	4.7	71.9	71.3	0.6

Correct and Erroneous Classification Results of Logit Models

Figure 3.3 is a graphic representation of expectancy statistics from Table 3.5, depicting ASAP-attributable incremental utility from three perspectives: (a) true positive rates, (b) false negative rates, and (c) incremental attrition cost savings. The ASAP-attributed cost savings considered the difference in expected true positive rates between the institutional model and the ASAP-included model. This difference was multiplied by the number of FY 1991 DoD active duty first enlistments ($N = 184,875$). This product estimates the additional number of personnel expected to complete service annually as a function of the ASAP screen.

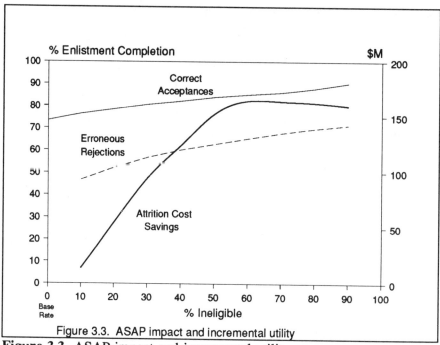

Figure 3.3. ASAP impact and incremental utility

Figure 3.3 ASAP impact and incremental utility

This number was multiplied by an estimated attrition cost of $18,400 per individual (GAO, 1979)[5]. For example, in an Armed Services drawdown scenario that excluded the bottom 20 percent of scorers based on the ASAP-included model, roughly 3,000 additional personnel (of the 184,875 accessions) would successfully complete their contracts each year, saving over $54 million annually in attrition-related costs. This projected savings is predicated on the size and quality of the Armed Services' applicant pool and on associated marginal costs of recruiting remaining constant while the active duty force is reduced. More realistically, the estimated attrition-reduction cost savings would be reduced in proportion to the recruiting costs associated with replacing otherwise qualified applicants who were excluded on the basis of the new selection algorithm.

---

[5]This attrition cost estimate was adjusted for inflation to a 1989 metric.

Fairness of the ASAP

Table 3.6 compares attrition rates, ASAP scores, and ASAP validity coefficients for three sets of subgroups: branch of service, educational attainment, and race by gender. Attrition rates ranged from a low of 21 percent for Air Force personnel to a high of 46 percent for non-high school diploma graduates. Hispanic males, Asian males, and all female subgroups had lower attrition rates than white males, whereas American Indian males had higher attrition rates than white males. Relatedly, ASAP mean scoring was highest for Air Force personnel, high school diploma graduates, Asian males, and most female subgroups.

Table 3.6						
Subgroup Attrition Rates, ASAP Scores, and Validity Coefficients						
			ASAP		Point-Biserial	
	N	Attrition %	Mean	SD	r	SE
Total Sample	49,779	26	116.9	10.1	.28	.004
Service						
Army	22,303	26	115.4	10.3	.28	.006
Navy	10,992	30	115.8	10.5	.30	.014
Air Force	11,191	21	120.8	8.7	.23	.009
Marine Corps	5,293	28	116.8	9.5	.24	.013
Education						
H. S. Diploma	44,003	23	118.2	9.5	.24	.004
Alt. Credential	3,082	46	107.9	9.7	.18	.017
No Credential	2,694	46	106.1	9.2	.17	.019
Males						
White	32,290	27	116.4	10.6	.30	.005
Black	8,355	28	117.4	8.9	.24	.009
Hispanic	1,627	22	116.9	10.1	.21	.024
Asian	633	15	119.0	9.6	.21	.037
Amer. Indian	251	39	112.9	10.5	.26	.057
Females						
White	3,766	25	118.3	9.3	.27	.015
Black	1,813	18	118.7	8.3	.15	.023
Hispanic	187	22	118.4	8.6	.16	.070
Asian	117	10	119.7	8.6	.26	.082
Amer. Indian	56	21	116.3	9.2	.36	.106

Note. All validity coefficients were statistically significant (p < .02).

The uncorrected point-biserial ASAP validity coefficient was .28 for the total accession sample. The predictive validity of the ASAP was lower for Air Force and Marines Corps personnel, non-high school diploma graduates, and non-white Service members. Nonetheless, the ASAP proved to be a valid predictor of first-term enlistment completion for all subsamples.

Adverse Impact. Interest in the utilization of biodata for preemployment screening has been renewed as the Equal Employment Opportunity Commission's (1978) Uniform Guidelines on Employee Selection Procedures, concerning the avoidance of adverse impact in personnel selection, are increasingly germane to Federal Civil Service and Armed Services hiring procedures. For example, a GAO report (1990) has questioned the validity of the Armed Services Vocational Aptitude Battery (ASVAB) and challenged the ASVAB's adverse impact on women and minority recruits in determining eligibility for technical military occupations.[6]

Recent implementation of the Individual Achievement Record (IAR) (MacLane, 1990) for screening Federal Civil Service applicants was intended to equalize selection ratios across races.[7] The IAR is a biodata instrument similar to the ASAP, which also demonstrates little adverse impact on "protected groups." In fact, Table 3.7 shows that, relative to a white male reference group, black males and females, Hispanic males and females, and white females have lower exclusion rates for all but the highest potential ASAP cutting scores. On the other hand, American Indian males demonstrate higher ineligibility rates across the full range of potential cutting scores.

---

[6]In response to the GAO audit, the Personnel Testing Division of the Defense Manpower Data Center (DMDC) together with Service personnel research laboratory representatives conducted an extensive analysis of the equity of the ASVAB. Results showed compelling evidence that the ASVAB subtests are fair and sensitive to women and minorities (see Wise et al., 1992). DMDC's analyses and conclusions were reviewed by the Defense Advisory Committee on Military Personnel Testing, a rotating group of independent, reknowned testing experts, which concurred (see *Biennial report of the Defense Advisory Committee on Military Personnel Testing*, 1992).

[7]Following the *Leuvano v. Horner* 1979 consent decree, the Professional and Administrative Career Examination (PACE) was eliminated on the basis of discrimination against Hispanic and black applicants.

Table 3.7

Percentages of Applicant Subgroups Excluded at ASAP Cutting Score Levels

Total Applicants (120,175)	Males				Females		
	Whites (70,919)	Blacks (21,926)	Hispanics (1,751)	American Indians (734)	Whites (13,187)	Blacks (6,787)	Hispanics (232)
10	13	8	6	17	6	5	5
20	23	17	13	32	14	11	9
30	33	28	22	46	24	20	17
40	42	39	31	54	33	29	25
50	52	50	41	64	44	41	37
60	61	62	54	74	55	55	48
70	70	74	65	84	67	68	65
80	79	84	77	90	78	81	77
90	90	93	88	96	90	92	90

Note. Numbers of applicants are shown in parentheses.

A moderated regression procedure (Pedhazur, 1982) revealed intercept differences that were statistically significant but had less than small effect-sizes (Cohen, 1988) for non-white males (blacks, Hispanics, and American Indians) and black females. No intercept differences were found for white females and Hispanic females. Slope differences were found for Hispanic males and nonwhite females.

Relative to the white males' regression line, the Johnson-Neyman procedure (Johnson & Neyman, 1936) indicated that the ASAP underpredicted the enlistment completion probabilities of 69 percent of the Hispanic male applicants and 79 percent of black females. However, the practical significance of the observed differential validity and prediction does not outweigh the goal of a uniform application of a single ASAP scale across all groups.

89

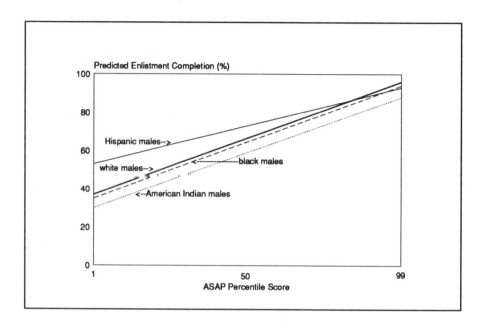

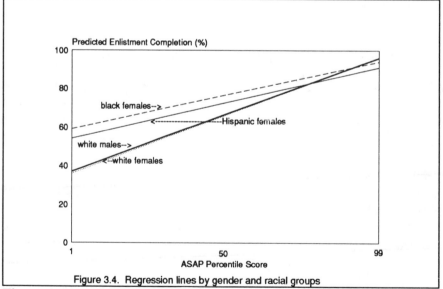

Figure 3.4. Regression lines by gender and racial groups

Figure 3.4 Regression lines by gender and racial groups

Lessons Learned

In nonmilitary applications, self-reported biographical data have outperformed other types of preemployment assessment instruments (cf. Cascio, 1978; Ghiselli, 1966; Reilly & Chao, 1982). The ASAP was a cross-Service distillation of many years of research and development to apply biodata technology to military personnel screening. In a nonoperational mode, the ASAP demonstrated practical incremental validity when it was added to the existing institutional screens (AFQT and educational attainment) to predict first-term enlistment completion.

Crawford and Trent (1987) also found the ASAP to be useful as a prescreening inventory for identifying individuals who are likely to be disqualified from receiving top secret or sensitive information clearances. The composite ASAP score was associated with personal reliability dimensions: nondelinquency, work ethic, independence, academic achievement, athletic involvement, and social adaptation.

Biodata have utility in measuring an array of personal attributes and motivations that are somewhat independent from cognitive aptitude and educational status. This characteristic is especially useful when screening military applicants in high-risk target groups such as non-high school diploma graduates (NHSDGs). In fact, the Navy has begun operational screening of NHSDGs with an old-fashioned "weighted application blank" (Trent, Folchi, & Sunderman, 1991) that includes several biodata variables (e.g., employment status and police record). Yet, DoD has declined to implement the ASAP for operational use. The overriding concern in military application has been the reliability of the ASAP in an operational context that includes thousands of professional military recruiters and the potential for test compromise.

In general, previous research has found the predictive validity of biodata to degrade over time. This instability may be explained by item compromise, capitalization on chance in the empirical scoring procedure, changes in characteristics of the applicant pool, and changes in personnel policies and performance assessment criteria (Hough, 1989). The literature indicates that the long-term stability of empirically keyed biodata requires periodic revalidation and the development of additional items and new scoring keys (Mumford & Owens, 1987). For example, Walker (1988) reported that after a decade of use in screening NHSDG applicants to the Army, the Military Applicant Profile (MAP) was withdrawn because of lack of maintenance and validity failure.

Indeed, many military manpower accession policy managers are avowedly skeptical about the long-term efficacy of biographical and temperament inventories. This concern was formally expressed by the Defense Advisory Committee (DAC) on Military Personnel Testing to the Office of the Assistant Secretary of Defense for Force Management and Personnel (OASD/FM&P). The DAC warned that adaptability screening under operational conditions would likely result in substantial score inflation. The DAC further stated that the development of the ASAP and the Compensatory Screening Model (see Chapter 5) from applicant data that were not obtained under operational conditions would lead to "systematic errors" that would rival the infamous misnorming of the ASVAB (F. Draskow, DAC chair, personal communication to W. S. Sellman, Director for Accession Policy, within OASD/FM&P, May 29, 1991). Given the fact that the ASAP was developed from a military applicant administration (no cutting score was applied), it is unclear how to complete the ASAP's development without using it for operational screening.

This "Catch-22" notwithstanding, results of faking experiments have tended to diminish fears about biodata's susceptibility to applicant dissimulation (see Hough, Eaton, Dunnette, Kamp, & McCloy, 1990). Trent, Atwater, and Abrahams (1986) compared the responses of Navy recruits to ASAP items under a simulated "applicant-fake-good" condition at Time-1 and an "honest-not-for-attribution" condition at Time-2. The "applicant" response simulation resulted in mean ASAP scores that were one-third of a standard deviation higher than the "honest" simulation. Yet, this "applicant" group showed restrained score inflation when compared to a control group that was instructed to fake good. Compared to rational scoring, a criterion-referenced empirical scoring key was found to minimize the impact of response distortion on score inflation.

In addition, these applicant-simulated response scores were significantly reduced by verification warning statements in the test administration instructions. Verifiable items were found to be less susceptible to faking. Asher (1972) has also recommended the use of verifiable items to encourage authentic self-reporting. ASAP items vary in the extent to which they are perceived by the respondent to be potentially verifiable (Hanson, Hallam, & Hough, 1989).

Social desirability and fake-good scales were developed and applied to the ASAP responses of 25,860 applicants for military enlistment (Trent, 1987). As measured by these scales, the magnitude of response distortion was found to be relatively modest for the group as a whole. From a test-retest perspective,

Shaffer, Saunders, and Owens (1986) have also reported that biodata are substantially reliable. Despite the fact that social desirability responding is positively correlated with criterion success, the validity of the ASAP to forecast successful completion of military service was significantly compromised in the subgroup that scored above the mean on the fake-good scale.

It should also be pointed out that other studies have found more clear-cut evidence of applicants' propensity to fake-good on pre-employment tests. In particular, Pannone (1984) found that one-third of applicants for employment as an electrician falsified a job experience item on a biographical questionnaire. Hough (1986) has reported that a validity (unlikely virtue) scale can detect unrestrained, but not subtle, response distortion. With respect to a validity scale embedded in the Army's ABLE, a similar finding is reported in the following chapter.

The development of the ASAP is somewhat at odds with a biodata literature that increasingly emphasizes the importance of construct reference and the job-relatedness of item content. Pace and Schoenfeldt (1977), for example, have suggested that lack of job-relatedness defies the intent of the 1964 Civil Rights Act. Similarly, Pannone (1984) has argued that specific job-referenced and rationally scored biographical inventories are necessary to meet Equal Employment Opportunity Commission guidelines and to control for applicant faking. The job-content validity of the ASAP, however, was constrained by the fact that the Armed Forces screen applicants for hundreds of distinctly different occupational specialties. For this reason, the ASAP is conceptually broad, relatively amorphous, and less operationally transparent compared to more content-specific scales. This last advantage is diminished by the fact that respondents coached on subtle biodata items can distort scores on externally developed scales (Meehl & Hathaway, 1946; Schrader & Osburn, 1977).

The DoD decision to abandon a decade of research and development on the ASAP has alleviated the concern that biographical and temperament inventories will foster an undesirable climate of applicant faking, military recruiter coaching, test compromise, and misnorming of military eligibility standards. However, this decision also abandons the two primary strengths of such inventories. First, a large amount of personal background and temperament data is captured in an economical fashion. Second, many of these data elements are uniquely associated with military performance criteria and cannot be captured by another medium. For these reasons, the love-hate relationship with biodata for military personnel assessment is likely to continue.

References

Aamodt, M. G., & Kimbrough, W. W. (1985). Comparison of four methods for weighting multiple predictors. *Educational and Psychological Measurement, 45*, 477-482.

Aldrich, J. H., & Nelson, F. D. (1984). *Linear probability, logit, and probit models* Beverly Hills, CA: Sage.

Asher, J. J. (1972). The biographical item: Can it be improved? *Personnel Psychology, 25*, 251-269.

Atwater, D. C., & Abrahams, N. M. (1983, December). *Adaptability screening: Development and initial validation of the Recruiting Background Questionnaire (RBQ)* (NPRDC TR 84-11). San Diego, CA: Navy Personnel Research and Development Center.

Atwater, D. C., Skrobiszewski, M., & Alf, E. F. (1976, May). *A preliminary selection of biographical items for predicting recruit attrition* (NPRDC Technical Note 76-6). San Diego, CA: Navy Personnel Research and Development Center.

Barnes, J. D., Gaskins, R. C., III, Hansen, L. A., Laurence, J. H., Waters, B. K., Quenette, M. A., & Trent, T. (1989, March). *The Adaptability Screening Profile (ASP): Background and pilot test results* (IR-PRD-89-06). Alexandria, VA: Human Resources Research Organization.

Bell, D. B., Kristiansen, D. M., & Seeley, L. C. (1974, July). *Initial considerations in the development of the Early Experiences Questionnaire (EEQ)* (ARI Research Memorandum 74-10). Arlington, VA: Army Research Institute for the Behavioral and Social Sciences.

Biennial report of the Defense Advisory Committee on Military Personnel Testing. (1992, November). Washington, DC: Office of the Assistant Secretary of Defense, Force Management and Personnel.

Boldt, R. F. (1984). *Sensitivity analysis of the Joint Service Adaptability Profile.* Princeton, NJ: Educational Testing Service.

Campbell, J. P. (1990). An overview of the Army Selection and Classification Project (Project A). *Personnel Psychology, 43*, 231-239.

Carleton, F. O., Burke, W. A., Klieger, W. A., & Drucker, A. J. (1957, May). *Validation of the Army Personality Inventory against a military adjustment criterion* (PRB Technical Research Note 71). Washington, DC: The Attorney General's Office, Department of the Army.

Cascio, W. F. (1978). *Applied psychology in personnel management.* Reston, VA: Reston Publishing Company.

Cleary, T. A. (1968). Test bias: Prediction of grades of Negro and white students in integrated colleges. *Journal of Educational Measurement, 5*, 115-124.

Cohen, J. (1988). *Statistical power analysis for the behavioral sciences* (2nd ed.). Hillsdale, NJ: Lawrence Erlbaum and Associates.

Crawford, K. S., & Trent, T. (1987). *Personnel security prescreening: An application of the Armed Services Applicant Profile (ASAP)* (PERSEREC TR-87-003). Monterey, CA: Defense Personnel Security Research and Education Center.

Devlin, S. E., Abrahams, N. M., & Edwards, J. E. (1992). Empirical keying of biographical data: Cross-validity as a function of scaling procedure and sample size. *Military Psychology, 4*, 119-136.

Eaton, N. K., Weltin, M., & Wing, H. (1982, December). *Validity of the Military Applicant Profile (MAP) for predicting early attrition in different educational, age, and racial groups* (ARI Technical Report 567). Alexandria, VA: Army Research Institute for the Behavioral and Social Sciences.

Equal Employment Opportunity Commission. (1978). Uniform guidelines on employee selection procedures. *Federal Register, 43*, 38290-38315.

Erwin, F. W. (1984, March). *Development of new Military Applicant Profile (MAP) autobiographical questionnaires for use in predicting early Army attrition* (ARI Research Note 85-11). Alexandria, VA: Army Research Institute for the Behavioral and Social Sciences.

Fiedler, E. R. (1990, November). The Air Force Medical Evaluation Test, basic military training, and character of separation. In *Proceedings of the 32nd Annual Conference of the Military Testing Association* (pp. 392-397). Orange Beach, AL: Naval Education and Training Program Management Support Activity.

General Accounting Office. (1979). *High cost of military attrition can be reduced* (FPCD-79-28). Washington, DC: Author.

General Accounting Office. (1982). *Service programs to reduce costly attrition by developing and using biodata inventories* (FPCD-82- 27). Washington, DC: Author.

General Accounting Office. (1990). *Military training: Its effectiveness for technical specialties is unknown* (PEMD-91-4). Washington, DC: Author.

Ghiselli, E. E. (1966). *The validity of occupational aptitude tests.* New York, NY: John Wiley & Sons.

Glennon, J. R., Albright, L. E., & Owens, W. A. (1966). *A catalog of life history items.* Washington, DC: American Psychological Association (Division 14).

Guinn, N., Johnson, A. L., & Kantor, J. E. (1975, May). *Screening for adaptability to military service* (AFHRL-TR-75-30). Brooks Air Force Base, TX: Air Force Human Resources Laboratory.

Guion, R. M. (1965). *Personnel testing.* New York, NY: McGraw-Hill.

Hanson, M. A., Hallam, G. L., & Hough, L. M. (1989, November). Detection of response distortion in the Adaptability Screening Profile (ASP). *Proceedings of the 31st Annual Conference of the Military Testing Association,* 422-427.

Harman, H. H. (1967). *Modern factor analysis.* Chicago: University of Chicago Press.

Hough, L. M. (1986, June). *Utility of temperament, biodata, and interest assessment for predicting job performance: A review and integration of the literature* (PDRI Report #145). Minneapolis: Personnel Decisions Research Institute.

Hough, L. (1989). *Implementation issues for biodata measures* (Institute Report No. 175). Minneapolis: Personnel Decisions Research Institute.

Hough, L. M., Eaton, N. K., Dunnette, M. D., Kamp, J. D., & McCloy, R. A. (1990). Criterion-related validities of personality constructs and the effect of response distortion on those validities. *Journal of Applied Psychology, 75,* 581-595.

Kaiser, H. F. (1958). The varimax criterion for analytic rotation in factor analysis. *Psychometrika, 23,* 187-200.

Johnson, P. O., & Neyman, J. (1936). Tests of certain linear hypotheses and their applications to some educational problems. *Statistical Research Memoirs, 1,* 57-93.

Lawley, D. A. (1943-4). A note on Karl Pearson's selection formulae. *Royal Society of Edinburgh, Proceedings, Section A, 62,* 28-30.

Lindsay, C. A., & Prichard, M. A. (1971). An analytical procedure for the equipercentile method of equating tests. *Journal of Educational Measurement, 8,* 203-207.

MacLane, C. N. (1990, August). *Issues in scoring the Individual Achievement Record.* Paper presented at the Convention of the American Psychological Association, Boston.

Meehl, P. E., & Hathaway, S. R. (1946). The K factor as a suppressor variable in the MMPI. *Journal of Applied Psychology, 30,* 525-564.

Mumford, M. D., & Owens, W. A. (1987). Methodology review: Principles, procedures, and findings in the application of background data measures. *Applied Psychological Measurement, 11,* 1-31.

Owens, W. A., & Schoenfeldt, L. F. (1979). Toward a classification of persons [Monograph]. *Journal of Applied Psychology, 64,* 569-607.

Pace, L. A., & Schoenfeldt, L. F. (1977). Legal concerns in the use of weighted applications. *Personnel Psychology, 30,* 159-166.

Pannone, R. D. (1984). Predicting test performance: A content valid approach to screening applicants. *Personnel Psychology, 37*, 507-514.

Pedhazur, E. J. (1982). *Multiple regression in behavioral research* (2nd ed.). Fort Worth, TX: Holt, Rinehart, and Winston.

Perry, D. K. (1965, July). *Percentage difference vs. regression in constructing application-blank keys* (SP-1963). Santa Monica, CA: System Development Corporation.

Peterson, N. G., Hough, L. M., Dunnette, M. D., Rosse, R. L., Houston, J. S., Toquam, J. L., & Wing, H. (1990). Project A: Specification of the predictor domain and development of new selection/classification tests. *Personnel Psychology, 43,* 247-276.

Reilly, R. R., & Chao, G. T. (1982). Validity and fairness of some alternative employee selection procedures. *Personnel Psychology, 35*, 1-62.

Schrader, A. D., & Osburn, H. G. (1977). Biodata faking: Effects of induced subtlety and position specificity. *Personnel Psychology, 30*, 395-404.

Shaffer, G. S., Saunders, V., & Owens, W. A. (1986). Additional evidence for the accuracy of biographical data: Long-term retest and observer ratings. *Personnel Psychology, 39*, 791-809.

Sympson, J. B., & Candell, G. (1988). *MVCOR correction for multivariate restriction of range* [computer program]. San Diego, CA: Navy Personnel Research and Development Center.

Trent, T. (1987, August). *Armed Forces adaptability screening: The problem of item response distortion.* Paper presented at the Convention of the American Psychological Association, New York.

Trent, T., Atwater, D. C., & Abrahams, N. M. (1986, April). Biographical screening of military applicants: Experimental assessment of item response distortion. *Proceedings of the Tenth Psychology in the DoD Symposium*, 96-100.

Trent, T., Folchi, J., & Sunderman, S. (1991). Compensatory enlistment screening: A nontraditional approach. *Proceedings of the 33rd Annual Conference of the Military Testing Association*, 565-570.

Trent, T., & Quenette, M. A. (1992, February). *Armed Services Applicant Profile (ASAP): Development and validation of operational forms* (NPRDC-TR-92-9). San Diego, CA: Navy Personnel Research and Development Center.

Walker, C. B. (1988, October). *The U. S. Army's Military Applicant Profile (MAP)*. Paper presented at the meeting of the Defense Advisory Committee on Military Personnel Testing, New Orleans.

Waters, B. K. (1989, April). *ASP 01A and 01B equating*. Paper presented at the meeting of the Joint Services Selection and Classification Working Group, Washington, DC.

Wise, L. L., Hough, L. M., Szenas, P. L., Trent, T., & Keyes, M. A. (1989, September). *Fairness of the Armed Services Applicant Profile (ASAP): Final report*. Washington, DC: American Institutes for Research.

Wise, L., Welsh, J., Grafton, F., Foley, P., Earles, J., Sawin, L., & Divgi, D. R. (1992, October). *Sensitivity and fairness of the Armed Services Vocational Aptitude Battery (ASVAB) technical composites* (DMDC Technical Report 92-002). Monterey, CA: Defense Manpower Data Center.

Chapter 4

The Assessment of Background and Life Experiences (ABLE)

Leonard A. White,
Roy D. Nord, Fred A. Mael, and Mark C. Young[1]

There is mounting evidence that enlisted job performance is multidimensional. Success on the job is the joint product of "can-do" components, such as skills and knowledges, and "will-do" components of effort, discipline, and adaptability. The Services use the Armed Services Vocational Aptitude Battery (ASVAB) and educational attainment as primary preenlistment tools for managing performance after enlistment. While the ASVAB strongly predicts skilled performance, being a high school diploma graduate (HSDG) does not. In contrast, being a HSDG is related to discipline and attrition during the first term of enlistment, while ASVAB is less strongly related to these performance components (Brady, Busciglio, White, & Young, 1991; Eitelberg, Laurence, Waters, & Perelman, 1984; McHenry, Hough, Toquam, Hanson, & Ashworth, 1990).

[1]U.S. Army Research Institute for the Behavioral and Social Sciences, Alexandria, VA 22333-5600. The statements expressed in this chapter are those of the authors and do not necessarily reflect the official opinions or policies of the U.S. Army Research Institute (ARI) or the Department of the Army. The authors give special thanks to Betty Shelly for her assistance in preparing this chapter.

Development of ABLE

This chapter describes the development, validation, and utility of a new temperament inventory called the Assessment of Background and Life Experiences (ABLE; Hough, Eaton, Dunnette, Kamp, & McCloy, 1990), which can supplement both ASVAB and the high school diploma as predictors of job performance. It was developed as part of a long-term personnel research program sponsored by the U.S. Army. This project, known as Project A, was to provide a basis for improving the selection, classification, and job assignment of Army enlisted personnel (Campbell & Zook, 1991). Nearly 60,000 soldiers in 22 Military Occupational Specialties (MOS) have participated in Project A.

Construction of Temperament Inventory for Project A

When research on ABLE began in 1982, temperament measures were generally regarded as poor predictors of job performance criteria. The results of three separate literature reviews (Guion & Gottier, 1965; Pearlman, 1985; Schmitt, Gooding, Noe, & Kirsch, 1984) concluded that personality tests have low validity. Pearlman rank ordered different types of predictors according to their criterion-related validity, and personality measures were at the bottom of the list, with an average correlation of .10.

Hough and her associates (Hough, 1992; Kamp & Hough, 1988) argued that the validity of temperament measures was low because the reviews focused on overall validity without differentiating among criteria. She hypothesized that stronger relationships, both positive and negative, would be found if the correlations between temperament and job performance were averaged within each predictor and criterion construct, rather than across constructs. However, testing this hypothesis requires a taxonomy of temperament and job performance constructs. Unfortunately, despite the widespread use of personality tests, there was no well-accepted taxonomy for these constructs. Recently, though, the five basic dimensions of temperament advanced by Goldberg (1981) and Norman (1963), have received empirical support and acceptance. A sixth component has also been identified by Hogan (1982), yielding the dimensions of Surgency, Agreeableness, Adjustment, Dependability, Affiliation, and Intellectance.

Using Hogan's six dimensions as a starting point for the taxonomic analysis, a total of 146 temperament scales were reviewed and sorted into construct categories. Eighty percent of the scales fit into one of the six dimensions

102

proposed by Hogan and the remaining 20 percent were classified into the additional categories of Achievement, Masculinity, or Locus of Control. (See Kamp & Hough, 1988, for more details on the development of this taxonomy.)

To determine relationships between these temperament constructs and job performance, criterion-related validity studies conducted between 1960 and 1984 were reviewed (Hough et al., 1990). A total of 237 studies involving 339 independent samples were examined in this analysis. Five types of criteria were identified for the first stage of this analysis: job proficiency, training success, educational success, delinquency in the workplace, and commendable job behaviors such as awards and job effort. Table 4.1 presents the validity of the nine temperament constructs against these five criteria.

The average correlation between temperament and job proficiency, the performance measure used in the earlier literature reviews (Pearlman, 1985), was low, with $r=.08$. However, Table 4.1 shows that temperament constructs have validities higher than .08 for predicting other aspects of job performance and training success. Achievement and Locus of Control had the highest correlations with commendable behavior, education, and performance in training. Temperament measures were also strongly predictive of delinquency criteria in the workplace. In a complementary, concurrent study, subject matter experts estimated the likely relationships between these temperament constructs and 72 different criteria of successful soldiering that emerged from a comprehensive job analysis of enlisted occupations (Wing, Peterson, & Hoffman, 1984).

Based on the encouraging results from this literature review and the expert judgments, preliminary temperament measures were developed. An initial battery of items assessing the most promising constructs for predicting enlistee job performance was administered to 11,000 Army trainees in four MOS. Guided by the results from the Preliminary Battery, 10 new temperament scales were developed to form the ABLE: Dominance, Work Orientation, Self-Esteem, Energy Level, Emotional Stability, Cooperativeness, Traditional Values, Nondelinquency, Conscientiousness, and Internal Control. The scales and their underlying construct definitions are shown in Table 4.2 (Hough, et al., 1990).

Table 4.1

Summary of Criterion-Related Studies That Used Temperament Predictors

Construct	Education		Training		Job Effort		Job Proficiency		Delinquency	
	No. of Predictors	Mean r	No. of Predictors	Mean r	No. of Predictors	Mean r	No. of Predictors	Mean r	No. of Predictors	Mean r
Surgency	42	.15	47	.08	21	.04	175	.04	8	-.29
Affiliation	5	-.04	0	---	4	.06	16	-.01	0	---
Adjustment	44	.26	44	.16	21	.13	146	.13	10	-.43
Agreeableness	9	.01	5	.10	4	.02	48	-.01	1	-.31
Dependability	24	.15	26	.11	18	.17	102	.13	10	-.27
Intellectance	6	.18	7	.14	8	-.10	32	.01	1	.24
Achievement	8	.30	4	.33	4	.24	0	---	4	-.35
Masculinity	8	-.16	3	.09	10	.10	0	---	3	.02
Locus of Control	1	.32	2	.29	7	.25	0	---	0	---

Note. Correlations are not corrected for unreliability or restriction in range. Time period covered is 1960 to 1984.

Source: "Criterion-related validities of personality constructs and the effect of response distortion on those validities" by L. M. Hough, N. K. Eaton, M. D. Dunnette, J. D. Kamp, & R. A. McCloy, 1990, in Journal of Applied Psychology, 75, pp. 581-595.

Table 4.2	
Summary of ABLE Temperament Scales and Related Constructs	
Dominance	**Surgency:** The tendency to enjoy positions of leadership and influence over others.
Work Orientation Self-Esteem Energy Level	**Achievement:** The tendency to strive energetically for competence in one's work.
Emotional Stability	**Adjustment:** The tendency to have an even and positive affect and the ability to perform well under stress.
Cooperativeness	**Agreeableness:** The tendency to show pleasantness in interpersonal relationships. A cooperative person is easy to get along with, and a team player.
Traditional Values Nondelinquency Conscientiousness	**Dependability:** The tendency to be discplined, obey and be respectful of rules and regulations, and accepting of authority.
Internal Control	**Locus of Control:** The tendency to perceive reinforcements as being under one's own control.

Source: Hough et al. (1990).

Another scale, Physical Condition, was next added to ABLE. Items on this scale ask about the frequency and degree of one's participation in sports, exercise, and other physical activities. Physical ability tests were considered for measuring this domain; however, this approach was beyond the scope of the project.

Four validity scales were developed as a check on the quality of information from these 11 content scales. A Social Desirability measure was developed to detect inaccuracy in examinees' responses caused by intentional or subconscious attempts to look good. The Nonrandom Response scale, comprised of items with obvious correct answers, is used to detect inaccuracy in one's responses due to random/careless responding. The Poor Impression scale is used to detect faking in an undesirable direction, as might occur during a military draft. Finally, a Self-Knowledge scale was developed to assess differences in how well people "know themselves," based on the hypothesis that self-awareness would improve the accuracy of the self-reports and moderate the validity of ABLE scales. The 11 content scales and four validity scales together make up the 199-item form of ABLE.

The items on the ABLE content scales contain three response options that are rationally scored on a 1-3 scale. Table 4.3 presents descriptive statistics for the 15 ABLE scales from the Project A Longitudinal Validation (LV) sample of FY86/87 Army recruits. (Note: The LV is described in a subsequent section). Intercorrelations among the content scales ranged from .15 to .76, with a mean of .46 (Campbell & Zook, 1991). The alpha coefficients and test-retest reliabilities (1-2 week interval) had medians of .81 and .78, respectively. The test-retest reliability for ABLE scales over a 3-month interval was somewhat lower, with a median of .62 (Wiskoff, Zimmerman, Parker, & Sherman, 1989).

Table 4.3					
ABLE Scale Statistics					
Scale	Number of Items	M	SD	Alpha[a]	Test-Retest[b]
Content Scales					
Dominance	12	27.2	4.65	.84	.79
Energy Level	21	50.5	6.10	.85	.78
Self-Esteem	12	28.8	3.99	.79	.78
Work Orientation	19	45.3	6.22	.87	.78
Emotional Stability	17	40.2	5.61	.84	.74
Cooperativeness	18	44.4	4.99	.81	.76
Traditional Values	11	29.0	2.95	.64	.74
Nondelinquency	20	47.6	5.61	.79	.80
Conscientiousness	15	36.6	4.16	.73	.74
Internal Control	16	41.8	4.45	.77	.69
Physical Condition	6	13.5	3.02	.82	.85
Validity Scales					
Nonrandom Response[c]	8	7.4	1.23	---	.30
Social Desirability	11	16.9	3.38	.66	.63
Poor Impression	23	1.2	1.66	.64	.61
Self-Knowledge	11	26.3	3.18	.61	.64

Note. Analyses based on cases screened for missing data and random responding. N = 44,188-44,371 unless noted otherwise.
[a]N = 39,695-39,904
[b]Based on n = 408-414 with 1 to 2 week test-retest interval.
[c]Data (N = 48,378) were not screened for random responding.

Analyses of subgroup differences on mean ABLE scores indicate that the race and gender effects slightly favored minorities (Campbell & Zook, in press). Blacks scored an average of .23 standard deviation higher than whites on 10 of the 11 ABLE content scales. Hispanics and "other" minorities also scored higher than whites on most ABLE scales. Women obtained higher scores than men in the areas of Dependability, Work Orientation, and Cooperativeness, while men scored higher on Emotional Stability, Dominance, and Physical Condition. Overall, these gender and race differences are small.

ABLE Validation Research

Validation Samples

Concurrent Validation (CV). In 1985, a 209-item ABLE was administered as part of the Army's Project A CV research. A total of 9,430 first-term enlisted personnel in 19 MOS participated in the CV. These 19 MOS constituted a representative sample of the population of Army job requirements.

The data collection took place at 15 continental United States (CONUS) posts and in United States Army Europe (USAREUR). The first-term soldiers in the sample had completed basic and MOS training and averaged 1.5 to 2 years of service. All were informed that the data were being collected for research purposes and would not affect their Army careers in any way. During the CV, soldiers completed a battery of tests developed to predict enlisted job performance. The battery included ABLE, computerized tests of psychomotor ability, measures of spatial ability, and vocational interests (see Peterson et al., 1990, for a more complete description of the predictor battery).

To assess the validity of these new predictor tests, the performance of job incumbents in nine of the 19 MOS was assessed using a broad array of criterion measures (Campbell et al., 1990). These included written tests of job knowledge, hands-on performance tests, supervisory and peer ratings of MOS-specific and Army-wide performance dimensions, and administrative criteria (e.g., awards, disciplinary infractions). Due to budget constraints, the job-specific hands-on tests could not be developed for 10 MOS in the sample. The performance of soldiers in these occupations was measured using the administrative indices, rating scales, and written tests of training knowledge.

107

Longitudinal Validation (LV). The Project A LV began with the administration of a predictor battery to 50,235 new recruits who were entering the Army in FY86/87. Of these, 48,731 soldiers were administered a 199-item ABLE. Ten items were dropped from the ABLE used in the CV. In addition, two MOS were added to the LV sample, for a total of 21, in order to provide better coverage of the ASVAB Aptitude Areas. To determine relationships between these predictor tests and performance, these soldiers were followed and their performance assessed at the end of training and later on the job. At the end of training, a written measure of training achievement was administered and drill instructor and peer ratings of performance were obtained. These soldiers were tracked through their first term of enlistment, and were later administered an updated version of the performance measures used in the CV.

At the time this chapter was written, new measures of second-tour performance were being administered to soldiers in the LV sample, many of whom had been promoted to sergeant. These second-tour measures included tests of job knowledge, hands-on performance tests, administrative criteria, and rating scales covering supervisory and nonsupervisory behaviors in combat and non-combat situations. In addition, two new methods were developed for assessing second-tour performance: role-play exercises and a paper-and-pencil situational leadership measure. The role-plays were used to assess one-on-one interpersonal skills required for counseling and training, and the situational test measured supervisory skill and decision making. Because most soldiers in the original sample did not reenlist, and others transferred to MOS for which performance measures were not developed, it is expected that only a small percentage of those tested on the predictor battery as new recruits will be available for second-tour criterion testing.

Validation Results: First-Term Performance

Analyses of the first-term performance measures indicated that enlisted job performance comprises of five dimensions (Campbell, 1988; Campbell, McHenry, & Wise, 1990). These job performance constructs and their definitions are listed below. These dimensions, along with attrition (discussed below), served as the primary criteria for first-term job performance.

Core Technical Proficiency. This is the skill with which the soldier performs the tasks that are specific to his or her MOS. The score for this construct was derived from written tests of job knowledge and job sample tests representing the core content of the job.

General Soldiering Proficiency. This is proficiency in performing tasks that are common to a wide variety of MOS, such as determining grid coordinates on maps and first aid. The score for this construct was based on job sample and job knowledge measures of general soldiering proficiency.

Effort and Leadership. This reflects the degree to which the soldier exerts effort over the full range of job tasks, perseveres under adverse or dangerous conditions, and demonstrates leadership and support toward peers. Supervisory and peer ratings of performance and the number of commendations and awards received by the soldier were combined to score performance in this area.

Personal Discipline. This reflects the degree to which the soldier adheres to Army rules and regulations and does not create disciplinary problems. Scores for this dimension were based on supervisor and peer ratings of discipline and two indices of disciplinary actions (Articles 15 and Flag Actions) from the soldier's personnel file.

Physical Fitness & Military Bearing. This represents the degree to which the soldier maintains military bearing and stays in good physical condition. Scores on this dimension were based on supervisor and peer ratings of physical fitness and military bearing and the individual's physical fitness qualification score.

The initial table in this section (Table 4.4) summarizes relationships in the LV sample between ABLE (screened for missing data and random responding) and first-term performance in nine MOS. The mean and standard deviation (*SD*) of the validity coefficients across the nine MOS was computed using unit weighting, as opposed to weighting by sample size. These correlations were not corrected for range restriction or unreliability in the predictor or criterion measures. Significance levels for the mean correlations were tested using 95 percent confidence intervals. To compute these confidence intervals, sampling error variance was estimated by dividing the variance of the observed correlations by the number of MOS (see Osburn & Callender, 1992).

Table 4.4

Relation Between ABLE Scales and First-Term Performance Criteria (CV Sample)

Construct	Core Technical Proficiency		General Soldiering Proficiency		Effort & Leadership		Personal Discipline		Physical Fitness & Military Bearing	
	Mean r	SD$_r$	Mean r	SD$_r$	Mean r	SD$_r$	Mean r	SD$_r$	Mean r	SD$_r$
Dominance	.03	.03	.02	.05	.09	.08	-.02	.06	.12	.09
Energy Level	.06	.05	.06	.03	.11	.06	.05	.06	.21	.04
Self-Esteem	.07	.07	.05	.07	.12	.09	.08	.06	.19	.06
Work Orientation	.05	.04	.05	.05	.13	.07	.09	.06	.19	.04
Emotional Stability	.06	.06	.06	.04	.07	.06	.03	.06	.15	.05
Cooperativeness	.05	.07	.05	.07	.11	.05	.11	.04	.11	.04
Traditional Values	.07	.06	.07	.09	.10	.04	.13	.05	.11	.05
Nondelinquency	.05	.06	.09	.06	.12	.08	.21	.05	.12	.06
Conscientiousness	.03	.05	.04	.04	.10	.04	.11	.05	.16	.04
Internal Control	.07	.07	.09	.06	.08	.06	.08	.07	.11	.06
Physical Condition	-.05	.06	-.04	.05	.09	.05	.03	.08	.29	.07
Social Desirability	-.09	.09	-.08	.05	.03	.05	.06	.06	.09	.04
Poor Impression	-.10	.06	-.10	.06	-.07	.06	-.07	.03	-.11	.05
Self-Knowledge	.01	.05	-.04	.07	.04	.07	.01	.05	.09	.04

Note. N=3,236-4,195. p<.05 for all mean correlations except those in italics.

Results show that the Dependability construct scales had the highest correlations with Personal Discipline. Soldiers scoring in the lower third on ABLE Nondelinquency had 66 percent more Articles 15 and Flag Actions than those in the upper third on this measure. By contrast, ASVAB does not differentiate among soldiers regarding discipline. Most ABLE scales had a significant, positive correlation with job effort. The Physical Condition scale predicted physical fitness best. Additionally, ABLE scales generally had small, significant relationships with general and MOS-specific technical skills. It is noteworthy that the correlations in Table 4.4 were typically 25-40 percent lower than the relationships obtained in the CV. Possible explanations for this unexpectedly large disparity in validity are being investigated.

Path-analytic techniques were applied to the CV data (n=4,362) to estimate causal relationships between temperament, cognitive ability, and job performance (Borman, White, Pulakos, & Oppler, 1991). In the model, Dependability had a direct effect and two indirect effects on job effectiveness. Soldiers high in Dependability (as opposed to low) had fewer disciplinary problems, which led to higher performance ratings. In addition, Dependability was positively related to a soldier's knowledge of the facts and procedures required to do his or her job. Job knowledge was the most important determinant of performance capability as measured by hands-on tests of job proficiency. Achievement also had a direct and indirect effect on supervisory ratings. Soldiers higher in Achievement (as compared to low) had more recognized accomplishments (awards, letters of commendation) on the job, which in turn, caused higher performance evaluations. It is noteworthy that Achievement and Dependability show low correlations with cognitive ability, which had its strongest influence on job knowledge.

In other research, ABLE was examined as an indicator of accident propensity. Records of at-fault, ground accidents were obtained from the U.S. Army Safety Center, for cases in the LV sample. Overall, 4.0 percent of the soldiers were responsible for causing an accident during their first three years of service. Results showed that temperament constructs of Adjustment, Dependability, and Achievement were predictive of accident involvement (Matyuf & White, 1991). For example, Infantrymen classified as least dependable (lowest 20%) caused 69 percent more accidents than those in the upper 20th percentile on this measure. By contrast, the ASVAB failed to differentiate among those personnel who caused more accidents.

The ABLE was also used to identify characteristics of successful Marine Security Guards (MSG) who provide security services at U.S. diplomatic and consular facilities throughout the world. National concern over MSG qualifications was heightened in December 1986 after Marine SGT Lonetree admitted that he provided information to the Soviet Union while serving as a MSG in Moscow. Most ABLE scales were significantly related to success in MSG training and the performance of MSG duties in the field (Wiskoff, et al., 1989). As a result of this research, ABLE is being used by the Marine Corps as a diagnostic tool to inform embassy assignment decisions for MSG school graduates.

Validation Results: Supervisory Performance

Results from a field test of the second-tour measures in nine MOS provided an opportunity to examine ABLE's validity for predicting entry-level non-commissioned officer (NCO) performance. The ABLE was administered concurrently with the performance measures to approximately 45 percent of the sample (n=590). Analysis of the criterion scores indicated that a model with six performance dimensions provided the best overall fit to the data (Campbell & Zook, 1991). These six components of second-tour performance are: (a) general soldiering knowledge and skill, (b) technical knowledge and skill specific to the Army MOS, (c) leadership and achievement, (d) personal discipline, (e) physical fitness and bearing, and (f) skill at training and counseling subordinates.

A mean correlation was computed to estimate relationships between ABLE scales (screened for missing data and random responding) and the six performance constructs. The ABLE scales correlated significantly with all six NCO effectiveness dimensions. Leadership and Achievement was best predicted by Dominance and Work Orientation, with mean uncorrected validities from .30 to .34, all p<.05. Within the set of temperament measures, Self-esteem, Dominance, Internal Control, and Conscientiousness showed the strongest positive relationships with effectiveness in training and counseling subordinates, with mean r = .15-.20, all p<.05. The ABLE Physical Condition scale was the most predictive of the Physical Fitness criterion, with mean r = .31, p<.05. The Internal Control and the Achievement scales were the best overall predictors of MOS-specific and general soldiering skills, with mean r = .13-.17, p<.05. In other research to develop measures of supervisory potential for Army civilians (Kilcullen, White, Mumford, Mack, & Rigby, 1991), similar relationships of job performance with Achievement and Dependability were reported, with validities as high as .33.

Summary

Overall, this research shows that temperament constructs have their highest validity against leadership, job effort, and personal discipline and are less strongly predictive of technical proficiency. The ABLE scales have a near zero correlation with the ASVAB and educational attainment, which are the primary measures the Services use in preenlistment screening. Therefore, almost all of ABLE's criterion-related validity is incremental above ASVAB and level of education as a predictor of job performance (McHenry et al., 1990).

Joint-Service Adaptability Screening Program

Attrition of first-term recruits continues to be a concern for the Services. It adds substantially to the cost of recruiting and training, limits the pool of candidates for NCO leadership roles, and has a disruptive effect on unit cohesion and morale (Hosek, Antel, & Peterson, 1989). Researchers have investigated a number of factors that influence attrition during the first term of enlistment. These include personal characteristics, such as educational-credentials, gender, age, and race, and organizational variables, such as one's enlistment term and MOS.

The most important of these variables is educational attainment. The first-term attrition rate for non-high school graduates is nearly double that of high school diploma graduates. In addition, attrition rates are typically higher for females, for recruits with low scores on the Armed Forces Qualification Test (AFQT), and for certain MOS. Blacks and other non-whites have been found to have lower attrition rates than whites, though differences are not always statistically significant (Baldwin & Daula, 1984).

Table 4.5 shows attrition rates in the LV sample for various levels of these variables. Aptitude Categories (i.e., CAT I-IIIA, CAT IIIB, CAT IV) are based on scores on the AFQT. The AFQT is a composite of the ASVAB subtests of Mathematical Knowledge, Arithmetic Reasoning, and Verbal, which is comprised of Paragraph Comprehension and Word Knowledge. It is used for selection into the Armed Services and reported as a percentile score with a median of 50.

		Table 4.5			
		36-Month Attrition Rates for Selected Independent Variables (LV Sample)			
Variable	N	Attrition Rate	Variable	N	Attrition Rate
Age (HSDG)			Age (Non-HSDG)		
17	1,708	.22	17	597	.54
18-20	24,430	.23	18-20	1,630	.47
21-25	7,387	.27	21-25	466	.42
26+	1,976	.33	26+	120	.39
AFQT Aptitude Category			Term of Enlistment		
CAT I-IIIA	23,991	.25	2 Yrs	4,881	.12
CAT IIIB	10,561	.28	3-4 Yrs.	33,433	.28
CAT IV	3,762	.27			
HS Degree			Gender		
HSDG	35,501	.24	Female	3,824	.34
GED	857	.43	Male	34,490	.25
None	1,956	.49			
Race					
White	27,749	.27			
Black	7,904	.24			
Hispanic	1,445	.20			
Other	1,216	.19			

Note: HSDG = High School Diploma Graduate
AFQT = Armed Forces Qualification Test
GED = General Educational Development

Information regarding predictors of attrition is used by the Services to reduce total attrition by modifying recruiting missions and job enlistment standards. The Army places a premium on recruiting high school graduates because earning a high school diploma is the best single measure of a person's potential for adapting to military life. Still, roughly a third of recruits fail to complete their first-term of enlistment (Hosek et al., 1989).

In recent years, there has been increasing Congressional interest in identifying applicants without a high school diploma who can perform effectively. Concurrently, advocates of non-traditional education credentials and alternative diplomas have criticized the policy of using the high school diploma without considering other factors that might relate to attrition. In response, research has been carried out to identify background and other personal characteristics of recruits who are most likely to complete their first-term of enlistment. A Joint-Service biodata measure called the Armed Services Applicant Profile (ASAP) was developed and administered to applicants for all Services in FY85. Scoring keys were generated for the ASAP that can identify applicants in all educational tiers who are likely to complete their first-term of enlistment. A detailed description of the ASAP is presented in Chapter 3 of this volume.

During this same period, data from the Army's Project A longitudinal sample provided a first-time opportunity to examine the validity of ABLE vis-a-vis the high school diploma as a predictor of first-term attrition. Many trainee discharges are attributed to poor adjustment, lack of effort, or lack of discipline. These reasons for attrition fit conceptually with ABLE constructs (e.g., Adjustment and Dependability) which were expected to be predictive of attrition. Within the set of ABLE scales, Emotional Stability was the best predictor of one-year attrition, while Nondelinquency had the highest correlation with 36-month attrition. In other research on attrition, ABLE scales were predictive of the successful completion of the Ranger course and the Special Forces Assessment System which is used to select volunteers for Special Forces training (White, Mael, & Sachs, 1991; DeMatteo, White, Teplitzky, & Sachs, 1991).

Results from these validation samples show that the ABLE and ASAP have incremental validity over educational attainment as a predictor of attrition. Subsequently, shorter versions of the ABLE and ASAP were combined to form a new Joint-Service screening instrument called the Adaptability Screening Profile (ASP). The ASP can supplement the high school diploma and ASVAB in assessing applicants' potential for completing their service contracts. One reason for including the ABLE in the ASP is that it contains a scale to detect faking good. Socially desirable responding may increase if the ASP is used for large-scale operational screening in the Services, and could lead to validity degradation over time (Walker, 1985).

In the remainder of this section we describe the ABLE portion of the ASP and its relationship to attrition. Following this discussion, a cost-benefit methodology is developed for setting enlistment standards on the ABLE. In a later section, the use of the ABLE Social Desirability scale to detect and counter faking is discussed.

Development of ABLE Forms for the ASP

Two 70-item alternate forms of ABLE (ABLE-70) were prepared for the ASP. The ASP has two scored sections: a section with 50 items from the ASAP, and a section with 70 items from the ABLE. Results from a trial administration (Barnes et al., 1989) indicated that respondents could easily finish the 70 items in the 20 minutes available for ABLE testing at Military Entrance Processing Stations (MEPS) and Mobile Examining Team Sites (METS). Within this item limitation, the primary test development goal was to develop two forms that had criterion-related validities comparable to those obtained with the longer, 199-item form. In addition, the new forms were designed to have similar score distributions with a minimum number of common items.

At the time the ASP was developed, factor analyses of the ABLE content scales (excluding Physical Condition) revealed three primary temperament dimensions of Achievement, Dependability, and Adjustment (Campbell & Zook, 1991). Work Orientation, Energy Level, Self-Esteem, and Dominance clustered together to form a broad Achievement factor. Traditional Values, Conscientiousness, and Nondelinquency had unique, high loadings on a single factor of Dependability; and Adjustment was marked by Emotional Stability. Due to limitations in testing time, measures of the ABLE factors of Internal Control, Cooperativeness, and Physical Condition were not included on the ASP.

Two ABLE-70 forms were constructed to measure these three factors. The general scale construction strategy was to select items with unique and high loadings on the factors of Achievement, Dependability, and Adjustment. The correlation of each item with its target scale and all other scales was also examined to estimate the linkages between items and constructs. Items showing

116

low convergent and discriminant validity were eliminated on this basis. Based on previous research (Taylor, 1953), it was suspected that several items on the Energy Level and Cooperativeness scales would have a higher correlation with Emotional Stability than their target scale. This hypothesis was confirmed, and these items were added to the pool of items for measuring Adjustment.

Items for the Achievement scale were chosen from Dominance, Self-Esteem, Energy Level, and Work Orientation. The Dependability scale covered three content areas; Conscientiousness, Traditional Values, and Nondelinquency. The Adjustment scale contained items pertaining to Emotional Stability, Energy Level, and Cooperativeness. The entire Social Desirability scale was included on both forms. Several items were reworded to make them appropriate for applicants to all Services.

Table 4.6 presents summary statistics from the LV sample for ABLE-70 Forms A and B. Although LV examinees responded to the 199-item ABLE, only the ABLE-70 items were scored for the results shown in Table 4.6. These cases had complete data on the three ABLE-70 content scales and were screened for random responding. Raw scores on Achievement, Dependability, and Emotional Stability were added to form a total ABLE score (ABLE-T). The scales on the two forms were closely balanced in terms of content and had nearly identical means and standard deviations.

| Table 4.6 ||||||
| ABLE-70 Scale Statistics ||||||
Scale/Composite	Number of Items	M	SD	Skew	Alpha
Achievement - Form A	23	54.3	7.40	-.28	.87
Achievement - Form B	23	54.3	7.35	-.31	.87
Dependability - Form A	22	54.5	5.93	-.57	.80
Dependability - Form B	22	54.5	5.94	-.62	.81
Adjustment - Form A	14	33.3	4.68	-.62	.80
Adjustment - Form B	14	33.4	4.75	-.58	.80
ABLE-T - Form A	59	142.1	15.27	-.37	.92
ABLE-T - Form B	59	142.2	15.29	-.35	.92
Social Desirability	11	16.8	3.38	.67	.65

Note. N = 40,809. Analyses based on cases screened for missing data and random responding.

A total of 18 items, 6 per content scale, were common to both forms. The ABLE-70 content scales were moderately intercorrelated (r=.48 to .66) and closely related to their target composites on the full ABLE, with r=.93 to .94. This high degree of shared variance was a hopeful sign that the criterion-related validity of the shorter scales would approximate the validities obtained with the longer scales.

Linear equipercentile equating with smoothing at the extreme lower tail was used to equate ABLE-T scores on Forms A and B. The results showed that the standard error of equating was greater than the error that would otherwise exist. Thus, the ABLE-T raw scores provide greater accuracy than the use of equated scores.

The ABLE-T score can be understood as measuring a broad construct of adaptability. It sacrifices some of the interpretability of the individual content scales in exchange for greater reliability, the simplicity of a single score, and less elaborate equating. The Joint-Service ASP program focused on first-term attrition; however the ABLE-T scales are not optimally weighted to predict attrition. A slight gain in the relation of ABLE-T to attrition would result from increasing the relative weights on Adjustment and Dependability in the composite. However, this would reduce the correlation of ABLE-T with overall job performance, which has a relatively higher relationship with Achievement. Thus, weighting of the component scales balances the prediction of job performance and attrition.

An examination of race and gender effects on ABLE-70 showed that, as with the 199-item version, minorities and females did not fare worse than their counterparts. Rather, as shown in Table 4.7, whites generally scored lower than minority group members on the three content scales. As shown in Table 4.8, male recruits scored slightly higher than females in Achievement and Adjustment, while females scored higher than males in Dependability. As a result, using ABLE-T to screen new recruits would not have adverse impact on women or minorities.

Table 4.7					
ABLE-70 (Form-A) Scale Means and Effect Sizes by Race					
	White (n = 29,265)		Black (n = 8,383)		
Scale	M	SD	M	SD	Effect Size
Achievement	53.9	7.60	55.6	6.60	.23
Dependability	54.0	6.12	55.8	5.15	.30
Adjustment	33.1	4.82	34.1	4.14	.21
ABLE-T	141.0	15.72	145.6	13.27	.30
Social Desirability	16.6	3.17	17.1	3.65	.15
	Hispanic (n = 1,530)			Other (n = 1,299)	
Scale	M	SD	Effect Size	M	SD	Effect Size
Achievement	54.9	7.01	.13	54.1	7.36	.02
Dependability	55.8	5.33	.30	54.7	5.62	.11
Adjustment	33.5	4.37	.08	33.0	4.60	-.02
ABLE-T	144.2	13.94	.20	141.8	14.91	.05
Social Desirability	18.8	3.97	.68	18.5	3.89	.59

Note. Effect size is the difference in group means divided by the pooled group standard deviation. Positive effect sizes indicate that whites score lower than the minority comparison group.

Table 4.8					
ABLE-70 (Form A) Scale Score Means and Effect Sizes by Gender					
	Male (n = 36,304)		Female (n = 4,505)		
Scale	M	SD	M	SD	Effect Size
Achievement	54.4	7.40	53.6	7.37	-.11
Dependability	54.3	5.95	55.9	5.62	.27
Adjustment	33.4	4.67	32.9	4.72	-.11
ABLE-T	142.1	15.30	142.3	14.97	.01
Social Desirability	16.8	3.37	16.7	3.39	-.03

Note. Effect size is the difference in group means divided by the pooled group standard deviation.

Relation of ABLE to First-Term Attrition

Logistic regression analysis was the technique used to relate ABLE and other independent variables to 36-month attrition. The sample consisted of 38,362 soldiers with complete data on all variables used in the estimation. Attrition information was obtained from automated enlistment records and merged with the LV database. The records of 277 soldiers who died or separated from the enlisted force to become officers were excluded from the analyses. The attrition variable was coded as 1 when a soldier separated before 36 months of service and as 0 otherwise. Thus a value of .26 means that 26 percent of the sample failed to complete 36 months of service.

Logistic regression was used for this analysis because we wish to model the *probability* of an event (attrition) as a function of various individual characteristics (age, education, etc.). The logit specification is preferred to linear regression for this problem because (a) unlike linear regression, it will always generate predicted probabilities of attrition that range from 0-1, and (b) it will provide unbiased estimates of the standard errors of the coefficients.[2] The general form of the model is:

$$prob(attrit_i=1) = P(a_i) = \frac{1}{1+\exp(-\beta x_i)} , \qquad (1)$$

where x_i is a vector of individual characteristics, $P(a_i)$ is the probability of attrition during a specified time period, and the βs are the parameters to be estimated relating the independent variables to the likelihood of attrition. The use of multiple variables rather than ABLE alone allows us to isolate the effect of the temperament characteristics reflected in ABLE from that of the other factors affecting attrition behavior.

Table 4.9 presents the means, standard deviations, and a brief description of the independent variables used in the estimation. The expected direction of their effect on attrition is also shown. All of the variables are nominal except ABLE-T, ABLE Social Desirability (ABLE-SocD), age, MOS Aptitude Area Composite (MOSAA), and months in the DEP. The MOSAA is a job-specific composite of ASVAB subtests that is used for classification into enlisted occupations. The DEP is a U.S. Army program in which recruits are permitted to contract for a job and then delay enlistment until a training seat becomes available. The DEP gives flexibility to the recruiting system and helps the Army to schedule training evenly throughout the year.

The correlations of explanatory variables in the model with ABLE and 36-month attrition are shown in Table 4.10. The ABLE-T composite has uniformly low correlations with all but one other predictor variable in the model. Age is moderately related to ABLE-T with $r = .20$. Thus, ABLE-T provides information in addition to that contained in currently used predictors of attrition. Most notably, ABLE-T is uncorrelated with educational attainment. The correlation,

---

[2]Probit analysis, which assumes a normal, rather than logistic distribution, would be equally appropriate. We used a logit specification here because it is somewhat more convenient computationally. A third alternative would be to use a duration model to estimate the determinants of time served. There are some difficulties with this approach, primarily due to the fact that attrition is defined as occurring prior to the end of the first term, while most formulations of the duration model assume an unlimited time horizon. Nevertheless, this is an alternative worthy of further exploration.

$r = -.19$, between AFQT and the Social Desirability scale indicates greater faking on ABLE-T by examinees in the lower aptitude categories.

Table 4.9				
Variables in the Attrition Models				
Variable	M	SD	Description	Expected Effect on Attrition
ABLE-T	51.50	28.61	ABLE-T Percentile	-
ABLE-SocD	16.82	3.37	ABLE Social Desirability	-
Age	20.31	2.86	Age in Years	+
CAT IIIB	.28	---	Aptitude Category IIIB=1; Else=0	+
CAT IV	.10	---	Aptitude Category IV=1; Else=0	+
MOSSAA	108.96	11.77	MOS Aptitude Area Composite	-
Combat MOS	.52	---	Combat=1; Noncombat=0	+
DEP	3.85	3.19	Months in DEP	-
ETERM2	.13	---	2 Yr Term=1; 3-4=0	-
GED	.02	---	GED=1; Else=0	-
HSDG	.93	---	HSDG=1; Else=0	-
Female	.10	---	Female=1; Male=0	+
White	.72	---	White=1; Nonwhite=0	+
ATT36	.26	---	Attrition Within 3 Yrs=1; Else=0	NA

Table 4.10			
Correlations of ABLE Scores and 36-Month Attrition with Selected Variables in the Model (N=38,362)			
Variable	ABLE-T	ABLE-SocD	36-Month Attrition
Age	.20	.11	.05
AFQT	.07	-.19	-.06
MOSAA	.07	-.14	-.06
DEP	-.09	-.10	-.09
ETERM2	-.05	-.09	-.12
Combat MOS	.04	.03	.03
HSDG	*.00*	*.00*	-.14
Female	*.01*	-.01	.06
White	-.11	-.13	.04
36-Month Attrition	-.06(.10)[a]	*.01*	---

p < .05 for all coefficients except those in italics.
[a]Adjusted R with ABLE-T^2 and ABLE-T^3 in the model to predict attrition.

Attrition Estimation Results

Estimates of two attrition models, one including all variables, and one excluding ABLE-related variables are presented in Table 4.11. The difference in chi-squares between the two models is 297 (4 df), p<.001, indicating that the addition of ABLE to the model provides a highly significant increase in explanatory power.

Note also that the coefficients on variables in both models are very similar--all differences except that for race are clearly insignificant. The difference on the race coefficient is roughly .08, more than twice the standard error of the beta. Thus, it appears ABLE-T may be accounting for some variance in attrition behavior that would otherwise be mistakenly associated with race. This is consistent with the fact that blacks, who have generally lower attrition rates than whites, also tend to score somewhat higher than whites on the ABLE-T.

123

Table 4.11

Table 4.11		
Logistic Regression Coefficients for 36-Month Attrition (N = 38,362)		
Independent Variables	With ABLE	Without ABLE
Intercept	*.4758 (.4831)*	*.3995 (.4745)*
ABLE-T	**-.0480** *(.0040)*	---
ABLE-T^2/100	**.0748** *(.0095)*	---
ABLE-T^3/10,000	**-.0361** *(.0063)*	---
ABLE-SocD	*.0066 (.0041)*	---
Age	**.0974** *(.0396)*	*.0587 (.0393)*
Age^2	*-.0011 (.0008)*	*-.0004 (.0008)*
CAT IIIB	*.0253 (.0355)*	*.0395 (.0352)*
CAT IV	*-.0514 (.0525)*	*-.0257 (.0519)*
MOSAA	**-.0139** *(.0015)*	**-.0155** *(.0015)*
Combat MOS	**.2438** *(.0267)*	**.2252** *(.0265)*
DEP	**-.1367** *(.0158)*	**-.1349** *(.0157)*
DEP^2	**.0078** *(.0013)*	**.0077** *(.0013)*
ETERM2	**-.9462** *(.0484)*	**-.9029** *(.0481)*
GED	**-.2771** *(.0842)*	**-.2350** *(.0835)*
HSDG	**-1.041** *(.0511)*	**-1.0382** *(.0507)*
Female	**.6935** *(.0422)*	**.6744** *(.0420)*
White	**.4227** *(.0315)*	**.5023** *(.0310)*
Attrition Model X^2	.26 2434 (17df)	.26 2137 (13df)

Note. Standard errors are shown in parentheses. p < .05 for all coefficients except those in italics.

Both the linear and higher order ABLE terms are clearly significant, indicating that the attrition effect of a small change in ABLE score is generally larger for low scorers than for high scorers. Figure 4.1 provides a graphic depiction of this result. The effect of the Social Desirability scale is nonsignificant, indicating that, at least in this sample, the effect of faking on the validity of ABLE as a predictor of attrition is negligible.

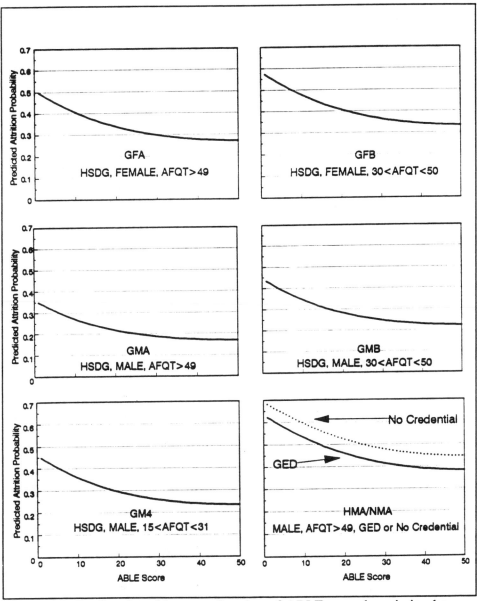

Figure 4.1 Predicted attrition as a function of ABLE score by mission box

In addition to ABLE, most other explanatory variables in the models are also significant. Aptitude category is the primary exception. The nonsignificance of this variable is due primarily to the more powerful effect of job specific aptitude (MOSAA), combined with the high correlation between AFQT and MOSAA. (Note: We tested specifications using both continuous and noncontinuous variables for AFQT, with and without MOSAA. These tests indicated that MOSAA is clearly superior to AFQT alone as a predictor. We retained the categorical form of AFQT in the model because it is the predictor that is used in practice).

The effect of age is more problematic. While the estimated coefficient on the linear term is positive and significant, it should be noted that the interaction between age and education was not included in the model. As shown in Table 4.5, attrition is positively related to age for HSDG recruits, but negatively related to age for non-high school graduates. Thus, the positive coefficient on age in the model may be due simply to the larger percentage of HSDGs in the sample.

The estimated effects of the remaining variables in the model are generally consistent with the results of other research discussed above:

(1) Soldiers in combat MOS are more likely to attrit than soldiers in non-combat jobs.
(2) Soldiers who spend more time in the DEP are less likely to attrit, but this effect diminishes as time in DEP increases.
(3) Soldiers who enlist in the Army for two years are less likely to attrit than those enlisting for three or four years.
(4) Soldiers with a GED are somewhat less likely to attrit than are those with no high-school credential, but considerably more likely than those with a conventional high school diploma.
(5) Whites and females are more likely to attrit than minorities and males.

Relative Strength of Coefficients. Comparison of *magnitudes* across coefficients in this model is less straightforward. Differences in units of measurement among the variables, combined with the inherent nonlinearities of the specification, make it difficult and/or misleading to apply the conventional formula for the partial derivatives of the predicted probability. Nevertheless, an important issue--the relative size of the effect of ABLE compared to other key variables--requires that magnitudes be compared. To do this, we focus on the predicted effect of using each of the selected variables as a selection criterion, and

126

compare the effect of "screening" an additional 5 percent of applicants using each of several variables in turn.

The results of this analysis are shown in Table 4.12. It shows that screening the bottom 5 percent of ABLE scorers (while maintaining current levels on all other variables in the model) would increase the mean ABLE score among accepted recruits from 51.4 to 54.4 and reduce attrition by .86 percent. If, instead, the proportion of non-HSDG accessions were reduced from .08 to .02 and replaced by HSDG accessions, the attrition rate could be expected to drop by 1.17 percent. A similar policy involving replacement of non-credentialed accessions by recruits with GEDs would produce a reduction of .34 percent in the attrition rate. Thus, by this measure, the effect of ABLE in predicting attrition is roughly 75 percent as strong as that of a conventional high school diploma, and more than twice as strong as the effect of a GED.

Table 4.12 Predicted Change in 36-Month Attrition Rate Resulting from a 5 Percent Screen on Selected Independent Variables		
Independent Variable	Change in Mean	Change in Attrition Rate
ABLE-T	51.4 to 54.4	-.86
MOSAA	109.0 to 110.2	-.21
HSDG	.92 to .98	-1.17
GED	.02 to .08	-.34
COMBAT MOS	.52 to .57	+.23

Note. An attrition rate of 1 percent = 1.

The predicted attrition rates as a function of ABLE scores are shown in Figure 4.1 for each of seven categories of recruits. The categories are defined by high school degree status, AFQT category, and gender. These are the "mission boxes" used to define recruiting missions. Within each group, all variables other than ABLE in the model are set at the group means for the mission box. These curves demonstrate that the effect of ABLE on attrition probabilities is most noticeable for scores in the bottom 15 percentiles, with almost no effect in the range from the 40th percentile upward. The curves also reinforce the finding that ABLE and educational credentials provide independent contributions to the prediction of attrition.

Evaluating Model Fit. Evaluating the "fit" of a logit model is troublesome. While the log likelihood ratio and the chi-square statistics are useful for comparing properly "nested" models to each other, there are no convenient and intuitively appealing statistics (like R^2) to measure how well the model predicts what actually occurred in the sample. Most measures rely on rounding probabilities to either 0 or 1. Since this is not the way this model would be used in practice, this approach seems unnecessarily arbitrary. In practice, we are interested in how well the model predicts *on average* for particular subgroups within the population. In particular, we wish to know how accurate its predictions would be within subgroups defined by education, AFQT category, gender, and ABLE score.

To estimate the accuracy of the model, we subdivided the sample into groups defined by these measures, and then calculated the means of actual and predicted rates within each subgroup. The weighted correlations between these means range from .83 (for HSDG male CAT I-IIIA) to .39 (GED male CAT I-IIIA). The average within-group correlation is approximately .73. Thus, the model explains an average of 53 percent (i.e., $.73^2$) of the variance in mean attrition rates when the sample is grouped on ABLE percentile scores.

Cost-Effective Selection Standards

The gain to any organization from using a selection device is simply the reduction in operating costs (and/or the dollar-valued gain in output) due to the use of the selection device, minus any increased costs associated with the selection process. For the purposes of this analysis, we assume that all gains from the use of ABLE are realized in the form of reduced costs--that is, using ABLE to select recruits will lower the average attrition rate among selected applicants. Such a reduction would mean that fewer recruits will be needed to obtain the same fixed level of operating strength. The reduction in the volume of recruits translates into reductions in training and recruitment costs. On the other hand, the use of ABLE to screen applicants will generate new costs of two kinds--a relatively small fixed cost per applicant screened, plus a larger cost to

128

recruit additional applicants to replace those who are screened out because of low ABLE scores.

The objective of this analysis is twofold: First, to determine the optimal (that is, the most cost-effective) minimum ABLE score for each of seven kinds of recruits; and second, to analyze the sensitivity of the optimal level to changes in recruiting costs.

For the purposes of this analysis, we focused exclusively on the use of ABLE as a screen to reduce first-term attrition. Additional benefits of the ABLE screen, such as reduced disciplinary problems and improved job performance, were ignored, primarily because of the difficulty in quantifying these benefits in terms that could be compared to the costs of screening additional applicants. As a result, our recommendations with respect to minimum selection standards are conservative--that is, if the ancillary benefits of ABLE screening were considered, higher minimum standards than those recommended here would be justified. (Note: We do provide an estimate of the expected effects on job performance of implementing the selection standards derived from the cost-benefit analysis, but these benefits were not considered directly in the analysis.)

The difficulties in implementing this procedure have to do with obtaining reasonable estimates of expected attrition and replacement costs, and developing a workable algorithm for evaluating the difference between them under alternative selection policies. We make a number of simplifying assumptions to do this. These will be noted as they become relevant in the following discussion.

Attrition Probabilities

The specifics of the basic attrition model have already been described. We begin here with a more general model to clarify the assumptions inherent in the basic model and show how the actual estimates were used in the cost-benefit analysis.

Denote the probability that an individual (i) with a vector of observable characteristics x_i will be an attrition in job (j) as a_{ij}. Then $a_{ij}=f(x_i;\beta_j)$ represents a set of job-specific equations relating applicant characteristics to the probability of attrition in each job.

129

The first simplification we make is to eliminate the subscript j in this equation, *i.e.*, $a_i=f(\mathbf{x}_i;\beta)$. While previous research suggests that there are important differences both in mean rates and in the effect of certain individual characteristics on attrition across jobs, the data to estimate separate equations for all Army jobs, using ABLE, are not currently available. Furthermore, for purposes of initial selection this simplification has no effect, as long as the assignment of applicants to specific jobs is not affected by changes in the minimum selection standard.

To use the predicted probabilities to evaluate alternative minimum standards, two additional steps are needed. While it would be theoretically possible to calculate a different a_i for each applicant and make eligibility dependent directly on the predicted attrition probability, this approach would be impractical within the Army's current selection and assignment system.

One alternative to direct use of the predicted probabilities is to assume that all elements of $\mathbf{x}$, with the exception of the ABLE score, are at their means, and derive a single minimum ABLE score for all applicants. This approach is undesirable not only because of large and systematic differences in the predicted probabilities among recruits who differ on other elements of $\mathbf{x}$ (high school attainment, for instance), but also because there are significant differences in the replacement costs among groups of applicants.

The approach we take is a compromise between these two extremes. We carry out a separate analysis for each of seven major categories of recruits, where the criteria defining the categories are those used by the U.S. Army Recruiting Command to define major segments of the recruiting market ("mission boxes")-- high school diploma status, AFQT category, and gender.

This treatment of individual differences can be represented as a partition of $\mathbf{x}_i$ into three components indexed by mission box m={1,2, ... 7}. The first, denoted w, contains the ABLE score, the second, $\mathbf{y}_m$, includes the values for the variables that define mission box (m), and the third, $\mathbf{z}_m$, contains the means for mission box m of the other variables in the attrition equation. This yields an equation that can be used to predict the mean attrition probability for each possible ABLE score for each mission box:

$$a_{km} = f_m(w_k, y_m, z_m; \beta) ,$$ (2)

where k={1,2,...99} indexes ABLE percentile scores.

The final step in obtaining the attrition rate prediction needed for the analysis is to calculate mean predicted survival rates for accepted applicants (denoted s_{km}) for each potential ABLE cutoff score. Since ABLE scores are distributed differently within different mission boxes, each a_{km} must be weighted by the percentage (p_{km}) of mission box m falling in the kth ABLE percentile. That is,

$$s_{km} = 1 - \frac{\sum_{j=k+1}^{99} p_{jm} a_{jm}}{\sum_{j=k+1}^{99} p_{jm}} .$$ (3)

Attrition Costs

Attrition imposes significant costs on the Army, including some that are not easily quantified. These include disruptive effects of personnel turbulence, increased administrative requirements, and the discipline-related problems that often precede attrition. These are not accounted for in our analysis, which focuses only on two directly measurable costs associated with first-term attrition-- excess training costs, and increased recruiting needs.

For this analysis, we treat all training costs for a recruit who attrits within the first 36 months of service (the time frame used for the attrition model) as wasted resources. For those attritions that occur early in training, only a small portion of total training cost is saved, since most of these costs are not responsive to changes in class size after a class has started. Even when attrition occurs later, the portion of the training investment that is recouped through subsequent productive service may be relatively small. In the LV sample, 298 (10.7%) soldiers who were tested on the first-term performance measures failed to complete their enlistment terms. The overall level of job performance for these cases was about .8 SD below the mean.

Attrition increases recruiting requirements. In order to maintain fixed levels of trained and deployed manpower, soldiers who fail to complete their tour must be replaced. This requires an increase in recruiting missions. Currently, expected attrition rates are factored into both recruiting missions and training requirements. Thus, a reduction in expected attrition rates due to improved selection is likely to take some time to be reflected in reduced accessions and training loads. In this sense, our analysis is a "steady state" approach, reflecting the savings that accrue after the system has adjusted to the lower loss rates.

Training Costs

The data used to compute training costs were obtained from the Army's Manpower Cost Model (AMCOS). AMCOS is an automated system containing estimated variable costs of Army training, broken down by type of training, budget category, and MOS. For the purposes of this analysis, we extracted only those *variable* costs commonly incurred during basic and advanced individual training. Variable costs (as opposed to fixed costs) are responsive to changes in class size and can be reduced if lower attrition rates lead to reduced training loads. The estimated variable costs include pay and allowances for trainees, operation and maintenance costs for training facilities, and costs for training devices, instructional materials, and travel. The data upon which the AMCOS estimates are based are extracted from the ATRM-159 report compiled by the Resource Management Office of the U.S. Army Training and Doctrine Command (TRADOC).

To obtain average training costs for this analysis, we computed weighted mean costs across all entry-level MOS from the AMCOS data base, using 1986 accessions by MOS as the weights. The resulting estimate of average training cost was $14,130.

Recruiting Costs

The costs of using a selection device include not only the minimal costs of actually administering the selection instrument, but also the cost of attracting and processing the applicants required to replace those screened out by the device. While in some cases these costs may be negligible, for the Army they are not. A substantial proportion of the recruiting budget is spent to attract applicants, and, for the most desirable recruit categories, these costs escalate at an increasing rate as the total number of needed applicants rises. Thus, any policy that increases the required number of these applicants will increase not only total recruiting costs, but also the average cost per applicant.

In addition to this effect, estimation of replacement costs must account for the substantial processing costs incurred prior to determining an applicant's eligibility under a proposed selection device. In the case of ABLE, this determination will probably be made only after the recruit reaches the Military Entrance Processing Station (MEPS). At this point, most of the costs of a signed contract will already have been incurred. It is not feasible to determine a precise value for the proportion of total recruiting costs that should be charged to a rejected applicant. For the purposes of this analysis, we assume a proportion of 80 percent.

To estimate either replacement costs or the value of reductions in recruiting loads due to reduced attrition, reasonable estimates of recruiting costs are necessary. For these, we have relied on estimates produced by Kearl and Nord (1990) for their analysis of cost-effective recruit selection policy. Their approach varies from previous work in this area primarily in that they develop estimated non-constant marginal cost (MC) curves for all categories of recruits (i.e., "market segments"). Previous research has generally assumed that costs are constant for all groups other than high-school graduates in the upper half of the AFQT distribution (i.e., mission boxes GMA and GFA). Recent evidence from the difficult recruiting year of FY89 suggests that this assumption may not be valid.

The general approach used by Kearl and Nord (1990) assumes that, for each market segment, there exists some number of recruits (designated Q_m^0) that can be obtained at a constant marginal cost, P^0. P^0 represents the basic costs of screening and processing applicants, and is assumed to be the same for all market segments. Q^0 varies across market segments, and is assumed to depend on the population within each segment, the "taste for military service" within each segment, and external economic conditions (e.g., youth unemployment).

In order to attract applicants in excess of Q^0, the Army must expend additional resources in the form of added recruiters, advertising, bonuses, and other incentives. The amount of these resources needed to attract each new applicant is assumed to rise as the number of needed recruits increases. Thus, if the required number of recruits is $Q^* > Q^0$, the first Q^0 recruits can be obtained at a constant cost of P^0, but the remaining $Q^* - Q^0$ recruits can be obtained only at an increasing average cost.

Nord and Kearl assumed that the elasticity of marginal cost with respect to changes in demand was constant (i.e., that a 1% increase in demand would produce a constant percentage increase in marginal costs). They relied on the results of previous research on enlistment supply (e.g., Daula & Smith, 1986) for their estimate of 1.25 as the marginal cost elasticity for high quality recruits. (Note: The marginal cost elasticity is the inverse of the supply elasticity, so this implies an assumed supply elasticity of .8.) They developed their estimate of the elasticity for non-quality groups by finding the rate that would minimize the mean square error (MSE) when the marginal cost function was used to "backcast" the Army recruiting budget for the period 1984-1990. The resulting value was .83 (implying a supply elasticity of 1.2), producing a mean square error (MSE) of less than 4.2 percent for the six budget years. The resulting equation for marginal recruiting cost in the case of $Q^* \geq Q^0$ is:

$$MC_m = P^0 + \frac{P^0(Q^* - Q^0)}{Q^0}e^{\eta} = P^0(1 - e^{\eta}) + \frac{P^0 Q^*}{Q^0}e^{\eta}. \qquad (4)$$

Note that, for $Q^* < Q^0$, $MC_m = P^0 = \$3,270$ for all market segments.

Table 4.13 shows the values of Q^0, Q^*, and η used for each mission box ("market segment"), as well as the resulting estimate of marginal cost at Q^*.

These estimates of recruiting costs seem quite reasonable. They generate fairly accurate estimates of actual recruiting budgets, and the differences in costs across mission boxes are sensible. Nevertheless, there is clearly a great deal of uncertainty associated with these costs, and a key issue that will be addressed later in this section is the sensitivity of the "optimal" selection standard to errors in recruiting cost estimates.

Determining the Optimal Cut Score

For this analysis, we define the "optimal" cut score for each mission box to be the one that provides the largest total reduction in training and recruiting costs for that mission box. Since total recruiting costs vary as a function of the number of recruits accessed within each mission box, this approach does *not* say anything about the most cost-effective distribution of recruits across mission boxes. Instead, it starts with two assumptions: (a) the total number of "successful" (that is, non-attriting) recruits is fixed; and (b) the proportions of accessions within each mission box are also fixed. The first assumption allows us to measure the benefits of an ABLE screen in terms of the reduction in the total number of recruits needed to produce the target level of non-attritees. The second allows us to treat each mission box separately, and avoid the difficult problem of simultaneously evaluating tradeoffs among cost, attrition, and other aspects of performance across all recruit categories.

Table 4.13 Recruiting Market Characteristics					
Market Segment	Description	Q^o	Q^*	η	$MC(Q^*)$
GMA	Grad, Male, I-IIIA (AFQT>49)	22,000	48,000	.8	$16,758
GFA	Grad, Female, I-IIIA (AFQT>49)	5,000	10,000	.8	$14,683
GMB	Grad, Male, IIIB (AFQT=31-49)	10,500	15,000	1.2	$ 6,494
GFB	Grad, Female, IIIB (AFQT=31-49)	1,700	2,000	1.2	$ 4,598
GM4	Grad, Male, IV (AFQT=10-30)	20,000	5,000	∞	$ 3,270
HMA	Grad, Male, I-IIIA (AFQT>49)	4,700	5,000	1.2	$ 3,750
NMA	Nongrad, Male, I-IIIA (AFQT>49)	4,700	5,000	1.2	$ 3,750

Note: Q^o = number of recruits available at constant marginal cost
Q^* = total number of recruits needed
η = elasticity of marginal cost with respect to changes in Q^*
$MC(Q^*)$ = marginal cost of Q^*

The key variables in the analysis are (a) the number of *recruits* needed to yield the target level of successful completions, which depends on the predicted attrition rate of acceptees; and (b) the number of *applicants* required to find enough qualified recruits, which depends on the selection standard.

Let Q_m^* represent the initial mission for recruits of type m, and ρ_{km} denote the proportion of Q_m^* needed to achieve the same number of successful completions as that provided by Q_m^* at the baseline survival rate (s_{0m}). Then where s_{km} is

$$\rho_{km} = \frac{s_{0m}}{s_{km}}, \tag{5}$$

the predicted survival rate with an ABLE screen at the kth percentile. Thus, if the initial mission is 1,000 recruits, the "baseline" attrition rate is 30 percent, and predicted attrition among acceptees at a cut score of 20 is 25 percent, then $\rho_{20,m}$ is (.70/.75)=.933. Out of the initial mission of 1,000 recruits, 700 will complete their tours. By screening out the 20 percent of applicants with the highest attrition risk, the same number of completions can be obtained with only 933 recruits.

The number of *applicants* per accepted recruit is denoted by

$$\lambda_{km} = \frac{1}{r_{km}} \quad k=\{1,2,\cdots,99\}, \tag{6}$$

where r_{km} is the selection rate associated with a cut score at the kth percentile (*i.e.*, $r_{km}=1-.01k$).

We can now use these two quantities to arrive at an expression for average recruiting cost. First, we can simplify notation by dropping the subscript m and defining a constant $C=\exp(\eta)P^0/Q^0$. Then (4) can be rewritten as $MC=P^0(1-\exp(\eta))+CQ^*$.

The number of recruits needed when an ABLE screen at the kth percentile is imposed is $Q_k^r=\rho_k Q^*$, and the associated number of applicants required is $Q_k^a=\lambda_k \rho_k Q^*$.

The average cost *savings* per recruit resulting from reduced accession requirements is simply the total cost savings divided by the reduction in requirements. Since total cost is the integral of the marginal cost function, average cost (when $Q^* \geq Q^0$) can be expressed as

136

$$AC_k^r = P^0 (1-e^{\eta}) + \frac{1}{1-\rho_k} \int_{x=\rho_k}^{1} CQ^* x\, dx$$

$$= P^0(1-e^{\eta}) + \left.\frac{CQ^*}{2(1-\rho_k)}x^2\right|_{x=\rho_k}^{1} \qquad (7)$$

$$= P^0(1-e^{\eta}) + \frac{CQ^*}{2}(1+\rho_k).$$

Similarly, the average cost per recruit *added* to replace rejected applicants is

$$AC_k^a = P^0(1-e^{\eta}) + \frac{\alpha}{\rho_k(\lambda_k-1)} \int_{x=\rho_k}^{\rho_k\lambda_k} CQ^* x\, dx$$

$$= P^0(1-e^{\eta}) + \left.\frac{CQ^*\alpha}{2\rho_k(\lambda_k-1)}x^2\right|_{x=\rho_k}^{\rho_k\lambda_k} \qquad (8)$$

$$= P^0(1-e^{\eta}) + \frac{\alpha CQ^*}{2}\rho(\lambda_k+1),$$

where α is a scaling factor indicating the proportion of recruiting costs that must be expended to attract an applicant (we shall use $\alpha=.8$ for this analysis). In the case of constant marginal costs (i.e., $Q^* < Q^0$), these average costs are equal to P^0 and αP^0, respectively.

We can now use (7) and (8) to produce an expression for the net cost or benefit of any given selection standard. Let *TRN* denote per capita training costs, *TEST* be the cost per applicant for test administration (assumed constant for all recruit types), and V_k be the savings per accession at a cut score of k. Then the savings (which may be negative) of applying the selection instrument using a cut score of k can be expressed as:

$$V_k = (1-\rho_k)(TRN+AC_k^r) - (\lambda_k-1)AC_k^a - \rho_k\lambda_k TEST. \tag{9}$$

Using (7) and (8) we can rewrite (9) in terms of the original marginal cost as follows:

$$V_k = (1-\rho_k)TRN - \rho_k\lambda_k TEST + P^0(1-\rho_k)(1-e^\eta)$$

$$+ \frac{CQ^*}{2}(1-\rho_k^2) - \alpha P^0(\lambda_k-1)(1-e^\eta) - \frac{\alpha CQ^*}{2}\rho_k(\lambda_k^2-1)$$

$$= \left[TRN(1-\rho_k)\right] - \left[\rho_k\lambda_k TEST\right] + \left[P^0(1-e^\eta)(1+\alpha-\rho_k-\alpha\lambda_k)\right] \tag{10}$$

$$+ \left[\frac{CQ^*}{2}\left(1-\rho_k^2+\alpha\rho_k-\alpha\rho_k\lambda_k^2\right)\right],$$

for $Q^*{\geq}Q^0$.

For the case of constant marginal costs ($Q^*{<}Q^0$), this expression is simplified to:

$$V_k = (1-\rho_k)TRN - \rho_k\lambda_k TEST + P^0(1+\alpha-\rho_k-\alpha\lambda_k). \tag{11}$$

In spite of being somewhat messy, this expression provides useful insights into the effect of changes (or errors in estimating) training, recruiting and testing costs on the value of the selection device. First, it may help to note that $0{\leq}\rho{\leq}1$. (Even a useless predictor will not *reduce* the baseline survival rate.) Second, note that $\lambda{\geq}1$ (the selection ratio cannot be less than 1). Examining the bracketed terms from left to right we see that:

(a) The effect of an increase in training costs will always be an increase in savings, since $(1-\rho){\geq}0$. The magnitude of the change will depend on the effectiveness of the predictor--that is on the ratio S_0/S_k.

(b) Increases in processing costs will, of course, always reduce savings. This effect is dampened when the selection device is highly accurate (producing small values for ρ). This occurs because an accurate selection device tends to lower the number of applicants that must be processed. The effect is amplified as λ

becomes large (i.e., as the selection ratio becomes smaller), because a low selection ratio increases the processing burden. However, as will be seen in the graphs of this function, this term can sometimes generate negative savings for high selection ratios, even when a lower selection ratio produces positive savings. The reason for this is that high selection ratios can, at best, produce only small reductions in the attrition rate, but in order to achieve those reductions, the costs of testing all applicants must be incurred.

(c) The effect of changes in recruiting costs on savings is more difficult to discern. This is to be expected, since these costs act simultaneously in opposite directions in the savings function, increasing savings via reductions in the number of recruits, and reducing savings via increases in the number of applicants. To gain a sense of this relationship, it is easiest to examine equation (11). Here we can see that the effect of an increase in P_0 will depend on the values of λ_k, ρ_k, and α. In terms of the underlying variables, the effect will depend on the baseline survival rate S_0, on the validity of the predictor--that is, on the ratio of S_0 to S_k, and on the selection ratio r. An increase in P^0 will increase savings if and only if $(1+\alpha)>(S_0/S_k+\alpha/r)$. For the case of $\alpha=1$, this condition becomes $(1/r+S_0/S_k)<2$. Using this expression, we can see that the lower the baseline survival rate (low values of S_0) and the higher the validity of the predictor (high values for S_k), the broader the range of selection ratios over which increases in recruiting costs will increase savings.

Note, however, that even for favorable values of S^0 and S_k, this range is relatively restricted. First, note that the maximum range is $.5 \leq r \leq 1$. This formula can also be rewritten in terms of the "true negative" rate for the predictor, β (i.e., β is the proportion of rejected applicants who would have been attritions if accepted). This makes explicit the direct relationship between r and the maximum attainable reduction in the attrition rate, and allows us to replace S_k with $S_0+\beta(1-r)$. For a 75 percent attrition rate among rejectees ($\beta=.75$), and a low initial survival rate of .5, increases in P_0 will increase savings only for selection ratios greater than .84. In addition, if the baseline survival rate is increased to the level of .7 observed in our sample, the required selection ratio rises to .975. If the cost of attracting applicants is significantly lower than that of obtaining recruits (i.e., α is small), these ranges will expand. On the other hand, the effect of increasing marginal recruiting costs (as in (10)) will be to narrow the ranges. Thus, in general, the effect of increased recruiting costs will be a reduction in savings, and consequently, an increase in the optimal selection ratio.

Results

Perhaps the implications of these equations are best understood by examining their graphs. These are shown in Figure 4.2. The dotted curve on each graph shows the total savings at each cut score resulting from reductions in training and recruiting costs due to reduced accession requirements. The solid curve shows the *net* savings after the costs of testing and attracting additional applicants are accounted. The optimal cut score is the one coinciding with the maximum point on each of the net savings curves. Table 4.14A summarizes the optimal cut scores, savings per applicant, and total potential savings for each group.

Clearly the greatest savings can be obtained by screening applicants who do not possess a high school diploma. The optimal ABLE-T cut score for applicants with no credentials is 11, providing savings of $165.80 per accession. For applicants who possess an alternative credential such as a GED, the optimal cut score is 10, only 1 point lower, but the savings per applicant at that level are significantly less--only $109.20. The relatively high savings for these groups result from the combined effect of a low baseline survival rate, the strong relationship between ABLE scores and attrition rates at the low end of the ABLE range, and relatively low recruiting costs.

The graphs also show that a slight saving can be achieved by screening applicants in the lowest aptitude category (i.e., CAT IV). The recommended cut score for this group is 7, producing a savings per accession of $10. This recommendation is driven primarily by the low (and constant) marginal recruiting costs for this group. The graphs also show a potential savings of $27.00 per accession by imposing a cut score of 7 on CAT IIIB HSDG females. In practice, however, it is unlikely that a screen that differentiates purely on the basis of gender would be used. The results reported in Table 4.14A are based on 36 month attrition propensities. A similar pattern of findings was obtained in an analysis of the utility of ABLE screening to reduce 21-month attrition (White, Nord, & Mael, 1989).

140

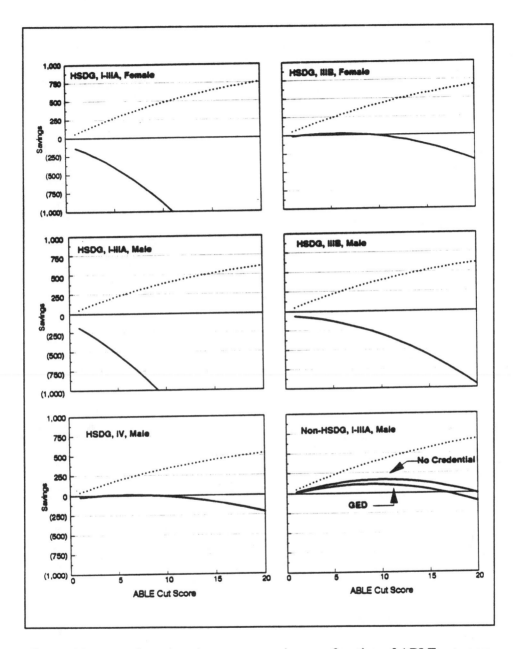

Figure 4.2 Net and gross savings per accession as a function of ABLE cut score. (Solid curve shows estimated net savings per accession at each ABLE score. Dotted curve shows estimated "gross" savings - that is, savings due to reduced accession requirements, not accounting for costs of attracting and processing additional applicants.)

Table 4.14A				
Proposed ABLE-T Cut Scores and Associated Savings				
Group	Cut Score	Attrition Rate of Rejectees	Savings Per Accession	Total Savings
HSDG, I-IIIA	0	---	---	---
HSDG, IIIB	0	---	---	---
HSDG, IV	7	.39	$ 9.80	$ 49,000
GED, I-IIIA	10	.57	$109.20	$546,000
NHS, I-IIIA	11	.63	$165.80	$829,000

Additional benefits of implementing ABLE selection standards are derived from improved job performance, such as increased job effort and reduced indiscipline for recruits. Regression analyses were applied to the LV data to estimate the relationship between ABLE-T and overall job performance by mission box. The overall performance score was a weighted composite of the performance construct scores, with weights obtained from military personnel working in each MOS (Sadacca, Campbell, White, & DiFazio, 1989). Table 4.14B shows the predicted effect of imposing the optimal cut score on expected overall job performance for the one mission where that effect on performance is statistically significant.

There has been considerable research in the civilian sector to estimate the dollar value of changes in job performance; however, its relevance to military performance has been questioned. Nord and Kearl (1991) argue that because a volunteer Army must compete with civilian markets to attract manpower, the value to society of the output produced by that manpower must be approximately equal to its price. The cost of first-term performance was estimated to be $56,580 over 39 months, which is the average term of first enlistment (Nord & Kearl, 1991). This cost includes basic military compensation, and average recruiting and training costs. To estimate the dollar value of one standard deviation increase in performance, we used the conservative rule that it is equal to 40 percent of salary

(Hunter & Schmidt, 1982). Applying this rule to the GED, CAT I-IIIA mission, the average performance gain of .08 SD is valued at $1,810 per accession over the average enlistment term. Thus, the cut score recommendation for this group is conservative and could be slightly higher if the gains from improved performance were considered.

Table 4.14B				
Expected Change in Performance Associated with Proposed ABLE-T Cut Scores				
Group	Cut Score	SD Change in Mean ABLE Score	Standardized Regression Weight	SD Change in Performance
HSDG, I-IIIA	0	---	.18*	---
HSDG, IIIB	0	---	.15*	---
HSDG, IV	7	.13	.08	---
GED, I-IIIA	10	.28	.29*	.08
NHS, I-IIIA	11	.26	.11	---

*$p<.05$.

Sensitivity Analysis

Equation (10) could be used directly to identify the most cost-effective selection ratio by simply calculating values of V_k over a selected range of k, and then selecting the k that produced the maximum value of V_k. A more computationally efficient method is to find an expression for the derivatives of (10) and (11) with respect to changes in the selection ratio. The maximum of V will occur at the point where the derivative is 0, so we can solve directly for the "optimal" cut score. We do this by noting that the survival rate S_k is a function of the inverse selection ratio (λ). Thus, the derivative of (10) can be written as: and, for the case of $Q^*<Q^0$,

143

$$\frac{\partial V}{\partial \lambda} = TRN\frac{S_0}{S_k^2}\frac{\partial S_k}{\partial \lambda_k} - TEST\left(\frac{S_0}{S_k} - \frac{S_0}{S_k^2}\frac{\partial S_k}{\partial \lambda_k}\lambda_k\right)$$
$$+ P^0(1-e^\eta)\left(\frac{S_0}{S_k^2}\frac{\partial S_k}{\partial \lambda_k} - \alpha\right) - \alpha\lambda CQ\frac{S_0}{S_k} \qquad (12)$$
$$+ \frac{CQ}{2}\frac{\partial S_k}{\partial \lambda_k}\frac{S_0}{S_k^2}\left(\frac{2S_0}{S_k} + \alpha(\lambda^2 - 1)\right),$$

$$\frac{\partial V}{\partial \lambda} = TRN\frac{S_0}{S_k^2}\frac{\partial S_k}{\partial \lambda_k} - TEST\left(\frac{S_0}{S_k} - \frac{S_0}{S_k^2}\frac{\partial S_k}{\partial \lambda_k}\lambda_k\right)$$
$$+ P^0\left(\frac{S_0}{S_k^2}\frac{\partial S_k}{\partial \lambda_k} - \alpha\right). \qquad (13)$$

Again, these equations are messy, but useful. In addition to their value as a means of calculating the optimal cut scores, they provide a convenient way of evaluating the sensitivity of the results to errors or changes in the key variables affecting the estimated savings. By straightforward algebraic manipulations, (12) and (13) can be solved for any of the right-hand side variables. The result is an expression for the value of the selected variable at the point where the savings function is maximized. For example, by solving for marginal cost, we obtain a function describing the marginal cost that would make any given cut score optimal. By comparing this value to the estimate of marginal cost actually used, we can see how the optimal level would change if the baseline estimate were changed. Figure 4.3 shows the results of this exercise for each mission box.

By examining Figure 4.3, we see that the recommendation of no screen for high quality accessions is highly insensitive to errors in the estimated recruiting costs. Costs for male, CAT I-IIIA, HSDG recruits would need to be cut by more than half before a cut score greater than 0 was optimal. On the other hand, relatively small changes in the estimates for low quality groups could produce substantial changes in the recommended selection rate.

144

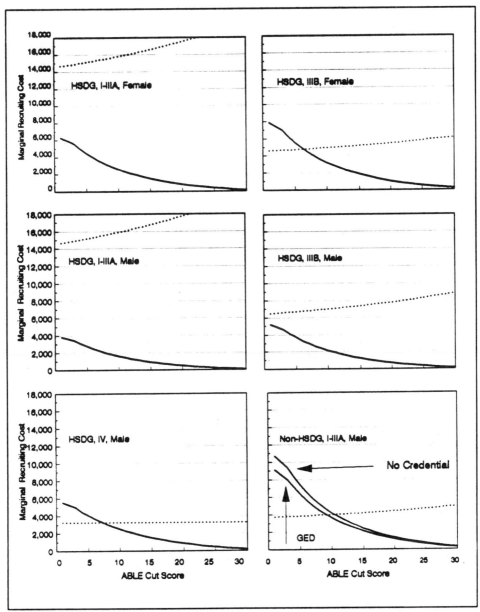

Figure 4.3 Sensitivity of optimal cut score to recruiting cost estimates. (Solid curve is maximum recruiting for which each ABLE cut score is cost-effective. Dotted curve shows estimated actual recruiting cost at each cut score.)

Equation 11 can also be used to compute the validity needed to make any given cut score optimal. Validity could be increased slightly by using all of the ABLE scales, optimally weighted to obtain the probability of attrition used in the analysis. Greater increases in validity could be obtained by using other variables (e.g., age, ASVAB) along with ABLE to predict attrition. The small validity gains from using the entire ABLE would raise the optimal cut score for the lower quality groups. However, given the assumptions in the model developed here, the validity of the screening composite would need to be increased substantially before a nonzero cut score was recommended for the HSDG CAT I-IIIA mission.

Use of ABLE for Classification

The cost-benefit analysis developed in this section shows the utility from ABLE screening. The ABLE can also be used for classification in a complementary way with selection, in order to account for MOS differences in ABLE's predictive validity and the cost of training new recruits. Preliminary analyses of Project A data provide some indication that ABLE's relationship to attrition and performance varies by job. If this differential prediction holds, performance gains would be obtained by using ABLE to place recruits into jobs where they are most apt to perform well. Additional savings would result from allocating recruits with a high probability of completing their enlistment into MOS where the cost of training is high.

An advantage of using ABLE for classification is that potential benefits from reduced attrition and improved performance can be achieved without incurring significant increases in recruiting costs. In addition, potential problems with faking and coaching might be reduced if ABLE were used to help applicants find jobs in which they were most likely to adapt successfully and perform well, rather than to screen candidates from service.

Fairness Issues

The fairness of ABLE as a predictor of first-term attrition and job performance was evaluated using data from Project A. Sufficient cases were available to examine the differential validity and differential predictability of ABLE for three comparisons: (a) blacks and whites, (b) Hispanics and whites and, (c) males and females. Research on whether the ABLE functions the same way for different race/ethnic and gender subgroups is summarized in this section.

For these analyses, the regression of the criterion on the predictor was calculated within and across the subgroups, and R was calculated for each regression. The slope, intercept, and standard error of estimate for the majority and minority group lines were compared and Johnson-Neyman significance boundaries were computed for the group regression line. Logistic regression analyses were used to relate the predictor scores to the dichotomous attrition criterion. Differences in predicted performance for the majority and minority groups were compared at two standard deviations below the mean, in the region of a feasible cut score. For each comparison, the mean and standard deviation of the predictor and criterion score were examined, overall and separately by group. For the regression analyses described in this section, ABLE-T is the predictor measure. Three CV criterion constructs (Effort and Leadership, Discipline, and Physical Fitness and Bearing) in the CV sample and one-year attrition in the LV sample were used as the first-term performance criteria.

We note here that the criterion construct scores are based, in part, on measures of rated effectiveness, which are susceptible to racial and gender bias. Specifically, there is some evidence that raters evaluate persons who are of the same race or sex as themselves higher than employees of another race or sex. Analysis of the Project A data showed that this source of race and gender bias was present, but the variance in ratings accounted for by these effects was extremely small (Pulakos, White, Oppler, & Borman, 1989).

As noted earlier, whites (as compared with blacks and Hispanics) scored lower on ABLE-T and had higher rates of attrition. For the attrition criterion, the black/white and Hispanic/white regression slopes were not significantly different. Slope differences were evaluated at five points on the regression line, since the relationship between ABLE and attrition is nonlinear and the slope is not constant. At two SDs below the mean predictor score, there was a slight underprediction of completion rates for minorities by the common regression line. This difference was of little practical significance, in part because so few minorities scored in the lower portion of the ABLE score range. With respect to the first-term job performance criteria, the black/white and Hispanic/white regression slopes were not significantly different for a vast majority of the comparisons. However, overall job performance of blacks was slightly overpredicted by the group regression line.

The ABLE-T scores did not vary by gender, but females (as compared with males) had significantly higher rates of attrition. The male/female regression slope differences were not significantly different. However, the use of a common prediction equation would result in overprediction of service completion rates for females. Examination of the male/female regression slope differences for predicting the CV job performance criteria showed few significant comparisons.

Adverse impact was examined by determining, for race/ethnic and gender subgroups, the percentages of new recruits who would be rejected by ABLE screening. These percentages were determined for the LV sample across a range of feasible cut scores, from the 5th to the 25th percentiles. Results consistently showed no adverse impact for women or minorities. Rather, white males and white females had the highest rates of rejection across the range of cut scores. Similar results were obtained when the analysis was limited to missions most likely to be screened using ABLE (i.e., non-HSDG, HSDG CAT-IIIB, and HSDG CAT-IV). Figure 4.4 shows the impact of a 10-percent ABLE-T screen by subgroup for these missions.

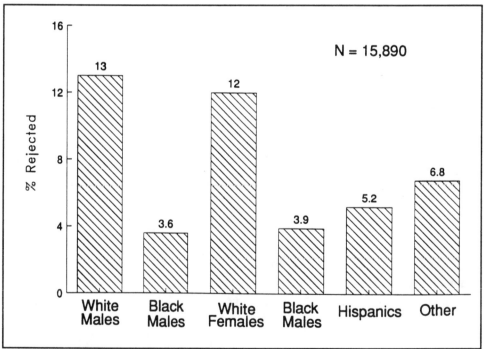

Figure 4.4 Impact of a 10-Percent ABLE-T screen by subgroup

As part of Project A, Army Research Institute researchers and Project A staff reviewed the ABLE test materials item by item for invasion of privacy, accusatory import, and offensiveness to protected groups and the general public. Based on this review, several potential items and scales were rejected as too sensitive. As for extramural review outside of Project A, at the request of the Office of the Assistant Secretary of Defense(Force Management and Personnel), the 70-item ABLE Forms A and B received a legal and sensitivity review by the Assistant General Counsel (Personnel and Health Policy). The General Counsel's review was favorable and found no legal or sensitivity objections to ABLE. It should also be noted that during pre-enlistment processing, applicants to all of the Services are asked questions about prior arrests, fines or convictions, and their use of drugs and alcoholic beverages. Compared with these examples, the ABLE items are not sensitive. However, the ultimate test of an instrument's sensitivity depends, of course, on subject reactions to the items that remain. Judging by the reactions of nearly 60,000 examinees in Project A, ABLE's items are not offensive and do not violate sensitivity norms.

Coaching and Faking Issues

In previous sections, evidence was presented for the validity and potential utility of ABLE in selection. This section addresses a concern common to many self-report measures, namely susceptibility to socially desirable responding and faking. Temperament scales such as ABLE require individuals to assess personal tendencies, often in areas in which people either portray themselves favorably ("impression management"), or actually see themselves in an unrealistically favorable light ("self-deception") (Paulhus, 1984). Although self-deceptive responses may provide criterion-related, valid variance to prediction, previous results have been conflicting. When positively related to a criterion, such responses have been interpreted as demonstrating self-esteem (Hogan & Stokes, 1989; Zerbe & Paulhus, 1987), and when negatively related, they have been interpreted as measuring defensiveness and approval-seeking (Crosby, 1990; Crowne & Marlowe, 1960). However, the Services are most concerned that respondents might attempt to raise their ABLE scores by responding with overt faking in choosing socially desirable responses. Such "faking good" might occur if the ABLE were to be used operationally for the screening of military applicants. A related concern is that respondents might receive outside guidance (i.e., coaching) on how to score well. Were faking and coaching to become rampant, the validity of the ABLE could become compromised, leading to the selection of applicants who might otherwise be rejected for military service.

Hough and her associates (Hough et al., 1990) have shown that ABLE respondents are capable of either raising or lowering their scores in the desired direction. These researchers found little evidence of faking among new Army enlistees who completed the ABLE in an "applicant-like" setting. However, this research took place under non-operational conditions, so that both some of the motivation to fake and the feasibility of coaching were lacking. It is quite possible that widespread faking could occur in an operational setting. Were ABLE to become widely known like the ASVAB, manuals might be written and marketed to applicants who wished to do well on the test. Recruiters under pressure to meet quotas might encourage or train applicants to respond in a particular manner (Hanson, Hallam, & Hough, 1989).

Therefore, as part of the ABLE research program, a body of inquiry was conducted to (a) determine the effects of faking and coaching on ABLE scores, and (b) explore alternative strategies for minimizing or managing the effects of faking and coaching, and their impact on validity. The findings regarding these questions are reported in this section. An alternative approach, that of measuring ABLE constructs with less fakable, objective biodata, is also introduced.

Effects of Faking and Coaching on ABLE Scores

In a series of experiments, new Army recruits were asked to complete the ABLE while imagining themselves as civilians applying to join the Army. These soldiers were assigned randomly to different testing conditions in which they were asked to make a good impression on the test or were coached on how to do so. The groups were then compared in terms of the elevation of their scores relative to uncoached respondents who were asked to respond honestly.

The coaching and faking manipulations examined in this research had varied effects on ABLE scores. In these experiments, similar to previous studies, soldiers told to fake by "looking good" showed elevated scores on ABLE. The most effective coaching strategy provided encouragement to "look good" with practice items and feedback on the best responses. This raised ABLE scores nearly 1.0 SD above the scores obtained in the honest condition (Young, White, & Oppler, 1991). The ABLE scores of coached examinees were also .5 SD higher than those of uncoached respondents who were simply asked to "look good."

To deter coaching and faking in the Joint-Service Adaptability Screening program, a mandatory retest was proposed for applicants whose score profiles indicated excessive faking. Retesting was intended to discourage unconstrained coaching to "look good," but it may also encourage coaching to avoid detection. One counter-detection strategy, coaching to "look average" was examined in our research. It was hypothesized that appearing average would yield an ABLE score that was high enough to exceed any reasonable enlistment standard without being identified as faking good. As predicted, mimicking an average person significantly reduced the number of records classified as faked. However, the mean ABLE score in this condition fell .9 SD below those answering honestly. Thus, this coaching was only partially effective and would not help applicants score well on the test. It is possible that more intensive training on avoiding detection coupled with practice identifying an "average" response might be effective in raising scores.

Persons high (in contrast to low) in cognitive aptitude were somewhat more successful in raising their ABLE scores after receiving coaching to look good (Young et al., 1991). There was also some indication that additional practice with feedback might result in even greater score increases, while possibly reducing the effects of individual differences. The data also demonstrate that coaching would be an even greater cause for concern than individual attempts at faking. It must be reiterated that these studies do not address whether applicants would actually fake under operational conditions.

Managing the Effects of Faking and Coaching on the ABLE

Although ABLE is susceptible to the effects of faking and coaching, at least three methods show promise for managing these effects. These include: (a) the detection of faking, (b) warning statements during test administration, and (c) the adjustment of scores for faking. In an operational context, some combination of these methods might be used together in a complementary fashion.

Detection of Faking. The accurate detection of faking could help to manage the effects of faking in an operational environment. Applicants identified as having inflated their scores on the ABLE might be asked to retest or the faking index could be used to adjust scores for socially desirable responding.

ABLE's Social Desirability scale was developed to detect faking good. This scale shows the largest increases of all the ABLE scales when examinees are distorting their responses in a positive direction (e.g., Hallam, 1990; Hough et al., 1990; Palmer, White, & Young, 1990). As a result, it can be used to detect moderate to high levels of faking among first-time examinees. Results show that the Social Desirability scale correctly identifies about 67 percent of examinees who were successfully coached to look good, while erroneously classifying only 5 percent of those responding honestly.

Warning Statements. Previous research with biodata inventories has shown that warning statements can effectively suppress faking. In some cases, respondents were warned of faking-detection scales (Doll, 1971; Schrader & Osburn, 1977). Other types of warnings have included the threat of response verification and consequences for detected faking (Trent, Atwater, & Abrahams, 1986).

In the current research program, the question was whether warnings would be effective with the ABLE. Examinees were told that the ABLE contained items to detect faking and therefore not to answer in "a way that could not possibly be true." Consistent with the research on biodata, subjects who were warned of faking detection items had scores comparable to those responding honestly (Palmer et al., 1990). However, the effectiveness of warnings needs to be evaluated when more intense coaching is provided. It must also be realized, as noted above, that operational coaching may include inoculation against the warnings, such as providing strategies to avoid detection.

Even if scale means under coached/warned conditions are comparable to those in the honest condition, *validities* may be adversely affected. It is possible that the warned applicant changes from a fake good stance to some other, albeit still invalid, one. The validity of ABLE scores under the coached/warned condition is currently under investigation.

Adjustment of Scores. The feasibility of adjusting ABLE content scores for the effects of faking is also being examined. One approach uses multiple regression to remove the variance in content scores that is predicted by the Social Desirability scale. These residualized content scores would then serve as the "corrected" scores for use in prediction.

An alternative approach, referred to as blocking, involves an extension of the first. Instead of using the same regression equation for all applicants to predict the criterion, one equation would be used for persons with low to moderate scores on the Social Desirability scale, while a separate equation would be used for those having high scores on this scale.

Preliminary results from the experiments provide some evidence that faked or coached ABLE scores provide valid prediction of first-term attrition (White & Young, 1991). However, the magnitude of these validities is lower than those for persons responding honestly. The greatest reduction in validity appears to be for examinees who are successfully coached to look good. Residualizing content scores for an entire sample improves the validity of faked or coached ABLE scores slightly. The blocking procedure is also being explored to enhance the validity of ABLE scores among individuals at both levels (i.e., low and high) of the Social Desirability scale.

Biodata Measurement of ABLE Constructs

A parallel research effort has been undertaken to develop biodata indicators that would allow for the measurement of the ABLE temperament constructs, yet still be potentially suitable for use in an environment in which faking and coaching are significant concerns (Mael & Schwartz, 1991). This would be accomplished by developing a biodata form limited to objective and verifiable items, items identified as being more resistant to faking and socially desirable responding (Mael, 1991).

The ABLE and a biodata instrument developed for this research were administered to members of the United States Military Academy class of 1994. Criterion measures were attrition from the six-week preliminary summer training period, leadership ratings from that summer period, and leadership ratings from the fall semester. The biodata items were coded in order to produce analogs to the five ABLE scales used in the research, as well as an analog to the overall ABLE. The methodology used in keying the biodata items used in this research is described in detail in Mael and Schwartz (1991).

The biodata analogs showed strong relationships to their equivalent ABLE scales, and a smaller relationship to the other ABLE scales. When compared to the ABLE scales regarding their relationship to the criteria, the biodata measures demonstrated comparable validities in 13 of 15 cases. Most germane to the current discussion is the finding that five out of the six biodata scales had significantly smaller correlations with a social desirability scale than did the equivalent ABLE scale. There is also some evidence that the biodata analogs demonstrate stability in their relationship to the ABLE scales upon cross-validation, based on findings with a sample of 1,002 enlisted cadets, even though the two samples were not wholly comparable (Mael & White, forthcoming).

In related research involving 229 Army civilian employees, rational biodata scales were constructed to measure temperament constructs and compared with corresponding ABLE scales (Kilcullen, et al., 1991; White & Kilcullen, 1992). The biodata items referred to past behaviors and life events thought to be indicative of the construct in situations that most individuals would have been exposed to by adulthood. Results from this preliminary research show that rational biodata scales can approximate the temperament constructs they are intended to measure, have comparable criterion-related validity, and are less fakable. In sum, biodata measures may provide an alternative way of measuring temperament constructs while reducing susceptibility to faking.

Summary

This chapter has described the development and validation of the Army test referred to as ABLE. ABLE reliably measures six temperament constructs that are predictive of attrition and various components of successful performance of Army jobs, such as job effort and discipline. A short form of the ABLE has also been developed and incorporated into the Joint-Service Adaptability Screening Profile (ASP), and retains the psychometric qualities of the longer version. In cases where one ABLE construct is most closely related to a criterion construct, there is a conceptually sound basis for that stronger relationship. Thus, Dependability shows the highest correlation with personal discipline, Achievement is the best predictor of leadership and achievement, and Adjustment is the best predictor of early attrition. A seventh construct, Physical Condition, was the best predictor of Physical Fitness and Military Bearing.

Moreover, the ABLE has little overlap with measures of cognitive aptitude and previous education, which currently serve as the basis for screening applicants to the Armed Services. This was demonstrated in research on the ASP, in which ABLE added unique predictive information over and above high school diploma, cognitive ability, and other factors affecting first-term attrition. Thus, ABLE can provide information that supplements, rather than supplants, typical selection methods. This is potentially noteworthy not only for military selection, but also for applications elsewhere in the public and private sector.

In addition, blacks and Hispanics score *higher* on ABLE than whites do, and there is little difference between the ABLE scores of males and females. Therefore, ABLE screening would have no adverse impact on females and minorities who would otherwise qualify for service. Faking and socially desirable responding, perennial concerns with temperament measures, have not proved problematic with ABLE, albeit ABLE has been used mostly in research settings. While faking and coaching in operational settings remains a concern, a number of possible antidotes to both faking and coaching have been proposed, and continue to be investigated.

A cost-benefit model was developed for setting enlistment standards on ABLE to reduce costs. The benefits of reduced training costs resulting from ABLE screening were balanced against the added costs of test administration and increased recruitment to replace the increased numbers of rejected applicants. Results with Army data show that ABLE has the greatest utility for screening Army missions where recruiting costs are relatively low. In higher quality market segments where the cost of recruiting is substantial, the payoff from ABLE screening was negligible. Selection utility for those missions could be increased by combining ABLE with other variables (e.g. age) to predict attrition. This approach is currently under development in the Joint-Service arena under the rubric of the Compensatory Screening Model (Trent, Folchi, & Sunderman, 1991). Use of ABLE as a classification tool, in order to capitalize on differences in ABLE's predictive validity by job family or MOS differences in training costs, is also being explored.

When research on ABLE was initiated in 1982, temperament constructs were regarded as generally poor predictors of job performance. The results of ABLE research, which are consistent with recently published reviews and meta-analyses (Barrick & Mount, 1991; Tett, Jackson, & Rothstein, 1991), present a more optimistic view of the use of temperament assessment in predicting job performance.

References

Baldwin, R. H., & Daula, T. V. (1984). The cost of high-quality recruits. *Armed Forces & Society, 11*, 96-114.

Barnes, J. D., Gaskins III, R. C., Hansen, L. A., Laurence, J. H., Waters, B. K., Quenette, M. A., & Trent, T. (1989). *The Adaptability Screening Profile (ASP): Background and pilot test results.* Alexandria, VA: Human Resources Research Organization.

Barrick, M. R., & Mount, M. K. (1991). The Big Five personality dimensions and job performance: A meta-analysis. *Personnel Psychology, 44*, 1-26.

Borman, W. C., White, L. A., Pulakos, E. D., & Oppler, S. H. (1991). Models of supervisory job performance ratings. *Journal of Applied Psychology, 76*, 863-872.

Brady, E. J., Busciglio, H. H, White, L. A., & Young, M. C. (1991, October). *The relationship of educational credentials to enlisted job performance.* Paper presented at the 33rd Annual Conference of the Military Testing Association, San Antonio, TX.

Campbell, J. P. (Ed.). (1988). *Improving the selection, classification, and utilization of Army enlisted personnel: Annual report, 1986 fiscal year* (ARI Technical Report 792). Alexandria, VA: U.S. Army Research Institute for the Behavioral and Social Sciences.

Campbell, C. H., Ford, P., Rumsey, M. G., Pulakos, E. D., Borman, W. C., Felker, D. B., DeVera, M. V., & Riegelhaupt, B. J. (1990). Development of multiple job performance measures in a representative sample of jobs. *Personnel Psychology, 43*, 277-300.

Campbell, J. P., McHenry, J. J., & Wise, L. (1990). Modeling job performance in a population of jobs. *Personnel Psychology, 43*, 313-333.

Campbell, J. P., & Zook, L. M. (Eds.). (1991). *Improving the selection, classification, and utilization of Army enlisted personnel: Final report on Project A* (ARI Research Report 1597). Alexandria, VA: U.S. Army Research Institute for the Behavioral and Social Sciences.

Campbell, J. P., & Zook, L. M. (Eds.). (in press). *Building the career force: New procedures for accessing and assigning Army enlisted personnel* (ARI Technical Report). Alexandria, VA: U.S. Army Research Institute for the Behavioral and Social Sciences.

Crosby, M. M. (1990, April). *Social desirability and biodata: Predicting sales success.* Paper presented at the Annual Conference of the Society for Industrial and Organizational Psychology, Miami Beach, FL.

Crowne, D. P., & Marlowe, D. (1960). *The approval motive.* New York: Wiley.

Daula, T. V. & Smith, A. D. (1984). Recruiting goals, enlistment supply, and enlistments in the U.S. Army. In C. Gilroy (Ed.). *Army manpower economics*, Chapter 3. Boulder, CO: Westview Press.

DeMatteo, J. S., White, L. A. Teplitzky, M. L., & Sachs, S. A. (1991, October). *Relationship between temperament constructs and selection for Special Forces training.* Paper presented at the 33rd Annual Conference of the Military Testing Association, San Antonio, TX.

Doll, R.E. (1971). Item susceptibility to attempted faking as related to item characteristic and adopted fake set. *The Journal of Psychology, 77*, 9-16.

Eitelberg, M. J., Laurence, J. H., Waters, B. K., & Perelman, L. S. (1984). *Screening for service: Aptitude and education criteria for military entry.* Washington, D.C.: Office of Assistant Secretary of Defense (Manpower, Installations and Logistics).

Goldberg, L. R. (1981). Language and individual differences: The search for universals in personality lexicons. In L. Wheeler (Ed.), *Review of personality and social psychology* (Vol. 2. pp. 141-165). Beverly Hills, CA: Sage.

Guion, R. M., & Gottier, R. F. (1965). Validity of personality measures in personnel selection. *Personnel Psychology, 18*, 135-164.

Hallam, G. L. (1990). Development and assessment of psychometric indices for the detection of faking on a biodata and temperament instrument. (Doctoral dissertation, University of Minnesota, 1990). *Dissertation Abstracts International, 51*, 5621B.

Hanson, M.A., Hallam, G.L., & Hough, L.M. (1989, November). *Detection of response distortion in the Adaptability Screening Profile (ASP)*. Paper presented at the 31st Annual Conference of the Military Testing Association, San Antonio, TX.

Hogan, R. (1982). A socioanalytic theory of personality. In M. M. Page (Ed.), *1982 Nebraska Symposium on Motivation* (pp. 55-89). Lincoln: University of Nebraska Press.

Hogan, J. B., & Stokes, G. S. (1989). *Influence of socially desirable responding on biographical data of applicant versus incumbent samples: Implications for predictive and concurrent research designs.* Paper presented at the annual meeting of the Society for Industrial and Organizational Psychology, Boston, MA.

Hosek., J. R., Antel, J., & Peterson, C. (1989). Who stays, who leaves? Attrition among first-term enlistees. *Armed Forces & Society, 15*, 389-409.

Hough, L. M. (1992). The "Big Five" personality variables - construct confusion: Description versus prediction. *Human Performance, 5*, 139-155.

Hough. L. M., Eaton, N. K., Dunnette, M. D., Kamp, J. D., & McCloy, R. A. (1990). Criterion-related validities of personality constructs and the effect of response distortion on those validities. *Journal of Applied Psychology, 75*, 581-595.

Hunter, J. E., & Schmidt, F. L. (1982). Fitting people to jobs: The impact of personnel selection on national productivity. In E. A. Fleishman and M. D. Dunnette (Eds.). *Human performance and productivity. Vol. 1: Human capability assessment.* Hillsdale, NJ: Lawrence Erlbaum and Associates.

Kamp, J. D., & Hough, L. M. (1988). Utility of temperament for predicting job performance. In L.M. Hough (Ed.), *Literature review: Utility of temperament, biodata, and interest assessment for predicting job performance.* (ARI Research Note 88-02, pp. 1-90). Alexandria, VA: U.S. Army Research Institute for the Behavioral and Social Sciences.

Kearl, C. E., and Nord R. D. (1990). How much soldier quality? Cost effective recruit selection policy for a smaller Army. Paper presented at the Army Science Conference, Durham, NC.

Kilcullen, R. N., White, L. A., Mumford, M. D., Mack H., & Rigby, C. K. (1991, October). *On the construct validity of rational biodata scales.* Paper presented at the 33rd Annual Conference of the Military Testing Association, San Antonio, TX.

Mael, F. A. (1991). A conceptual rationale for the domain and attributes of biodata items. *Personnel Psychology, 44,* 763-792.

Mael, F. A., & Schwartz, A. C. (1991). *Capturing temperament constructs with objective biodata* (ARI Technical Report 939). Alexandria, VA: U.S. Army Research Institute for the Behavioral and Social Sciences.

Mael, F. A., Schwartz, A. C., & McLellan, J. A. (1992, August). Antidotes to dustbowl empiricism with objective biodata. In Rumsey, M. G. (Chair) *Biodata advances: Bridging the rational and empirical perspectives.* Symposium presented at the annual meeting of the American Psychological Association, Washington, DC.

Mael, F. A., & White, L. A. (forthcoming). Dispositional and biographical antecedents of performance. Forthcoming chapter in H. O'Neill & M. Drillings (Eds.), *Motivation: research and theory.* Hillsdale, NJ: Laurence Erlbaum and Associates.

Matyuf, M. M., & White, L. A. (1991, October). *Individual differences in at-fault accident behavior.* Paper presented at the 33rd Annual Conference of the Military Testing Association, San Antonio, TX.

McHenry, J. J., Hough, L. M., Toquam, J. L., Hanson, M. A., & Ashworth, S. (1990). Project A validity results: The relationship between predictor and criterion domains. *Personnel Psychology, 43*, 335-354.

Nord, R. D., & Kearl, C. E. (1991). *The Army manpower selection and allocation model.* Paper presented at the OSRA/TIMS conference, Philadelphia, PA.

Norman, W. T. (1963). Toward an adequate taxonomy of personality attributes: Replicated factor structure in peer nomination personality ratings. *Journal of Abnormal and Social Psychology, 66*, 574-583.

Osburn, H. G., & Callender , J. (1992). A note on the sampling variance of the mean uncorrected correlation in meta-analysis and validity generalization. *Journal of Applied Psychology, 77*, 115-122.

Palmer, D. R., White, L. A., & Young, M. C. (1990, November). *Response distortion on the Adaptability Screening Profile (ASP).* Paper presented at the 32nd Annual Conference of the Military Testing Association, San Antonio, TX.

Paulhus, D. L. (1984). Two-component models of socially desirable responding. *Journal of Personality and Social Psychology, 46*, 598-609.

Pearlman, K. (1985). *Validity generalization: From theory to application.* Paper presented at the Center for Human Resources Programs, Institute of Industrial Relations,   University of California-Berkeley.

Peterson, N. G., Hough, L. M., Dunnette, M. D., Rosse, R. L., Houston, J. S., Toquam, J. L., & Wing, H. (1990). Project A: Specification of the predictor domain and development of new selection/classification tests. *Personnel Psychology, 43*, 247-276.

Pulakos, E. D., White, L. A., Oppler, S. H., & Borman, W. C. (1989). Examination of race and sex effects on performance ratings. *Journal of Applied Psychology, 74*, 770-780.

160

Sadacca, R., Campbell, J. P., White, L. A., & DiFazio, A. S. (1989). *Weighting criterion components to develop composite measures of job performance* (ARI Technical Report 838). Alexandria, VA: U.S. Army Research Institute for the Behavioral and Social Sciences.

Schmitt, N., Gooding, R. Z., Noe, R. A., & Kirsch, M. (1984). Meta-analyses of validity studies published between 1964 and 1982 and the investigation of study characteristics. *Personnel Psychology, 37*, 407-422.

Schrader, A.D., & Osburn, H.G. (1977). Biodata faking: Effects of induced subtlety and position specificity. *Personnel Psychology, 30*, 395-404.

Taylor, J. A. (1953). A personality scale of manifest anxiety. *Journal of Abnormal & Social Psychology, 48*, 285-290.

Tett, R. P., Jackson, D. N., & Rothstein, M. (1991). Personality measures as predictors of job performance: A meta-analytic review. *Personnel Psychology, 44*, 703-742.

Trent, T., Atwater, D.C., & Abrahams, N.M. (1986, April). Biographical screening of military applicants: Experimental assessment of item response distortion. In G.E. Lee (Ed.), *Proceedings of the Tenth Annual Symposium of Psychology in the Department of Defense* (pp. 96-100). Colorado Springs, CO: U.S. Air Force Academy, Department of Behavioral Sciences and Leadership.

Trent, T., Folchi, J., and Sunderman, S. (1991, October). *Compensatory enlistment screening: A nontraditional approach.* Paper presented at the 33rd Annual Conference of the Military Testing Association, San Antonio, TX.

Walker, C. B. (1985). *The fakability of the Army's Military Applicant Profile (MAP).* Paper presented the the Association of Human Resources Management and Organizational Behavior Proceedings, Denver, CO.

White, L. A. & Kilcullen, R. N. (1992, August). The validity of rational biodata scales. In Rumsey, M. G. (Chair) *Biodata advances: Bridging the rational and empirical perspectives.* Symposium presented at the annual convention of the American Psychological Association, Washington, DC.

White, L. A., Mael, F. A., & Sachs, S. A. (1991) *Selection of candidates for Ranger training.* Unpublished manuscript, Alexandria, VA: U.S. Army Research Institute for the Behavioral and Social Sciences.

White, L. A., Nord, R. D., & Mael, F. A. (1989, April). *Setting enlistment standards on the ABLE to reduce attrition.* Paper presented at the Army Science Conference, Durham, NC.

White, L. A. & Young, M. C. (1991, September). *Effects of coaching strategies on the Adaptability Screening Profile.* Presentation to the Manpower Accession Policy Working Group Technical Committee, Washington, DC.

Wing, H., Peterson, N. G., & Hoffman, R. E. (1984). Expert judgments of predictor-criterion validity relationships. In N. K. Eaton, M. H. Goer, J. H. Harris, & L. M. Zook (Eds.), *Improving the selection, classification, and utilization of Army enlisted personnel: Annual report, 1984 fiscal year* (ARI Technical Report 660) (pp. 219-269). Alexandria, VA: U.S. Army Research Institute for the Behavioral and Social Sciences.

Wiskoff, M. F., Parker, J. P., Zimmerman, R. A., & Sherman F. (1989). Predicting school and job performance of Marine Security Guards (PERSEREC Technical Report 90-003). Monterey, CA: Defense Personnel Security Research and Education Center.

Young, M. C., White, L. A., & Oppler, S. H. (1991, October). *Coaching effects on the Assessment of Background and Life Experiences (ABLE).* Paper presented at the 33rd Annual Conference of the Military Testing Association, San Antonio, TX.

Zerbe, W. J. & Paulhus, D. L. (1987). Socially desirable responding in organizational behavior: A reconception. *Academy of Management Review, 12,* 250-264.

Chapter 5_____

Compensatory Screening Model Development

James R. McBride[1]

This chapter describes the development and evaluation of several alternative compensatory models for screening prospective enlistees in the U.S. Armed Services. These models were developed as possible replacements for current enlistment eligibility criteria intended to reduce the incidence of first-term attrition from service. While such criteria vary from one Service to another, all of the current criteria have the effect of making enlistment difficult or impossible for applicants who have not attained a traditional secondary or post-secondary education credential.

---

[1]Human Resources Research Organization, Alexandria, Virginia. The opinions expressed here are those of the author, not necessarily those of the Department of Defense or the Military Services.

The development work described here was done by the Navy Personnel Research and Development Center (NPRDC), in its capacity as lead laboratory for the development of the Armed Services Applicant Profile (ASAP). Technical support and statistical analysis were provided by the Human Resources Research Organization (HumRRO) under contract to NPRDC. For NPRDC, Thomas Trent directed the project, and was assisted by John Folchi and Stuart Sunderman. Trent also monitored the contract effort. Janice H. Laurence directed the work by HumRRO; data analysis and model development were conducted by John Dempsey; Brian Waters, James McBride, and Bruce Belden also participated.

This chapter will describe in summary fashion the work of the Navy Personnel Research and Development Center (NPRDC) and the Human Resources Research Organization (HumRRO) to develop compensatory screening models for possible joint or separate use by the four Armed Services. The chapter will proceed in six parts. The first provides background for the project, including a summary overview of the policy issue that motivated the development of a compensatory screening procedure (discussed in more detail in Chapter 1). The second part describes, in general terms, the approach taken in that development. The third part summarizes details of the methods used to develop several alternative compensatory models, and the fourth presents the results that were obtained. The fifth part is an evaluation of the results, and a discussion of the potential practical value of the compensatory screening models. The final part summarizes the work done, and concludes with a discussion of some of its implications and limitations.

Background

The thrust of the Compensatory Screening Model (CSM) development project was to devise alternative criteria that would open up enlistment eligibility to individuals with alternative education credentials or none at all, without detriment to the Services' objective of keeping first-term attrition to a minimum. This would be accomplished by allowing positive indicants in an applicant's record to compensate for an education credential with a relatively high attrition risk. The remainder of this section summarizes current enlistment screening practices and the circumstances that motivated development of alternative screening procedures.

Enlistment Screening Practices in the Armed Services

The CSM Project resulted from a conflict between personnel screening procedures used by the Services, and certain educational interests. The screening procedures in question are employed by the four Armed Services to lessen the incidence of premature attrition among first-term enlistees. Each Service currently establishes its own screening procedures, but all of these procedures include educational attainment standards that have the effect of limiting the enlistment of applicants who have not graduated from high school with a traditional high school diploma.

The educational interests in question are those of individuals or groups who possess, grant, or advocate alternatives to the traditional high school diploma. Such alternatives include credentials received through correspondence schools, adult education programs, home study programs, and qualifying scores on educational equivalency examinations, among others. Advocates of such alternative education credentials are concerned that Department of Defense enlistment policies in effect bar enlistment to individuals who possess the alternative credentials.

Some proportion of the personnel who enlist in the Armed Services fail to complete their enlistment contract. These people must be replaced, and their replacements must be trained and equipped for service. Because the costs of recruiting, equipping, and training new recruits are substantial, the Armed Services have an interest in minimizing the incidence of first-term attrition, and each of the Services employs screening standards designed to reduce the number of enlistees who attrit. Specific policies and practices vary among the Services, but each is based on research (e.g., Sands, 1976) into the relationship of preenlistment variables and the propensity for attrition.

One long-established relationship is that of attrition and completion of high school. For years it has been known that nongraduates have about twice the attrition rate of high school graduates. More recently, it was established that enlistees with high school diplomas based on equivalency tests have attrition rates closer to nongraduates than to holders of traditional diplomas. This has led to enlistment screening procedures that discriminate, in one way or another, among the different education credentials. At one extreme is the Air Force, which in effect bars enlistment to all but those who possess traditional high school diplomas or even higher levels of educational attainment. A contrasting practice is that of the Navy, which distinguishes three levels, or tiers, of educational attainment, and sets more stringent enlistment standards for the lower tiers. Despite the differences in these practices, the effect is similar: An applicant is placed in a category on the basis of his or her educational attainment credentials, and a screening decision is made on the basis of category membership. It is nearly impossible for an applicant without a high school diploma to enlist in the Armed Services, and it is difficult for a holder of a nontraditional credential to do so.

Motivation for Developing Alternative Screening Procedures

This de facto discrimination against nontraditional diploma sources has led to complaints, and to some congressional interest in the issue. Advocates of alternative educational credentials argue, correctly, that more than half of enlistees holding such credentials have been successful in completing their terms of enlisted service. Defense enlistment policy advocates have maintained, also correctly, that holders of nontraditional diplomas have about twice the attrition risk of traditional diploma holders.

A compromise between these two positions may be possible. That compromise would be for the Services to discontinue the discriminatory practice of screening solely on the basis of educational credential category, and replace such procedures with a *compensatory* screening procedure. In such a procedure, each applicant's attrition risk would be estimated individually, and the screening decision would be based on the magnitude of that risk rather than on educational category alone. A compensatory screening procedure might weight all information about the applicant that is known to be relevant to attrition risk--or to its complement, the probability of completing the first term of enlistment. For instance, a compensatory screening procedure might include the applicant's age, aptitude test scores, marital status, number of dependents, and other things--including educational attainment--in a formula to predict completion of service.

Such a formula would be a mathematical or statistical model describing the relationship of all the information elements, in combination, to the likelihood of completing the enlistment term. A variable that suggested high attrition risk could be offset by other variables that serve to mitigate, or compensate for, such risk. Hence the term *compensatory screening model.*

Approach

In response to the urging of several members of Congress to discontinue screening solely on the basis of education credentials, the Department of Defense undertook to explore the possibility of developing compensatory screening procedures for controlling first-term attrition. Such procedures would be based on mathematical models relating service completion to applicant characteristics. The Navy was designated lead Service for this exploratory project. This section describes, in broad terms, the approach taken by the Navy in this effort.

166

The overall approach to developing the compensatory screening models was to develop mathematical models for forecasting first-term completion as a function of what is known about the applicant prior to enlistment. In principle, attrition risk can be evaluated on an individual basis, and the enlistment eligibility determination can be based on DoD or Service-specific policies establishing the magnitude of acceptable risk.

In short, the Compensatory Screening Model development project undertook a relatively straightforward statistical modeling problem--forecasting completion of service on the basis of individual attributes. However, the difficulty of the problem was materially increased by several complicating factors. These included the need for timely model development, the lack of fully appropriate data for analysis, and the absence of unanimity as to acceptable variables which could be used in making the statistical forecast.

The development of a model to predict service completion necessarily involves several key elements. First, the criterion variable must be made explicit, and useful predictor variables must be identified. Second, the nature of the statistical model--or alternative models--must be specified. Third, criterion and predictor variable data must be collected. Fourth, the parameters of all alternative models must be estimated, using statistical analysis techniques. The paragraphs below provide a general description of the approach taken to each of these elements of the project. The Methods section of this chapter will describe this approach in more detail.

Criterion and predictor variables. This and subsequent paragraphs discuss, briefly, considerations in the choice of variables to be used in the models.

Criterion variables. The purpose of the compensatory screening model or models is to predict the behavior of individual candidates for enlistment. The behavior of interest is a dichotomous variable: first-term attrition or its complement, completion of the first term. To place emphasis on the positive, we will treat service *completion* as the criterion of interest in what follows.

Predictor variables. The choice of what predictor variables to employ in the model should be guided by a theory or rationale, by previous research, and by practical and legal considerations.

167

Although there is not a well-developed theory that explains service completion as a function of individual differences, there is a loosely formed rationale that might be summarized thus: The propensity to complete the first term of service is a function of physical and mental ability, and of motivation and persistence. Variables that measure or indicate ability, motivation, and persistence ought to be useful in predicting service completion.

Previous research into first-term attrition has shown that, while there are no powerful predictors of service completion, there are some consistent relationships. Among the variables that are routinely available before enlistment, completion of high school is the best predictor of first-term completion (Department of Defense, 1978). Aptitude test scores, while not strongly related to enlistment completion, are the best predictors of success in military technical training (Welsh, Kucinkas & Curran, 1990). And variables such as age at enlistment, gender, marital status, and number of dependents all have a statistical relationship to the criterion, albeit a small one (Dempsey & Fast, 1976; Dempsey, Fast, & Sellman, 1977).

Another class of variables that appear promising are biodata questionnaires-- measures of background and experience, or biographical data. Indeed, a Joint-Services project recently developed and validated the Adaptability Screening Profile (ASP), a biodata instrument for use in screening for attrition (Barnes et al., 1989). ASP was scheduled for operational implementation in 1989, but its implementation was suspended due to lack of consensus among the Services about its long-term usefulness.

Practical and legal considerations serve to limit the range of information that is feasible or acceptable to include in a screening procedure. For example, prior employment history is thought to provide a useful indicator of an individual's propensity for completion, but such information is not systematically available for enlistment applicants at present, so it is not immediately practical to include it as part of a screening procedure. As to legal considerations, there are well-established but small relationships between service completion and membership in different gender and racial groups, but the use of race and gender in employment decisions is discriminatory and prohibited by law.

Alternative statistical models. The development and validation of personnel selection and screening systems is generally considered to be in the domain of applied psychology. For statistical prediction, psychologists have historically

168

favored the use of linear models (e.g., Cohen & Cohen, 1975), that is, mathematical models of the form

$$Y = \Sigma \ a_i X_i + \varepsilon$$

Linear models, however, are not especially well-suited to the problem of describing the probability of discrete events (Aldrich & Nelson, 1984; Dempsey, Sellman, & Fast, 1979) such as service completion or attrition. Such problems are more suitable for the application of nonlinear models--such as event history or survival models--more commonly used in other fields, including biometrics and econometrics. An example of the general form of such models is

$$Prob(Y) = \int_a^b f(X)$$

where f(X) represents any probability density function, such as a normal or a logistic function.

There are any number of nonlinear models that might be used to predict the probability of service completion. Aldrich and Nelson (1984, pp. 32-35) describe six nonlinear models that might be employed for this kind of problem. Of the six models they describe, two are most widely used: the logistic--or logit--model, and the normal--or probit--model. Kmenta discusses these alternative statistical models and notes that the logistic model is popular in practical applications because it is simpler to work with (Kmenta, 1986, pp. 548-555). The logistic function has the following form:

$$Prob(Y) = \frac{1}{1 + \exp(-Z)}$$

After considering the alternatives, the investigators chose the logistic function as the general form to be employed in developing the Compensatory Screening Model. As described later, several alternative logistic CSM models were developed and evaluated.

Data collection. Developing a statistical model for predicting service completion necessarily entails collecting and analyzing criterion and predictor variable data. In many cases, the preferred approach to this would be *prospective*. In such an approach, it would be necessary to collect predictor data over a prescribed period of time, then observe criterion behavior after the passage of time. Due to the nature of the criterion in this case, a prospective study would necessarily be a protracted one--perhaps five years or longer.

The alternative is a *retrospective* study, in which existing data are employed for analysis. Such an approach has the advantage that the analytical work can begin as soon as the data can be assembled for analysis--there is no need to wait for the criterion to mature.

Because of the need for timely development and evaluation of compensatory screening procedures, a retrospective approach was used in formulating alternative compensatory models. The latest annual accession cohort with recorded 24-month attrition (criterion) data was chosen for analysis. An additional, earlier data sample was also used in the study, for reasons explained below; that sample was the experimental group previously analyzed in the evaluation of the ASP (Trent & Quenette, 1992).

Model parameter estimation. As mentioned earlier, the developers of the compensatory models chose to employ a logistic regression model as the general form for model development. In all, ten alternative models were developed. The SAS LOGIST procedure was used to estimate the parameters of each logistic regression equation.

Method

The formulators of the compensatory screening models developed and evaluated a number of alternative models. All were logistic regression models for estimating individual propensity for service completion from information available prior to enlistment. All of the models were developed retrospectively, by analysis of existing file or research data. The sections below describe the selection of the variables used in the models; the data sets that were employed in the analyses; the statistical analyses that were performed in developing the models; and the analyses that were performed in evaluating them. This description is a summary of the methodology employed; a more detailed description is presented in a technical report prepared for the Navy Personnel Research and Development Center (Dempsey, Laurence, Waters, & McBride, 1991)

The Criterion Variable

Since the purpose of the compensatory screening models is to help identify enlistment candidates with relatively good prospects for completing first-term enlistment, the criterion employed in model development was the completion of a specified period of service. Terms of enlistment contracts range from as little as 24 months obligated active service, to 60 months and more in some cases. To ensure uniformity for purposes of this study, the criterion of interest was the completion of 24 months' service, a dichotomous or qualitative variable. Persons who completed 24 months of service were coded as "1" on the criterion variable. Persons who did not complete 24 months of service were divided into two groups: those with "pejorative" reasons for attrition, and those with non-pejorative reasons. Examples of pejorative reasons include desertion and failure to meet behavioral or performance criteria. Non-pejorative reasons include death, disability, and entry into officer programs. Non-pejorative attrition cases were excluded from the analyses reported here. (See Dempsey et al., 1991, for a listing of the pejorative and non-pejorative reasons for attrition that were employed.)

Predictor Variables

Two broad classes of predictor variables were of interest. The first included existing file data--individual information that was available prior to enlistment and recorded in accessible data files. The second included biodata measures in the Adaptability Screening Profile, a research instrument administered previously to a large sample of enlistment applicants.

File data variables. The file data included data elements from two sources: (a) Military Entrance Processing Reporting System (MEPRS) files, which consists entirely of preenlistment data; and (b) enlisted cohort files maintained by the Defense Manpower Data Center (DMDC), which include preenlistment data as well as some data elements that are maintained and updated after enlistment. The variables encompassed by these two sources included personal information about the applicants, measurements taken and observations made in the course of the enlistment application process, and information about the specific Service or enlistment program. The database developed from these two sources contained applicant identifying information and a number of potential predictor variables; those variables are listed in Table 5.1.

Table 5.1		
Data File Elements and Potential Predictor Variables		
Age at application	Years of education	Term of enlistment
Marital status	AFQT category	Moral waiver
Dependents	AFQT percentile	Youth program
Gender	Date of testing	Date of birth
Race	High school testing program	Entry/separation date
Ethnicity	ASVAB subtest scores	Height and weight
Education credential	Military job specialty	Medical examination date
Service	DoD primary duty/occupation	Criterion variable

Biodata predictor variables. In addition to the predictor variables listed in Table 5.1, there was considerable interest in evaluating the usefulness of biodata for predicting completion of service. (Chapter 2 provided a description of biodata, and a summary of research into their use for personnel selection.) Of specific interest was the Adaptability Screening Profile (ASP), which had been developed previously. The ASP includes six separate scales. As described in Chapter 3, ASP Scale 1--also known as ASAP--was developed specifically for purposes of predicting service completion. ASAP was included in the compensatory model, as a means of assessing the value of biodata as a component of the model. Because of the need for timely model development, it was not feasible to administer ASAP anew; instead, existing ASAP data had to be employed. Details of this treatment are discussed in a subsequent section below.

Predictor variables used in the models. The variables listed in Table 5.1 were scrutinized both rationally and analytically to come up with a smaller set of predictor variables for use in the compensatory model. Dempsey et al. (1991) describe the considerations that were used in choosing the file data predictor

172

variables for the compensatory model. The variables chosen are listed in Table 5.2, and discussed here briefly.

Table 5.2 CSM Project Predictor Variables		
Variables	Description	
	Age Group	Scale Value
Age	17	.793
	18	.818
	19-25	.790
	26-27	.764
	28-29	.725
	30+	.693
Adaptability Screening Profile	ASAP Score	
Cognitive Ability	Math Knowledge Standard Score	
Dependents	0 if single with no dependents 1 otherwise	
Educational Attainment	Credential of record at entry	
Service	Army, Navy, USAF, or USMC	

Age. Previous research has consistently shown a relationship between age at enlistment and propensity for service completion. That relationship is nonlinear; the proportion completing service declines from age 18 to age 30 and above, but it is also somewhat lower for 17-year-olds than for 18-year-olds.

Cognitive ability. Applicants' cognitive abilities are measured by 10 subtests of the Armed Services Vocational Aptitude Battery (ASVAB), four of which are used in the Armed Forces Qualification Test (AFQT) to determine eligibility for enlistment. Because the AFQT subtests are subject to range restriction (as a result of the explicit use of AFQT scores for selection) the ASVAB's Mathematics Knowledge (MK) test score was included in the compensatory model development as the sole measure of cognitive ability. (Recently, MK became part of the AFQT; the accession cohorts used for the present research, however, were selected on the basis of a composite that did not include MK.)

Number of dependents. Along with age, previous research has sometimes found the number of an applicant's dependents to be statistically related to completion of service. Because the number of dependents at time of enlistment could not be determined reliably from file data, a dichotomous substitute variable was constructed for these analyses. That variable was assigned a value of 0 if the individual was single with no dependents at time of enlistment, and a value of 1 if he or she was married or otherwise had one or more dependents.

Educational attainment. As mentioned earlier, earning a traditional high school diploma has repeatedly been found to be one of the best predictors of completion of first-term enlisted service. However, the usefulness of this information has been somewhat blurred in recent years by the administrative treatment of alternative education credentials. Current enlistment processing practice distinguishes 19 different educational credentials spanning the range from non-completion of high school to possession of an advanced post-baccalaureate degree. Those 19 credential categories are listed in Table 5.3. For statistical analysis purposes, it was necessary to combine some of these credentials into groups of two or more.

Table 5.3 also lists the 10 educational attainment categories that were employed. These were encoded into nine mutually exclusive dichotomous variables, in such a way that a traditional high school diploma was represented by a value of 0 on all 9 variables. Individuals with an educational credential other than a high school diploma were assigned a value of "1" on the variable corresponding to their education credential category.

Military Service. Rates of completing first term of service vary among the four Armed Services. The Air Force typically experiences the highest rates of completion, followed by the Marine Corps, the Army, and the Navy. From this, it seems clear that branch of Service is a useful variable in predicting first-term completion. This could be accomplished by developing separate model equations for each of the Services, or by incorporating branch of Service as a predictor or moderator variable in a comprehensive model. For purposes of analysis, branch

174

of Service was encoded as three mutually exclusive dichotomous variables--one each for the Air Force, Marine Corps, and Navy. An Army applicant was encoded as having a value of "0" on all three of these variables.

Table 5.3	
1988 Educational Credentials and Categories	
Education Credential Category	Educational Credentials
1	Doctorate Master's Degree First Professional Degree Bachelors Degree
2	Professional Nursing Diploma Associate Degree
3	Adult Education Diploma
4	Test-Based Equivalency Diploma
5	Home Study Diploma
6	Correspondence School Diploma
7	High School Certificate of Attendance
8	Occupational Program Certificate
9	No Diploma Currently in High School Diploma Near Completion
10	Traditional High School Diploma

Data

As noted earlier, the Compensatory Screening Models were to be developed by fitting mathematical models to existing data, since conducting a new prospective study would require a minimum of four years for the predictor data to accumulate and the criterion data to mature and become available for analysis. What was desirable was to analyze predictor and criterion data collected as recently as possible, consistent with the two-year lead time for the 24-month service completion criterion to mature. Since the project started at the beginning of fiscal year 1991, the most recent year for which accessions could have completed two years' service was fiscal year 1988.

Unfortunately, one important predictor variable was not available for FY88 accessions--the ASAP score--because that biodata instrument was not administered as part of the enlistment processing procedure in FY88. ASAP data were available for part of an earlier accession cohort; for several months during fiscal year 1985, ASAP had been administered experimentally to a sample of over 100,000 applicants for enlistment. That 1985 ASAP sample was attractive for use in developing the compensatory models, since a four-year service completion criterion could be observed, and all predictor variables of interest were available.

One key consideration made the 1985 ASAP sample less than ideal for analysis, however. That was a subsequent change in the recording of educational attainment. In late 1987, the number of DoD-recognized education credentials increased from 14 to 19; several credentials were added, and the definitions of some of the older credentials were changed. This posed a problem because of the important role that educational attainment was expected to play in any compensatory model, and the necessity for the model to embody the current educational credentials rather than an obsolete set of them.

In short, there was a dilemma: the 1988 data base lacked ASAP scores--a promising predictor of service completion--and the 1985 data base containing ASAP scores employed an obsolete set of education credentials. There were only two ways of resolving this dilemma. Either (a) some means of combining the 1985 and 1988 data sets had to be found, or (b) a new study involving ASAP administration to applicants would have to be undertaken. The latter course would be more satisfactory from a technical standpoint, but would take 4 or more years before the required compensatory models could be developed and evaluated.

Consequently, NPRDC and HumRRO undertook to develop models that combined the 1985 and 1988 data. The approach to this is described below.

Data Analyses

Although a number of different kinds of data analyses were performed in the course of the project, this report will focus on just three: (a) descriptive analyses, looking at marginal relationships between each predictor variable and the completion criterion; (b) predictive analyses, using the joint distributions among the predictor and criterion variables to develop multivariate models; and (c) evaluative analyses, using independent data to assess the usefulness of the models for predicting service completion.

Descriptive Analyses

Descriptive analyses were used to assess the relationship of each predictor variable to completion of 24 months of service. Except for the ASAP variable, all of the descriptive analyses were conducted in the 1988 data base; the ASAP analyses were necessarily limited to the 1985 data base. Conditional means for 24-month attrition are displayed in Table 5.4.

Predictive Analyses

The results of the descriptive analyses of univariate statistics and bivariate relationships were used to inform the development of the compensatory models, all of which were multivariate in their predictors but used the univariate criterion variable completion of 24 months of service.

In the end, the compensatory models reported here were developed by analyzing multivariate relationships in the 1985 data set, the only data available that included the biodata scores from ASAP. However, preliminary stages in the predictive analyses involved analysis of the 1988 data. The preliminary analyses are described here.

Preliminary analyses

To eliminate the nonmonotonic relationship of age to completion, the age variable was rescaled. Additionally, an education credential scale was developed using the 1988 data set; this was done in order to enable the compensatory models developed in the 1985 data to contain parameters for all 19 education credentials now in use. Development of the age and education scales is described in this section.

Education Category	Education Credential Group	N (FY1988)	Attrition Rate
Table 5.4 Relationships Between CSM Predictor Variables and 24-Month Attrition			
1	Bachelors Degree and Higher	3,434	.15
2	Nursing Diploma, Assoc. Degree	2,201	.16
2	High School Diploma	232,236	.19
3	Adult Education Diploma, etc.	2,279	.29
4	GED (Test-Based Equivalency)	9,715	.37
5	Home Study Diploma	46	.17
6	Correspondence School Diploma	79	.33
7	H.S. Cert. of Attendance	985	.27
8	Occupational Program Cert.	96	.21
9	No Diploma, or Near Completion	5,287	.40
AFQT	Percentile		
	93-99	10,942	.15
	65-92	91,686	.18
	50-64	67,879	.22
	31-49	72,603	.21
	21-30	12,737	.26
	16-20	32	.31

(Continued)

178

	Group	N	Attrition Rate
	Table 5.4 (Continued)		
	Relationships Between CSM Predictor Variables and 24-Month Attrition		
Age	17	8,977	.21
	18	47,159	.18
	19-25	67,176	.21
	26-27	2,497	.24
	28-29	1,155	.27
	30+	1,374	.31
Service	Army	99,533	.21
	Navy	86,058	.23
	Air Force	39,519	.15
	Marine Corps	33,084	.19
Martial Status	Single	235,290	.20
	Married	21,087	.23
Dependents	None	232,947	.20
	One or more	23,947	.24

Development of an age scale. Previous research, as well as the descriptive analyses reported above, found a nonmonotonic relationship between age at enlistment and service completion. Typically the completion rates of 17-year-old enlistees and those over 25 are lower than those of enlistees between 18 and 24. To avoid complicating the compensatory model with terms to express this non-monotonic relationship, NPRDC decided to rescale the age variable in a way that would make the final compensatory model more straightforward.

To this end, 24-month completion rates were determined for each year of age at enlistment. Ages with similar completion rates were grouped together; rescaling was accomplished by substituting the age group completion rate for the chronological age in subsequent model development analyses. The completion rates used in the rescaling were determined through analysis of the 1988 data; these rescaled values were applied in the later analysis of the 1985 data. The result was that a single term was used in the final equations to model the influence of age. The actual age scale values used are the ones listed previously, in Table 5.2.

Development of an education credential scale. Because educational attainment is one of the few consistently reliable predictors of service completion and attrition, it was deemed essential for the compensatory model to include a parametric coefficient for each currently recognized credential or group of credentials. However, several credentials recognized as distinct by current policy were not recognized when the 1985 data set was compiled, and it was not possible to deduce them or impute them in the 1985 data. For this reason analysis of the 1988 data set was employed to develop an education scale that could be applied in the model development analyses of the 1985 data. The steps in this process are described here.

First, the 19 current education credentials were grouped into 10 mutually exclusive categories based on rational analyses. This reduction of the number of categories was necessary because it was found that some education credentials, while important substantively, occurred only rarely in the data available for analysis. Grouping some of them together was intended to increase the statistical power available for fitting the predictive models to sparsely represented credentials. The reduced set of 10 educational attainment categories was displayed in Table 5.3, above, along with the actual credentials that comprise each category.

Second, nine dichotomous categorical variables were defined that completely accounted for the 10 education categories. High school diploma graduates in the 1988 data set were assigned a value of 0 on all nine categorical variables; holders of all other credentials were assigned a value of 1 on the appropriate variable, and 0 on all others. In subsequent model development, this had the effect of establishing the high school diploma as a default, or reference variable. The categorical education credential variables are listed in Table 5.5.

180

Categorical Variable	Education Credential Group	Scale Value (Regression Weight)
\multicolumn{3}{c}{**Table 5.5**}		
\multicolumn{3}{c}{**The Nine Education Categorical Variables Employed, and Their Scale Values**}		
1	Bachelors Degree and Higher	.2046
2	Nursing Diploma, Assoc. Degree	.2045
3	Adult Education Diploma, etc.	-.4453
4	GED (Test-Based Equivalency)	-.8803
5	Home Study Diploma	.1799
6	Correspondence School Diploma	-.3494
7	H.S. Cert. of Attendance	-.5741
8	Occupational Program Cert.	-.0844
9	No Diploma, or Near Completion	-1.0268

Third, the 1988 data were analyzed in order to fit a multivariate logistic regression model of 24-month completion as a joint function of age, aptitude test score, education, and dependents. For this analysis, age was defined as the scaled variable described above; aptitude was represented by the applicant's standard score on the ASVAB test of Mathematics Knowledge (MK); dependents was the dichotomous variable described earlier; and education was represented in the model by the nine dichotomous categorical variables just described. Thus, there were 13 variables in the logistic regression equation--the criterion variable and 12 predictor variables.

Fourth, after the parameters of the logistic regression equation had been estimated, the education scale was defined for use in subsequent model development. An education scale variable Z was created, and defined as follows: where the weights β_i are the regression coefficients resulting from the logistic regression analysis described immediately above. These regression coefficients are listed in Table 5.5, under the heading "Scale Value".

$$Z_j = \Sigma \ \beta_i \ Category_{ij}$$

This scaling procedure applies a unique regression coefficient to each education credential category. An individual applicant's "score" on the education scale is one of the nine values in Table 5.5, or 0 if he or she holds a traditional high school diploma. Since these nine regression coefficients were derived together with regression coefficients for age, aptitude, and dependents, the resulting education scale accounts for the relation of education category to service completion rate, adjusted for the influence of those three variables.

Final Analyses

After the 1988 data set had been used to establish scales to be applied to the age and education variables, the final versions of several alternative compensatory screening models were developed. This final model development phase used the 1985 data set, containing predictor and criterion data for over 120,000 non-prior service applicants who had taken the ASAP during an earlier project to develop and evaluate the usefulness of that instrument. Trent and Quenette (1992) have described the details of the ASAP validation effort. As described in more detail in Chapter 3, over 55,000 of those applicants accessed into the Military Services, and hence established themselves as either service completers or attrition statistics. The compensatory screening models described here were based on analysis of data from those 55,000+ 1985 accessions.

The development of the final models proceeded in several steps. First, the age and education scales derived from the 1988 data were calculated for the 1985 cohort. Second, the cohort was divided into a model development sample and an evaluation sample. Third, alternative models of service completion as a function of our predictor variables were derived in the development sample. And finally, the usefulness of the models was assessed. The methodology and results of each of those steps will be discussed below.

Rescaling age and education. Each enlistee's age was calculated from the records of his or her birthdate and enlistment processing date, then rounded to the nearest full year. Based on that age-in-years value, the age scale value was

182

determined by table lookup, using the data presented earlier in Table 5.2. Thus, the "age scale" predictor variable was the marginal rate of service completion, given the individual's age category.

Calculating the value for the education scale was more complicated, since not all of the current education credentials were in use in 1985. The first step in the process was to convert the enlistee's 1985 education credential code into the closest equivalent 1988 code. Table 5.6 contains a list of the equivalent codes, and the five 1988 codes for which there was no 1985 equivalent.

Following this "mapping" of the 1985 education credential code into its 1988 equivalent, the education scale value Z was computed for each enlistee, using the equation specified earlier.

Dividing the sample. After scale values for age and education had been calculated, the 1985 accession sample was divided into two equivalent-sized subsamples. The first step in this process was to assign accessions to one subsample or the other on the basis of the last digit of the social security number. There was an exception to this procedure, however, in the case of applicants with infrequently occuring education credentials: In order to increase the accuracy of estimation of model parameters for those categories, all accessions possessing the rarest credentials were included in both the development subsample and the evaluation subsample. Thus, the outcome of this process was a dataset divided into two largely independent subsamples with some overlap.

Developing alternative models. In all, 10 alternative models were developed from analysis of the 1985 development sample data. These were developed in two waves, using somewhat different procedures in each wave. The first wave of model development was more rigorous, and was intended to yield models that could be implemented for enlistment screening. The second wave was somewhat less rigorous, and was intended only as an expeditious means of answering some questions that were raised upon inspection of the results of the first wave. Both waves of the analyses and results are described below.

Table 5.6		
Education Credential Categories Treated as Equivalent		
Category	1988 Credentials	1985 Credentials
1	Bachelor's	Bachelor's
	Master's	Master's
	Post-Master's	Post-Master's
	Doctorate	Doctorate
	Professional Degree	Professional Degree
2	Associate Degree	Associate Degree
	Nursing Diploma	Nursing Diploma
3	Adult Ed. Diploma	
	1 Semester College	
4	Test-based Equivalency Diploma	H.S. Equivalency Certificate (GED)
5	Home Study Diploma	
6	Correspondence School Diploma	
7	H.S. Certificate of Attendance	H.S. Certificate of Attendance/Completion
8	Occupational Program Certificate	Occ. Prog. Cert. of Attendance/Completion
9	Less than H.S. Diploma	Less than H.S. Diploma
	High School Diploma	High School Diploma

First-wave analyses. All of the first-wave models were developed using maximum likelihood estimation of the logistic regression of 24-month completion on some or all of the predictor variables listed above in Table 5.2. The specific form of these logistic regression models is:

$$P = Prob(Completion) = \frac{1}{1 + \exp(-Y)}$$

where

$$Y = \alpha_0 + \alpha_1 \text{ } ASAP + \alpha_2 \text{ } Education + \alpha_3 \text{ } Aptitude + \alpha_4 \text{ } Age + \alpha_5 \text{ } Dependents + \Sigma \text{ } (\alpha_i \text{ } Service_i)$$

It is worth noting that, in this logistic model, the argument Y is equal to the log odds (natural logarithm of the odds) of the discrete event; that is,

$$Y = \log(\frac{P}{1 - P}).$$

Since **Y** is a weighted linear combination of the predictor variables, we see that although the logistic regression is a nonlinear function, the log odds is a linear function.

Six alternative logistic regression models were developed in the first wave. Two were based on analysis of data from all applicants who accessed; the other four were Service-specific models--one each based on separate analyses of Army, Navy, Air Force, and Marine Corps accessions. The reason for developing so many models is the observation that some Services consistently have somewhat higher rates of attrition, and hence lower rates of service completion, than others.

Of the two models based on all four Services' data, one model incorporated branch of Service as a predictor; the other did not. We will refer to these models as "DoD 1" and "DoD 2", with DoD 1 denoting the model that did not incorporate branch of Service. Model DoD 1 was developed to provide a single compensatory model that could be used for all applicants, regardless of the Service to which they applied. Model DoD 2 was developed to provide more accurate estimates of an applicant's propensity to complete the term of service; the additional accuracy is an expected consequence of incorporating branch of

Service in the model as a predictor variable. In effect, model DoD 2 applies an adjustment that reflects differences among the Services' average completion rates.

The four Service-specific models were developed in response to an anticipated desire for each Service to consider using a Service-specific compensatory screening equation. These Service-specific equations thus go a step beyond model DoD 2: instead of a common model with an adjustment for branch of Service, they provide a separate model for each Service. To the extent that there are Service-peculiar interrelationships among the compensatory model variables, the Service-specific models should permit somewhat more accurate estimation than either model DoD 1 or DoD 2.

Sample sizes used in developing these six models varied from one model to the other, except for the two DoD models. Table 5.7 indicates the sample sizes employed in developing each of the models. It also contains development sample summary statistics for the variables in each model, and their intercorrelations.

Second-wave analyses. The second wave of analyses was done after the preliminary results of the first wave had been briefed to interested groups, including the Manpower Accession Policy Working Group (MAPWG) and the Defense Advisory Committee on Military Personnel Testing (DAC). These groups offered questions, comments and suggestions for further analysis; the second wave of analyses were intended to address some of these.

For example, the possible use of ASAP in enlistment screening is controversial; some group members wanted to see models developed with ASAP eliminated or with its contribution minimized. One reviewer suggested developing a model with just two equally weighted predictor variables--Education Credential and ASAP. A DAC member expressed concern that the first wave-models might contain serious estimation bias because they were developed in a selected sample. A MAPWG member urged a completely different approach to model development, on the grounds that modeling based on the 1985 sample was inappropriate, was technically flawed, and would not pass a rigorous methodological scrutiny.

Tabe 5.7

Tabe 5.7

Summary Statistics and Intercorrelations of Variables in the CSM Model Development Sample

Sample	ASAP	MK	Age Scale	Dependents (0 or 1)	Educ. Scale	Completion
Army N = 12,115	115.27 (10.16)	50.58 (7.88)	.795 (.020)	.133 (.339)	-.126 (.326)	.781 (.414)
Navy N = 5,781	115.60 (10.41)	51.64 (8.26)	.795 (.020)	.070 (.255)	-.148 (.355)	.774 (.418)
Air Force N = 5,941	120.87 (8.58)	53.64 (7.66)	.797 (.014)	.120 (.325)	.000 (.062)	.827 (.379)
Marine Corps N = 2,976	116.68 (9.49)	50.64 (7.85)	.800 (.014)	.047 (.212)	-.062 (.215)	.765 (.423)
DoD (Combined) N = 26,813	116.74 (10.11)	51.49 (8.01)	.796 (.019)	.107 (.309)	-.096 (.290)	.788 (.409)

Intercorrelations						
ASAP	1.00					
MK	.308	1.00				
Age Scale	-.009	.034	1.00			
Dependents	-.007	-.034	-.216	1.00		
Education Scale	.365	.087	-.037	-.018	1.00	
Completion	.222	.115	.024	-.008	.153	1.00

Note: () indicates standard deviations.

With these and other matters in mind, the second-wave analyses were undertaken. They addressed all but the last of the points just discussed. In each case, a new logistic regression model was developed; however, in the interests of development time the second-wave analyses took a less rigorous approach than those of the first wave, and only one model of each kind was developed rather than six. Specifically, a linear approximation technique was used rather than maximum likelihood to estimate the logistic regression weights. Each model was developed by analyzing all four Services' 1985 accession data; no Service-specific models were developed in the second wave, nor was branch of Service incorporated as a predictor. Each of the second-wave models is described below.

A model with ASAP and education equally weighted. Research prior to the development of ASAP consistently showed educational attainment to be the best predictor of service completion. Although the first-wave DoD models had education and aptitude making almost equal contributions, there was some skepticism about the replicability of that result. One observer felt that an a priori model containing just education and ASAP might suffice for predicting the criterion, and that equally weighting those two variables would avert technical criticism of the methodology used to develop the compensatory screening model. To investigate that line of inquiry, NPRDC developed an equal weights model using just those two predictors. Their standardized regression weights were set equal to one another; with this done, the unstandardized regression weights were derived.

A model without ASAP. Because the ASAP questionnaire is controversial, there was a real possibility that ASAP would never be used operationally. That would invalidate all of the first wave of models, since they all contain ASAP. Some Service representatives wanted to know what a compensatory model without ASAP would look like, and how it would compare in terms of usefulness for predicting service completion. Consequently, a compensatory model without ASAP was developed. Because the dependents variable had been found not to make a significant contribution, it also was omitted from the model.

A model with ASAP minimized. Of all the predictor variables studied, ASAP has the strongest relationship to the criterion, and its domination of the first-wave compensatory models was a matter of concern to some observers. NPRDC was asked to develop a model containing ASAP, but with its relative contribution minimized. This model was developed by means of a two-stage logistic regression analysis. In the first stage, a model was developed without ASAP, and the residuals (individual errors of estimate) were computed for every case in the development sample. In the second stage, the logistic regression of those residuals on ASAP alone was estimated. The final model was formed as an additive combination of the regression parameters estimated in both stages. The effect of this was to minimize the influence of ASAP by restricting it to predicting the criterion variance that was not predictable by the other variables, education, age, and aptitude.

A model corrected for the effects of selection. The 1985 development sample consisted entirely of individuals who had entered service, and had therefore passed the enlistment qualification standards in effect at the time. These standards included education and aptitude requirements, among other things; therefore, the sample must suffer to some extent from restriction of range on the very variables we used as predictors in developing the compensatory models. The effect of range restriction on the models developed in the first wave is unknown; in a worst-case situation, the first-wave models could be seriously biased in their estimates of the probability of completing service.

To investigate this concern, NPRDC and HumRRO developed a version of the DoD 1 model corrected for the effects of explicit and incidental selection. This development began by correcting a sample correlation matrix for the effects of selection, using a procedure developed by Lawley (1943), and implemented in a computer program at NPRDC by Sympson and Candell (1983). The corrected intercorrelations of the criterion and the age, ASAP, aptitude, and education variables were then analyzed to produce a linear approximation of the logistic regression weights for the DoD 1 model (less the dependents variable).

Results

First-wave results. Each of the logistic regression models is fully specified by the estimated values of its regression parameters. The estimated regression parameters for the six first-wave models are listed in Table 5.8; the standard errors of the parameter estimates are listed there as well.

Inspection of the DoD 1 model regression parameters indicates that all predictor variables except the dependents variable had statistically significant regression weights; this was true for DoD 2 as well. In the latter model, branch of Service was significant for the Air Force and Marine Corps, but not for the Navy.

Looking at the Service-specific models shows less consistency across models in terms of which variables' regression parameters are significant. Only the ASAP score was significant in all four of these models. The education scale variable was significant in three of the Services' models, but not in the Air Force model. The aptitude variable was significant in all Services except the Marine Corps. The pattern for the age and dependents variables was inconsistent from one Service to another.

	Army	Navy	USAF	USMC	DoD 1	DoD 2
Table 5.8						
Six "First-Wave" Compensatory Models: Logistic Regression Weights for Predicting Completion						
Constant	-7.996* (.951)	-7.475* (1.40)	-.4803* (2.18)	-7.516* (2.61)	-7.370* (.704)	-7.888* (7.11)
ASAP Score	.039* (.002)	.048* (.004)	.508* (.004)	.034* (.005)	.043* (.002)	.043* (.002)
Education Scale	.679* (.065)	.471* (.089)	-.725 (.623)	.809* (1.86)	.560* (.048)	.588* (.050)
Math Knowledge Std Score	.014* (.003)	.028* (.004)	.028* (.005)	.011 (.006)	.020* (.002)	.020* (.002)
Age Scale	5.514* (1.11)	2.294 (1.64)	-2.989 (2.63)	5.605 (3.17)	3.531* (.834)	3.889* (.840)
Dependents (0 or 1)	-.099 (.066)	.060 (.129)	.317* (.121)	-.140 (.205)	.020 (.051)	.006 (.051)
Navy Adjustment						-.055 (.040)
USAF Adjustment						-.129* (.043)
USMC Adjustment						-.229* (.051)

Notes: * indicates significant regression weight ($p < .05$)
  () indicates standard error of the regression weight.

190

The regression parameters displayed in Table 5.8 are unstandardized regression parameters. Although appropriate for model specification, unstandardized regression parameters cannot be compared across variables to determine the relative importance of any variable in predicting service completion. These parameters can be standardized by multiplying each one by the ratio of a constant and the standard deviation of its variable. This procedure transforms all the regression parameters to a common metric, and permits them to be compared directly. Table 5.9 lists standardized regression weights for the six models. As an example, in the Army the education variable (.221) contributes approximately twice as much as age (.112) or MK score (.111).

Table 5.9 "Standardized" Regression Weights for First-Wave Compensatory Model Equations						
Variable	Army	Navy	USAF	USMC	DoD 1	DoD 2
Education Scale	.221*	.167*	-.045	.174*	.162*	.171*
ASAP Score	.397*	.500*	.495*	.318*	.432*	.439*
Math Knowledge	.111*	.234*	.218*	.085	.157*	.160*
Age Scale	.112*	.047	-.041	.080	.066*	.072*
Dependents	-.034	.015	.103*	-.030	.006	.002
Navy Indicator						-.022
USAF Indicator						-.054*
USMC Indicator						-.072*

Note: * indicates significant regression weights (p < .05).

Second-wave results. The estimated regression parameters for the four second-wave models are listed in Table 5.10; the standard errors of the parameter estimates are listed there as well.

The estimated regression parameters for the model with education and ASAP equally weighted are listed in the "equal weights" column. The parameters for

191

the model without ASAP are listed in the "No ASAP" column. The estimated parameters for the model with ASAP minimized are listed in the "ASAP Minimized" column. Finally, the parameters for the model corrected for the effects of selection are listed in the "Corrected DoD 1" column. All of the parameter estimates in Table 5.10 are unstandardized regression weights. Table 5.11 lists standardized weights for the four second-wave models.

Table 5.10
Four "Second-Wave" Compensatory Models: Approximate Logistic Regression Weights for Predicting Completion

Variable	Equal Weights	No ASAP	ASAP Minimized	Corrected DoD 1
Constant	-2.09* (.000)	-2.53* (.013)	-7.685* (.142)	-8.03* (.046)
ASAP Score	.031* (.000)		.034* (.000)	.046* (.000)
Education Scale	1.087* (.001)	1.042* (.001)	1.448* (.011)	.514* (.003)
Math Knowledge Std Score		.035* (.000)	.062* (.000)	.023* (.000)
Age Scale		2.777* (.017)	2.694* (.177)	3.744* (.055)

Notes: * indicates significant regression weight (p < .05)
() indicates standard error of the regression weight.

Table 5.11
"Standardized" Regression Weights for the Four "Second-Wave" Compensatory Model Equations

	Model			
Variable	Equal Weights	No ASAP	ASAP Minimized	Corrected DoD 1
ASAP Score	.500*		.344*	.465*
Education Scale	.500*	.302*	.420*	.149*
Math Knowledge Std Score		.280*	.496*	.184*
Age Scale		.053*	.051*	.071*

Notes: All these equations were developed in the combined DoD data set.
* indicates significant regression weight (p < .05).

Evaluation and Discussion

Evaluation of the Results

This section will focus on evaluation of the results presented above. Where it will be helpful to that evaluation, additional analyses will be reported. The evaluation will proceed in several steps. First, we will consider the predictor variables separately, focusing on evaluating which variables made the largest difference in the prediction of the completion criterion. Second, we will evaluate the effectiveness of the CSM models for their purpose: predicting service completion. Third, we will examine the effects of applying the CSM models. In these first three steps, all evaluation is based on accession data. In the fourth step, we will attempt to extrapolate some of the results to an applicant population, and to assess the value of a compensatory model for screening applicants.

Predictor Variables in the First-Wave Models

To this point, we have presented 10 alternative compensatory models. The 6 "first-wave" models were fully developed; the 4 second-wave models were based on approximations. This part of the discussion will focus on the first-wave models. The principal differences among these models were the data sets in which they were developed, and the identity of the predictor variables that constituted them. Five data sets were used for model development: an overall sample, and four Service-specific subsamples. Five predictor variables were evaluated in all the models: education, ASAP score, aptitude, age, and dependents. Service branch was also a predictor in one model (DoD 2). In evaluating the salience of the candidate predictor variables, at least two matters are of interest: statistical significance and relative importance.

Statistical significance. If a variable's regression coefficient is not statistically significant, that variable's place in the model is questionable. One predictor variable had a significant regression weight in all six first-wave models: that variable was ASAP score. Aside from the categorical branch of Service variables, all variables except dependents were significant in the two DoD models. Branch of Service was significant for the Air Force and Marine Corps categorical variables, but not for the Navy. (Since the reference Service in model DoD 2 is the Army, this indicates that, *ceteris paribus*, propensity to complete 24 months' service was not significantly different between the Army and Navy, but was somewhat different between the Army and each of the other two Services.)

As discussed earlier, the pattern of statistical significance was less consistent in the four Service-specific models than in the two DoD models. Education was not significant in the Air Force model, but was significant in the three other Service models. Aptitude--significant in the Army, Navy, and Air Force models-- was not significant in the Marine Corps model. Dependents was a significant variable only in the Air Force model. In the Service-specific models, age was significant only for the Army (although it was significant in the two DoD models as well).

Relative importance. If a variable is statistically significant, its relative contribution to the model is of interest. The magnitude of a variable's contribution to a model cannot be assessed from the relative size of the regression weights, because the weights are a function of the units of measurement, and are also influenced by the size of each variable's variance. One means of comparing

194

the contributions made by different variables is to inspect standardized regression weights; Table 5.9 contains standardized weights for the six first-wave models.

Within the two DoD models, by far the largest contribution to the prediction is made by the ASAP variable. The education credential scale and aptitude variables are approximately equal in their contributions, but their combined contributions do not equal that of ASAP. All the other variables make minor or negligible contributions compared to ASAP, education, and aptitude.

In the four Service-specific models, except for the consistent importance of the ASAP variable, the relative contributions of the predictors vary from one Service to another. In the Army and Marine Corps models, education appears to be twice as important as aptitude or age. In the Navy model, aptitude makes a somewhat greater contribution than education. In the Air Force model, aptitude scores also make the largest contribution after ASAP, followed by the dependents variable; the education variable received a negative (but nonsignificant) weight.

Age made a small contribution in some models. Branch of Service also made a small contribution in the one model--DoD 2--in which it was used. The dependents variable made almost no contribution, except in the Air Force model.

Predictor Variables in the Second-Wave Models

Statistical significance. The approximate values of the logistic regression weights obtained in the second-wave analyses are listed in Table 5.10. In the second-wave models, all variables' regression weights were statistically significant.

Relative importance. Standardized regression weights for the variables in the second-wave models are displayed in Table 5.11. The second column in that table lists the standardized weights for the Equal Weights model, which included only ASAP score and education as predictor variables; by design, these two regression weights were equal.

The third column of Table 5.11 contains standardized weights for the model that excluded ASAP scores ("No ASAP"); in that model, education and aptitude (Mathematics Knowledge) made approximately equal contributions, as shown by their standardized weights: .302 and .280, respectively. The age variable made a much smaller contribution (.053).

195

For the model in which ASAP was deliberately minimized--shown in fourth column of Table 5.11--the aptitude (Mathematics Knowledge) variable had the largest standardized regression weight (.496); education made a slightly smaller contribution (.420). Age made about the same contribution it did to the previous model--.051. ASAP scores, even though they entered the equation only after all other variables had been partialed out, still attained a standardized weight of .344.

The fifth column of the table contains the standardized weights for the Corrected DoD 1 model: ASAP made the largest contribution (.465), followed by Mathematics Knowledge (.184), education (.149), and age (.071).

Effectiveness of the CSM Models

The effectiveness of the alternative CSM models for predicting 24-month Service completion was evaluated in two ways: (a) by means of cross-validated correlation coefficients; and (b) by actual count of the relative frequency of service completion.

Cross-validated correlations. For each of the 10 alternative CSM models, the correlation of the model with the criterion was calculated in a cross-validation sample of 1985 accession cases (n=27,068) whose data were not used in the model development analyses. (There was an exception to this, as described earlier: all individuals with the rarest education credentials were included in both the model development and the cross-validation samples.) The results are shown in the column labeled "Accession Sample Correlation" in Table 5.12. These correlations summarize the strength of the linear relationship between service completion and the composite defined by each model.

The strength of those relationships in the applicant population is of greater interest, but unfortunately cannot be observed, because criterion data are not available for anyone but accessions. The population correlation can be inferred, however, by applying an adjustment for range restriction to the observed correlations' values. This was done by applying a multivariate correction for the effects of selection, using the MVCOR program (Sympson & Candell, 1983). These "corrected" correlations are listed in Table 5.12, labeled "Applicant Population Correlation."

196

Table 5.12

Cross-Validated Correlations of CSM Score With 24-Month Completion

	Sample Size	Accession Sample Correlation (Observed)	Applicant Population Correlation (Inferred)
First-Wave CSM Equations			
DoD 1	27,068	.239	.27
DoD 2	27,068	.237	.27
Army	12,134	.247	.28
Navy	5,880	.270	.31
Air Force	6,075	.196	.22
Marine Corps	2,979	.171	.19
Second-Wave CSM Equations			
Corrected DoD 1	27,068	.237	.27
Equal Weights (ASAP and Education)	27,068	.215	.25
ASAP Weight Minimized	27,068	.216	.25
No ASAP	27,068	.174	.22

Among the models developed in the all-DoD sample, the uncorrected correlations were approximately .24 for the three models that included ASAP in their equations and developed optimal weights. Two other models were also based on DoD accessions, but did not develop optimal weights for the predictors-- the "Equal Weights" model and the "ASAP Minimized" model; both of these models had uncorrected correlations of about .22 with the criterion. The last of the models based on DoD accessions excluded the ASAP variable; its uncorrected correlation with the criterion was .17.

The Service-specific models had uncorrected correlations ranging from about .17 to about .27, with the largest correlation observed in the Navy sample, and the smallest observed in the Marine Corps sample.

The corrected correlations showed a similar pattern of relative magnitudes. The DoD sample estimates ranged from .22 to .27; the Service-specific sample estimates ranged from .19 (Marine Corps) to .31 (Navy).

Squared correlations express the proportion of variance accounted for by the various models. For this purpose, we prefer to use the inferred population correlations, since the models are intended to be applied in that population. Proportions of variance accounted for by the Service-specific models ranged from 3.6 percent (for the Marine Corps model) to 9.6 percent (for the Navy model). DoD-wide, the proportion ranged from 4.8 percent (for the model without ASAP) to 7.3 percent (for all three full DoD models).

Relative frequency of Service completion. Each of the 10 models predicts the probability that an individual will complete 24 months of service; the computed probability estimate is the "score" assigned to an individual by means of a compensatory model. In operational use, the Department of Defense and the Services would establish minimum qualifying scores (cut scores) on the CSM probability scale, and would enlist only applicants whose CSM scores exceeded the minimum. The effectiveness of the CSM approach can be evaluated by tallying the number of qualified applicants who fail or succeed, as well as corresponding outcomes for unqualified applicants. Such a tally would take the form of a 2-by-2 table, an example of which is illustrated in Figure 5.1.

CSM Score	Service Outcome	
	Attrition	Completion
Qualified	Erroneous Selection	Correct Selection
Unqualified	Correct Rejection	Erroneous Rejection

Figure 5.1. A schematic for cross-tabulating results of using CSM scores to screen applicants

198

Since we have both CSM scores and completion/attrition data for the 1985 accession sample, we could tally the relative frequencies of correct and erroneous selections and rejections, if the minimum qualifying CSM scores were established. The results would be misleading, however, because absent from our sample are all of those 1985 applicants who, for one reason or another, did not enter the Service; 2-by-2 table analyses based on our accession sample are likely to yield a biased frequency count.

An alternative approach to evaluation is to limit the analysis to those accessions who would have qualifying CSM scores: How many of them completed 24 months of service? To answer this question, a CSM cut score must be established. We computed CSM scores for every case in the 1985 applicant sample, and set four different provisional cut scores. These scores would qualify 50, 60, 70, and 80 percent of the applicants to enlist. Table 5.13 displays, for each of the first-wave and second-wave CSM equations, and for individuals exceeding each of the four cut scores, the percentage of 1985 accessions who completed 24 months of service. Since these cut scores would qualify 50 to 80 percent of the 1985 applicants, Table 5.13 in effect shows 24-month completion rates as a function of CSM cut scores.

The data in Table 5.13 suffer from the same defect as the 2-by-2 tables discussed above: Because they are based only on accession data, not on applicants, they are biased. The completion rates cannot be interpreted as the rates that would occur if a CSM qualifying screen were applied in the applicant population. The data in Table 5.13 are useful, however, for evaluating the validity of the 10 different CSM equations. For a CSM equation to be useful for screening, the expected completion rate should increase as the qualifying standard becomes more stringent. This occurs in every row of Table 5.13: every one of the 10 CSM model equations has validity in this sense.

Table 5.13 can also be used to assess which of the 10 models are more effective. The more the completion rate increases as selection ratios decrease, the "better" the model. This concept can be summarized by the difference between the largest and smallest completion rates in each row; this value is listed in the column labeled "difference" in Table 5.13. Among the six models evaluated in the entire DoD sample, the values of delta ranged from 2.3 percent (for the model without ASAP) to 3.7 percent (for the DoD 1 and DoD 2 models). Among the four Service-specific analyses, the values of delta ranged from 1.7 percent (Marine Corps) to 4.5 percent (Navy).

	Table 5.13				
	Effects of Using the Models for Screening: Percentage of 1985 Accessions Completing 24 Months Service, at Four Cut Scores on Each Alternative CSM Equation				
	Selection Ratio				
Model	80%	70%	60%	50%	delta
Army	82.5	83.8	85.4	86.6	4.1
Navy	80.0	81.7	83.1	84.5	4.5
Air Force	85.2	86.3	87.0	88.1	2.9
Marine Corps	80.1	81.0	81.4	81.8	1.7
DoD 1	82.3	83.6	84.8	86.0	3.7
DoD 2	82.3	83.6	84.8	86.0	3.7
Corrected DoD 1	82.3	83.6	84.9	85.8	3.5
Equal Weights	82.2	83.5	84.7	85.8	3.6
Minimized ASAP	81.9	83.2	84.1	85.0	3.1
No ASAP	81.3	82.0	82.7	83.6	2.3

Applying the Model

After the CSM models had been developed, another matter of interest was the impact they would have on recruiting and accessions in each of the Services. This was assessed in two ways: (a) The distribution of CSM scores in each Service was calculated, and (b) the effects of different CSM cut scores on eligibility for enlistment were evaluated.

Distributions of CSM scores. Once the Compensatory Screening Model equations had been developed, their values were computed for each individual in the 1985 data base; these are the "CSM scores"--estimates of individual probability of service completion. The distributions of CSM scores could then be calculated. Figure 5.2 shows the relative frequency distribution of CSM scores for each of the four Armed Services, based on the DoD 1 equation; these data were computed in the 1985 accession samples.

Figure 5.2 displays four distributions; three are fairly similar, and one is markedly different. The three most similar distributions are those of the Army, Navy, and Marine Corps accessions; the outlier is the Air Force. The Army and Navy distributions are almost indistinguishable from one another; the Marine Corps distribution is somewhat more elevated for CSM scores above 70, but is otherwise similar.

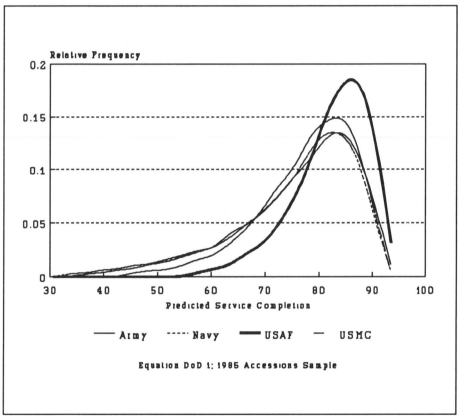

Figure 5.2 Distribution of CSM scores by Service

The Air Force CSM score distribution is strikingly different from the others. It shows a much lower frequency of CSM scores below 75, and a much higher incidence of scores above 80.

Effects of CSM cut scores. If a compensatory screening model were adopted for operational use, a minimum qualifying score would be used for applicant screening. This cut score would either replace current screening criteria or supplement those criteria in some way. Manpower policy officials will be concerned about the effect that any CSM cut score would have on the quantity of eligible individuals. To address this concern, the proportion of eligible individuals was calculated in the 1985 applicant sample. Figure 5.3 illustrates how the proportion of qualified applicants varies as a function of a CSM cut score; the graph is based on the 1985 Army applicant sample.

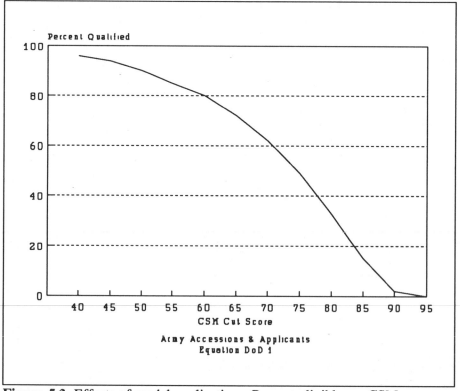

Figure 5.3 Effects of model application: Percent eligible vs. CSM cut score

As expected, the proportion of eligible applicants decreases as the qualifying CSM score increases. Reading from Figure 5.3, it is apparent that over 90 percent of 1985 Army applicants would be eligible at a CSM cut score of 40; the eligible proportion drops to 80 percent at CSM 60, to less than 40 percent at CSM 80 and almost to 0 percent at CSM 90. The data in Figure 5.3 are based on the DoD 1 equation. Although each of the other nine CSM models would yield slightly different results, the trend illustrated by Figure 5.3 is representative: as the minimum qualifying CSM score increases, the proportion of qualified applicants decreases from 100 percent to zero.

Discussion

In this section, we will interpret and qualify the results reported above. The discussion will address three topics: (a) the predictor variables included in the alternative CSM models, (b) Service-specific differences implied in the models, and (c) what difference the use of compensatory models might make in personnel selection.

The Predictor Variables. The effort to develop compensatory screening models to replace categorical screening decisions based largely on high school diploma is a worthy one. If successful, it could benefit the Services and applicants alike by providing a more equitable and more accurate means to identify those individuals with the greatest likelihood of completing their agreed terms of enlistment. The need to develop CSM models through analysis of available data, however, constrained the CSM models to include only legally and socially acceptable predictor variables that were recorded in existing data files.

The list of acceptable variables turned out to be a short one: educational attainment, mental aptitude, age at enlistment, and dependents; additionally, branch of Service was found to make a small but significant difference. The only promising variable in addition to these was the biodata instrument, ASAP. And because ASAP data were available only in a 1985 sample of applicants and accessions, the CSM model developers felt constrained to develop the models from that aging data set. The remainder of this section will discuss each of the six predictor variables, and attempt to interpret the role of each one in the prediction of service completion.

Based on the analyses summarized above, three of the six predictor variables made the largest contributions to predicting service completion: ASAP, education, and aptitude. Of these, ASAP clearly stood out: The correlation of 24-month completion with ASAP alone (.22) was higher than the correlation of the criterion with the best-weighted combination of all four of the other variables (.17). In addition to being the predictor variable that made the largest contribution to the equation, ASAP was the only predictor variable that was statistically significant in every CSM model that included it. Based on the data analyzed here, ASAP appears to be the single most powerful predictor of 24-month completion.

For the analyses reported here, education credential was rescaled from a categorical variable to a graded quantitative variable adjusted for the effects of most other predictor variables. This "education scale" variable made the second largest contribution to the compensatory screening models, in every instance except the Navy and Air Force-specific CSM equations. (Its nonsignificant contribution to the Air Force model may be misleading, however: As a result of Air Force selection practices, fewer than 2 percent of the 1985 Air Force accession sample had education credentials other than traditional high school diplomas or even higher degrees. Thus, there was severe range restriction on the education scale in the Air Force accession sample.) Based on the results obtained here, as well as the historical importance of education as the best predictor of service completion, education clearly has a role in any compensatory screening system.

Cognitive aptitude, as measured by the ASVAB Mathematics Knowledge standard score, made the third greatest contribution overall to the DoD equations, and was significant in every Service-specific CSM equation except that for the Marine Corps. Additionally, the Mathematics Knowledge score had a significant, but modest, zero-order correlation with the criterion (.11). We should note, however, that Mathematics Knowledge may be a proxy here for a broader aptitude measure, the Armed Forces Qualification Test (AFQT) score. Explicit selection on the basis of AFQT scores was influential in deciding who got into the Services in 1985, as it is today. In 1985, however, Mathematics Knowledge was not part of the AFQT composite; hence, its correlation with the criterion was less likely to be affected by range restriction than AFQT. Subsequent to 1985, the AFQT composite was redefined; it now includes the Mathematics Knowledge test score.

204

Age, as measured by the age scale variable, made the fourth largest contribution to the DoD prediction equations. The size of that contribution was considerably smaller than the first three variables, however. Furthermore, age was significant in only one of the four Service-specific equations--the Army. This suggests that its role in the DoD models may have been due to the large proportion of Army accessions in the overall sample; 45 percent of the cases in the model development sample were Army accessions. We are inclined to interpret the Service-specific data to suggest that age has a somewhat different role in attrition/completion in the Army than it does in the Air Force or the Navy. In addition, the similarity of the Army and Marine Corps Service-specific equations (specified in Table 5.8) leads us to conjecture that (a) a single compensatory model might serve equally well for both of those Services, and (b) the fact that age was not a significant variable in the Marine Corps equation may be an artifact of the small size of the Marine Corps model development sample.

The dependents variable was significant in only one of the six first-wave equations--that of the Air Force--and its contribution to that model was relatively small. We are inclined to dismiss the present dependents variable as a useful predictor. At the same time, however, we note that the dichotomous measure used here--Dependents vs. No Dependents--is a compromise substitute for the intended measure, the number of dependents at the time of application for enlistment. As noted earlier, that variable could not be assessed reliably in the available data; the dichotomous variable was used as a proxy.

The last predictor variable to be discussed here is branch of Service. Clearly, branch of Service makes a difference in predicting completion or attrition--witness the consistent differences in attrition rates from one Service to another. (As listed in Table 5.4, the Navy's 1988 attrition rate (.23) was over 150 percent of the Air Force rate of .15.) This will be discussed at greater length below.

Service-specific Differences in the Models. Branch of Service makes a difference in the relationship of the predictor variables to the probability of service completion. These differences could be taken into account in two different ways. The first is to include branch of Service as a predictor variable in a Joint-Service CSM equation, as was done in the case of the DoD 2 model. The other is to develop and use Service-specific compensatory model equations; this was also done in the preceding analyses.

If a Joint-Service equation is to be used, including in the CSM model an adjustment for branch of Service can be expected to improve predictive accuracy somewhat. This would be especially relevant for Air Force and Marine Corps applicants, since those two Service categories received statistically significant regression weights in the DoD 2 model.

Two additional matters will be noted here: (a) The Navy branch of Service regression weight was not statistically significant; this suggests that the estimated probability of completion is the same for Navy as for Army candidates, all other things being equal. (b) The regression weights for the Air Force and Marine Corps categorical variables had negative signs; this means that for each of those Services, the estimated probability of completion is *lower* than for the Army, all other things equal. (This may seem counterintuitive, given that the Air Force experienced a higher completion rate than the Army. The relatively favorable attrition record of the Air Force can be accounted for by the fact that they were somewhat more selective than the Army in terms of education and aptitude test scores. Additionally, a comparison of ASAP scores across Services shows that the 1985 Air Force accessions had considerably higher ASAP scores than the other Services' accessions--despite the fact that ASAP scores were not used for selection. (Figure 5.4 illustrates this graphically.)

The other alternative is to develop separate prediction equations for each Service. This alternative provides the possibility of greater sensitivity to differences among Services than a single equation can accommodate. However, this is achieved at the expense of some predictive accuracy, since fewer data are available for developing Service-specific equations than for a Joint-Service equation.

What Difference Do the Compensatory Models Make? To this point, the evaluation of the compensatory models has been limited to their statistical validity. Of much greater interest is the question of their utility: Is there any reason to believe that the use of compensatory models would improve personnel screening? The fact that all of the alternative models were correlated with service completion suggests that the answer is "yes." However, the magnitude of the correlations was modest: .17 to .24, uncorrected; approximately .22 to .31, corrected for range restriction. These numbers imply that a selection procedure that achieves them will be more effective in controlling attrition than no procedure at all; they do not, however, indicate whether such procedures might improve over present selection practices. To answer that question, we would need to have attrition data on the 1985 applicants who were not enlisted.

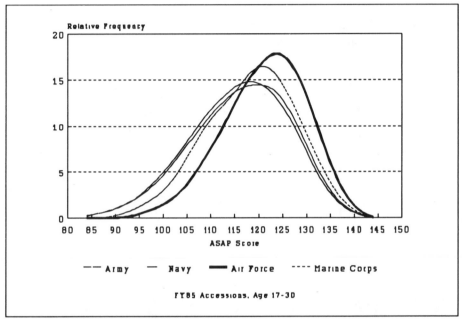

Figure 5.4 ASAP distributions by Service

Because we do not have these data, we will have to resort to statistical techniques to attempt an answer to the question. A statistical method of evaluating the usefulness of a selection procedure, developed by Taylor and Russell (1939), provided tables to allow a user to estimate the average level of employee productivity, if a selection procedure with specified degree of validity were employed. Abrahams, Alf, and Wolfe (1971) modified the Taylor-Russell tables for use with a dichotomous criterion variable--such as the service completion variable we are interested in; the user enters the tables with the test validity and the selection ratio, and reads out the expected proportion of successful employees.

Use of the tables also requires knowledge of the "base rate"--the proportion of successful employees that would occur in the absence of a valid selection procedure. In the present case, this would be the percentage of accessions who would complete service satisfactorily if the Services and DoD had no useful screening procedures for controlling attrition. That percentage is not known; to estimate it, we used the MVCOR program (Sympson & Candell, 1983) to correct the 1985 accession sample rate of successful 24-month completion for the effects of selection. The estimated completion rate in an unselected population was 76.8 percent; we used the nearest base rate in the Abrahams et al. tables, 75 percent, for the analyses that follow.

Table 5.14 illustrates the effect that valid selection procedures can be expected to have on service completion rates. The table displays expected completion rates as a function of two aspects of the situation: the selection ratio (the percentage of applicants selected) and the validity of the selection procedure. The range of selection ratios shown in Table 5.14--50 to 80 percent--was chosen because it is thought to contain the selection ratios typical in military personnel selection. The range of validity coefficients shown in the table includes the validity coefficients observed in this study, and extends below their levels slightly.

Table 5.14 Effects of Using the Models for Screening: Expected Completion Rate as a Function of Validity and Selection Ratio (Assumed Base Rate: 75 Percent Completion)				
Validity	Selection Ratio (Percentage)			
	50	60	70	80
.00	75.0%	75.0%	75.0%	75.0%
.10	78.4%	77.8%	77.2%	76.6%
.15	80.2%	79.3%	78.4%	77.4%
.20	81.9%	80.7%	79.6%	78.3%
.25	83.7%	82.2%	80.8%	79.2%
.30	85.4%	83.7%	82.1%	80.2%

Basis: Taylor-Russell tables, modified for dichotomous criterion (cf. Abrahams, Alf & Wolfe, 1971)

The data in Table 5.14 show that completion rate is unaffected by the selection ratio in the case of a selection procedure with 0 validity. The expected completion rate in that case is the base rate--75 percent--for every selection ratio. The table also shows, however, that completion rates can be expected to increase as (a) the validity of the selection procedure increases, and (b) the selection ratio decreases. The implication is that an organization that wants to improve its personnel attrition situation can do so by either or both of two means: Hire a smaller proportion of applicants, and/or use a selection procedure with higher validity than the current one. The former method can be achieved by either hiring fewer people or attracting a larger number of applicants. In most cases neither of these is practical; one results in personnel shortages, the other may entail unacceptable recruiting costs. If reducing the selection ratio is not an alternative, the organization can introduce a more valid selection procedure, or tolerate personnel attrition.

It should be of interest to read Table 5.14 with the results of the CSM study in mind, comparing completion rates for the current selection procedure with those that would be expected if a compensatory screening model were introduced. To make this comparison, one needs to know the validity of current selection procedures. Although the actual value is not precisely known, the correlations in Table 5.7 suggest it is between .11 and .15--the validities of the aptitude and education scale variables, respectively.

For purposes of discussion, we will assume that (a) DoD-wide, the selection ratio is 60 percent, and (b) current selection procedures have a validity between .10 and .15 in the applicant population. For these assumed values, Table 5.14 shows expected completion rates of 77.8 percent to 79.3 percent; these rates are close to the development sample completion rate of 78.8 percent listed in Table 5.7.

What completion rates should we expect if one of the compensatory screening models is implemented? To answer this question, we will assume (a) the same 60 percent selection ratio, and (b) that the validity of a selection procedure based on a CSM model is between .20 and .30. (The data in Table 5.12 show uncorrected CSM equation validity coefficients of .17 to .24. The range of the corrected DoD values is .19 to .31. The nearest tabled values are .20, .25, and .30.) For a validity of .20, the expected completion rate is 80.7 percent; for .25, it is 82.2 percent; for .30, it is 83.7 percent.

In summary, rate of service completion expected if one of the CSM models is used for selection is approximately 80 to 84 percent. This would be an increase of 1 to 5 percent at the DoD level. The expected increase is larger than this for the Army (2 to 6 percent) and the Navy (3 to 7 percent), the two Services for which the CSM models showed the highest validity. A smaller increase would be expected for the Marine Corps, the Service in which the CSM equation had the lowest validity. Only a small increase would be expected for the Air Force, which already had a completion rate of 82 percent in the 1985 sample.

Conclusions

The purpose of the research reported here was to evaluate the usefulness of compensatory screening procedures as an alternative to screening procedures based solely or largely on an applicant's attainment of a traditional high school diploma or an even higher degree credential. The analyses reported are very encouraging. The compensatory models developed in the course of the research appeared to offer improvements over the current procedures: Not only were they statistically valid alternatives to current procedures, but they also appeared to promise some increases in service completion rates.

All of these models were based on the logistic regression of several predictor variables--including education credential--on satisfactory completion of 24 months' enlisted service. In addition to education credential, the other variables were mental ability (as measured by ASVAB), personal background (measured by ASAP scores), age at enlistment, and dependents at enlistment. Of these predictor variables, all but one are currently recorded during enlistment processing. The one exception is the score on ASAP, a questionnaire that was administered experimentally during part of 1985, but has not been introduced into operational use.

The lion's share of the improvement potential demonstrated in this research was attributable to the contribution made by scores on the ASAP questionnaire. ASAP by itself showed a higher predictive relationship to 24-month completion than any other predictor variable; in fact, ASAP had a higher predictive validity than all the other variables in combination. Use of a compensatory screening procedure that includes ASAP could be expected to improve service completion rates appreciably, if the results here generalize to the present. Use of a compensatory procedure without ASAP would be expected to have less value, but still improve slightly over current screening practices.

Most of the improvement would be expected to occur in the Army and in the Navy; the compensatory procedure had the highest predictive validity for these two Services. It had its lowest validity for the Marine Corps, and consequently the expected improvement there would be small. The expected improvement was also small in the case of the Air Force, but for a different reason: The rate of service completion in the Air Force sample was considerably higher than that of the other Services, and little gain would be expected from the use of a compensatory screening procedure. In other words, the Air Force already appears to have highly effective selection procedures in effect, and the procedures evaluated here would probably make only a small improvement in Air Force personnel attrition.

The generally positive tone of the preceding paragraphs must be tempered with several important qualifications. First, the compensatory model equations developed in this research were based largely on analysis of data from a sample of 1985 accessions. There are two problems attendant on this fact: (a) Changes in applicant characteristics and Service environments since 1985 may have altered the relationships among the variables studied here. (b) Because of the highly selected nature of the members of the sample, the equations based on their data may contain substantial statistical bias (Biennial Report of the Defense Advisory Committee on Military Personnel Testing, 1992).

A second qualification has to do with the role of the ASAP questionnaire in the compensatory screening procedures. There are two problems here as well: (a) The use of the ASAP questionnaire is controversial because of the content of many of the questionnaire items. (b) The susceptibility of the questionnaire to faking, coaching, and other forms of response distortion threatens its validity in continued operational use. That faking can distort ASAP scores seems to be firmly established (e.g., see Chapter 4). The incidence of faking that would occur in operational use of an instrument like the ASAP is unknown.

At this writing, it appears doubtful that a compensatory model containing ASAP scores will be acceptable to all the Services; if a compensatory model is adopted at all, it probably will not include ASAP scores. In that event, the models developed in the research reported here will not be useful, and it will be necessary to develop a new model or models, without ASAP scores.

Model development should almost certainly be based on newer data than the 1985 data that were used in this research. Two reasons apply here, as well: (a) The use of newer data will permit regression parameters for the current set of education credentials to be fitted directly to the data, in contrast to the indirect fitting procedure that was used here (and criticized technically by D. R. Divgi, Manpower Accession Policy Working Group member, Personal Communication, June 1991, and others). (b) The passage of time since the present analyses were conducted means that the service completion criterion has matured in more recent enlisted cohorts, so data obtained in a more current social and military climate can be used to develop the new models.

References

Abrahams, N.A., Alf, E., & Wolfe, J.H. (1971). Taylor-Russell tables for dichotomous criterion variables. *Journal of Applied Psychology, 55,* 449-457.

Aldrich, J.H. & Nelson, F.D. (1984). *Linear probability, logit, and probit models* (Sage University Paper 07-045). Newbury Park, CA: Sage Publications.

Barnes, J.D., Gaskins, R.C., Hansen, L.A., Laurence, J.H., Waters, B.K., Quenette, M.A., & Trent, T. (1989). *The Adaptability Screening Profile (ASP): Background and pilot test results* (Interim Report PRD-89-06). Alexandria, VA: Human Resources Research Organization.

Biennial Report of the Defense Advisory Committee on Military Personnel Testing (1992, November). Washington, DC: Office of the Assistant Secretary of Defense (Force Management and Personnel).

Cohen, J., & Cohen, P. (1975). *Applied multiple regression/correlation analysis for the behavioral sciences.* Hillsdale, NJ: Lawrence Erlbaum and Associates.

Dempsey, J.R., & Fast, J.C. (1976). *Quality and requirements: A step toward reconciliation.* Paper presented at the 38th Annual Conference of the Military Operations Research Society, Fort Eustis, VA.

Dempsey, J. R., Fast, J. C., & Sellman, W. S. (1977, June). *A method to simultaneously reduce involuntary discharges and increase the available manpower pool.* Paper presented at the Office of the Secretary of Defense/Office of Naval Research Conference on First Term Enlisted Attrition, Leesburg, VA: In H. W. Sinaiko (Ed.), *First term enlisted attrition, Volume I: Papers,* Smithsonian Institution.

Dempsey, J.R., Laurence, J.H., Waters, B.K., & McBride, J.R. (1991). *Proposed methodology for the development of a compensatory screening model for attrition* (Final Report FR-PRD-91-17). Alexandria, VA: Human Resources Research Organization.

Dempsey, J. R., Sellman, W. S., & Fast, J. C. (1979, February). *Generalized approach for predicting a dichotomous criterion* (AFHRL-TR-78-84). Brooks Air Force Base, TX: Air Force Human Resources Laboratory.

Department of Defense (1978). *America's Volunteers*. Washington, DC: Office of the Assistant Secretary of Defense (Manpower, Reserve Affairs, and Logistics).

Kmenta, J. (1986). *Elements of Econometrics* (2nd ed.). New York: Macmillan.

Lawley, D.A. (1943). A note on Karl Pearson's selection formulae. *Royal Society of Edinburgh, Proceedings, Section A, 62,* 28-30.

Sands, W.A. (1976). *Development of a revised Odds For Effectiveness (OFE) table for screening male applicants for Navy enlistment* (NPRDC-TN-76-5). San Diego, CA: Navy Personnel Research and Development Center.

Sympson, J.B., & Candell, G. (1983) MVCOR. Unpublished computer program. San Diego, CA: Navy Personnel Research and Development Center.

Taylor, H.C., & Russell, J.T. (1939). The relationship of validity coefficients to the practical effectiveness of tests in selection. *Journal of Applied Psychology, 23,* 565-578.

Trent, T., & Quenette, M.A. (1992, February). *Armed Services Applicant Profile (ASAP): Development and validation of operational forms.* (NPRDC-TR-92-9). San Diego, CA: Navy Personnel Research and Development Center.

Welsh, J.R., Kucinkas, S.K., & Curran, L.T. (1990). *Armed Services Vocational Aptitude Battery (ASVAB): Integrative review of validity studies* (AFHRL-TR-90-22). Brooks Air Force Base, TX: Air Force Human Resources Laboratory.

Chapter 6 _____

Adaptability Screening:
Conclusions and Implications

Jack E. Edwards, James R. McBride, Brian K. Waters
& Janice H. Laurence[1]

In this chapter, we offer conclusions regarding the use of education credentials, biodata instruments, temperament measures, and compensatory screening models for screening military enlistment applicants. Our conclusions are based on the information provided in the five preceding chapters and our knowledge of both those content areas and the military. This approach, we hope, will give the reader a greater appreciation of the practical, technical, and political issues that must be addressed before any implementation of new adaptability screening measures is considered.

This chapter is organized around three major themes. The first theme examines the social and political problems that arise when the organizational needs of the Armed Services must be considered relative to the desires of potential military personnel. In the second section, numerous technical issues are

[1]Edwards is from the Navy Personnel Research and Development Center, San Diego, CA. McBride, Waters, and Laurence are from the Human Resources Research Organization, Alexandria, Virginia. The opinions expressed in this chapter are those of the authors, are not official, and do not necessarily represent those of the Department of Defense or the Armed Services.

215

identified. These issues outline a program of research that would be needed if biodata and temperament measures were to be a part of the military applicant screening process. In the third section, the practical issues of implementing the compensatory screening model are presented. Also, we address how the compensatory screening model might use biodata and temperament measures as an alternative to the traditional educational criterion.

Social and Political Concerns: The Conflict Between Organizational Needs and Applicant Desires

Adaptability screening of military applicants poses a dilemma that pits the organizational needs of the Armed Services against the desires of applicants who have had nontraditional educational experiences. At the root of this dilemma is the use of education credentials as a criterion for minimizing attrition. To date, the most useful selection procedure for controlling attrition has been screening applicants to determine if they have obtained a traditional high school diploma. Applicants who have not completed high school are twice as likely as diploma holders to "attrit." Similarly, applicants with alternative credentials (e.g., a GED or correspondence course diploma) are better prospects to finish their enlistments than are nongraduates, but are still less likely than high school graduates to complete their terms.

The Department of Defense (DoD) and the Armed Services have a legitimate interest in minimizing unplanned attrition. Such attrition is costly because it increases recruiting, training, travel, and other personnel expenditures. Also, early attrition reduces force effectiveness by leaving positions unexpectedly unfilled and diverting resources to process the actions needed to fill the positions. Another perspective on attrition is gained by focussing on the holders of alternatives to the traditional high school diploma. Through political and social pressure, advocates for these individuals have attempted to remove educational barriers to enlistment, arguing that denial of employment to individuals who have worked hard to attain a nontraditional diploma is unfair and discourages self-improvement. They have also noted that 50 percent or more of the enlistees who have alternative diplomas successfully complete their terms of service.

DoD and the Armed Services would like to be socially responsible and responsive to Congressional interests regarding this matter. At the same time, they are loath to institute policy changes that threaten to increase attrition, especially in a context of decreasing military budgets. In a good-faith attempt to resolve this dilemma, the Armed Services have conducted extensive research to develop alternative screening procedures that minimize attrition yet recognize the potential contributions of non-high school diploma applicants. So far, only the Navy has implemented an alternative applicant screening procedure. The Navy has adopted a CSM approach, which is in principle like the Joint-Service models proposed as alternatives to adaptability screening on the basis of education credential tiers. Like one version of the Joint-Service CSM, the Navy's does not include a formal biodata instrument. Unlike other models under development, the Navy's CSM is used to screen alternative credential holders and nongraduates (Tiers 2 and 3) only. Because of this limited scope, the predictors are tailored to these numerically small groups, thus offering the hope of greater validity among such attrition-prone accessions. As of yet, a firm empirical base is not available for studying the effect of the Navy's alternative system.

In general, however, none of the alternative instruments are ready for full implementation. This state of affairs is attributable to factors such as *bona fide* technical concerns about biodata and temperament measures, reluctance to sponsor a full-scale trial administration of a biodata or actuarial prediction system, institutional resistance to change, and fear of adversely affecting recruiting. The next section examines the primary technical concerns that must be addressed and overcome if biodata and temperament measures are to become a component of the applicant enlistment screening process.

Technical Issues

For many years, the only information available for use in preenlistment adaptability screening was application blank data (e.g., age, aptitude test scores, education, marital/dependent status, race, and gender). Some of this information cannot be used ethically for personnel decisions; of the usable information, the applicant's educational attainment has been the only strong indicator of attrition risk. If education had to be replaced as an adaptability screening variable, additional predictor variables would be needed. Two broad classes of variables have been considered: biodata and temperament measures. Biodata measures attempt to evaluate an applicant's background and experience, on the theory that the best predictor of future behavior is past behavior. Temperament measures assess personality traits thought to be related to attrition risk--traits such as reliability, emotional stability, and acceptance of authority.

The literature suggests that biodata are likely to be more useful than temperament measures for personnel selection. As summarized by Laurence and Waters (in Chapter 2), the validity of biodata instruments averages .35 whereas the average for personality measures is .10. Research on the Armed Services Applicant Profile (ASAP; recounted in Chapter 3 by Trent) has shown that a biodata instrument can be as valid as the education credential in predicting attrition. Recent advances in personality measurement research have suggested that temperament measures may be more useful than previously thought. White, Nord, Mael, and Young (in Chapter 4) reported research showing the Assessment of Background and Life Experiences (ABLE), a personality test battery developed for Army use, to be useful for predicting attrition.

The use of biodata and temperament in military settings raises many questions that have been voiced by researchers concerning the use of such non-cognitive self-report measures in civilian workplaces (e.g., see Hough, 1987; Mael, 1991; Mumford & Owens, 1987; Russell, Reynolds, & Campbell, 1992; Sparks, 1989; Steinhaus & Waters, 1991). These questions fall into three categories: faking issues, temporal stability, and validity concerns.

Faking Issues

Biodata, like other self-report assessments (e.g., self appraisal of performance), can be influenced by conscious and unconscious efforts to make a person appear different than he/she really is. As a result, some researchers have devised methods that attempt to detect faking. Foremost among these methods is the creation of fake and lie scales. Another method used in attempts to curb faking has been telling respondents that the information will be verified. For the most part, the success of these attempts is debatable.

Even if it were possible to detect which respondents had probably faked information on a biodata instrument, the user of the biodata information still faces other questions. The most pressing question is how to deal with that suspected faker's information: (a) eliminate the person from further selection and classification decisions, (b) force the person to take the biodata instrument again, or (c) adjust the person's score(s) relative to the lie or fake scale.

Suggested Strategies for Overcoming Conscious Faking. It is somewhat illogical to recommend that an applicant should be eliminated from further selection or classification decisions because his/her score is too high on a lie/fake scale. First, many fake scales are of limited usefulness (i.e., very low validity). Second, some methodologies used to establish lie scales are suspect. That is, no biodata instrument has been constructed with a fake scale that was developed and validated in an operational setting. Third, the problem of determining a cut score for labeling a respondent as a "faker" has not been resolved.

In regards to the second strategy for dealing with "faked" profiles, efforts to require respondents to repeat the biodata instrument may be of little use. Respondents who had high fake scores but told the truth may add measurement error by being over-cautious in reporting their past behaviors. Conversely, there is little reason to believe that respondents who consciously faked their answers will be more truthful during the second administration. Even if respondents are told that their answers will be verified, the test-wise respondent probably could identify those items that are potentially verifiable. In addition, the deliberate "faker" may not modify his/her responses because the different scores would indicate that the individual was untruthful--a characteristic that is not highly valued by organizations.

The third alternative, adjusting the respondent's scale score(s) relative to the individual's score on the fake scale also is not viable. The primary reason is that fake scales are of questionable validity. Another problem with adjusting the scores or eliminating the individual from further consideration is that the practitioner may be decreasing the validity of the biodata instrument. There are conflicting opinions and results regarding the effects of faking on criterion-related validity. Faking has been claimed to increase, decrease or have no effect on validity. Faking studies of the ABLE performed by Hough, Eaton, Dunnette, Kamp, and McCloy (1990) suggest that the problem of faking may be overstated since distortion was shown not to affect validity. This is not to say that faking potential should be ignored; instead, it is a warning that we need a valid system for identifying fakers before we attempt to do something with the scores for those individuals.

One method suggested for constructing a biodata system less susceptible to faking would be to concentrate more on verifiable items. Mael (1991) noted that little work has been done regarding determining the feasibility of verifying biodata responses under operational conditions. Although research evidence suggests that ostensibly verifiable items seem to work without actual verification, this may be risky particularly in an operational military setting. However, the use of actual verification for the military is probably a moot issue for several reasons.

First, negative information about applicants is difficult to obtain. Today, many organizations supply only dates of employment when they are contacted by other organizations seeking reference information. Second, the sheer number of applicants would make verification impossible. Third, the military has decreased its emphasis on pre-enlistment background checks. The military ceased conducting *thorough* criminal records checks *before* enlisting personnel when most local police departments began charging for this service.

Unconscious Faking. Most of the discussion to this point has pertained to conscious efforts to fake in some purposeful or socially desirable manner. Inaccurate information may also be obtained because of memory inaccuracies. Mael (1991) recommended that research examine the role of implicit theories in distorting recall. While this appears to be a potentially interesting area of investigation, the paucity of research makes such evaluation impossible.

Temporal Stability

Temporal stability pertains to whether biodata will be stable across time. This issue is a concern for all selection and classification research. As a matter of good scientific practice, personnel researchers should periodically revalidate operational selection systems. Thus, the importance of monitoring, revising, reweighting, and revalidating operational biodata measures exists with any selection system. The biodata instrument may, however, require more adjustment than systems based strictly on cognitive tests.

Across Respondents. The ongoing drawdown of the military could have effects on the validity of a biodata instrument. As the military gets smaller, the selection ratio will probably also get smaller. If this occurs, higher quality selectees (e.g., more educated and higher scoring on the Armed Services Vocational Aptitude Battery--ASVAB) will be taking the test. A result of this change could be a difference in the validity of the biodata items. For example, an item on a delinquency scale may have had 20 percent of the current selectees indicating some problem with delinquency when it was originally validated. In future administrations to higher quality applicants, the percentage among selectees may decrease to, say, 5 percent. This decreased discrimination index would translate into lower validity for that item.

220

Some critics of biodata research suggest that biodata items will become less valid over time. One hypothesized reason is that items will become compromised. That is, potential test takers will obtain information about the items and item scoring. Even if the items and item scoring are not explicitly known by the respondents, general coaching regarding how to respond in a socially desirable manner could influence biodata scores. Yet more damaging coaching could result from the issuance of test-preparation books that include strategies for specific biodata items.

There is no way to counter the severe negative effect that biodata preparation manuals would have. The picture is, however, less bleak for the other two temporal stability issues. While coaching and compromising the items and item scoring are concerns, they should not disqualify the use of biodata. Although the same criticism could be made for any cognitive test, tests with very limited item domains continue to be useful for selection and classification decisions. If the issue of test and item confidentiality is to be raised, it should be raised for all testing--not just biodata. The use of computerized biodata testing and scoring could remove the scoring algorithm from the hands of the recruiters and others who might have something to gain by allowing an applicant to enlist.

Within Respondents. The prior discussion of temporal stability dealt with the stability of validity across time. Mael (1991) identified another aspect of temporal stability, a person-based aspect. He suggested that the individual differences that cause one person's behavior to change from situation to situation, while another person's behavior is consistent across situations, need to be studied. If an organization attempted to verify some of the biodata information supplied by a high self-monitor (i.e., one who changes behavior depending upon the situation), the information might be judged correct or incorrect (or true or faked) depending upon comparability of the present and past situations. In essence, this issue questions the basis of biodata instruments--the assumption that past behavior is indicative of future behavior.

Validity Concerns

Predictive Validity. Regardless of why it works, biodata has been used successfully in many organizations. For example, Rothstein, Schmidt, Erwin, Owens, and Sparks's (1990) meta-analysis examined validity coefficients that were obtained using biodata from 11,000 first-line supervisors in 79 organizations. When the validity coefficients "were meta-analyzed across organizations, age levels, sex, and levels of education, supervisory experience, and company tenure...validities were generalizable. Validities were also stable across time..." (p. 175).

This ability to account for additional variance in a criterion is noteworthy. In Chapter 3, Trent showed that substantial savings could be gained from the moderate amount of incremental validity that would be supplied if the ASAP were adopted.

Content/Construct Validation versus Traditional Empirical Construction. In his summary of the criticisms of biodata, Fleishman (1988) noted that the traditional empirical keying which has been used to construct biodata scales lacks the content validity/job relatedness required in industrial selection. Others (e.g., Trent in Chapter 3; Hanson, Paullin, & Borman, 1990) have referred to this lack of a conceptual rationale for the biodata scales as an issue of construct validity.

Hanson et al. (1990) listed three advantages in using a construct-validation approach. Those advantages are (a) items will have a higher likelihood of being empirically related to the criterion, (b) increasing the internal consistency through the construction of *a priori* scales should add prediction, and (c) the conceptual framework provides a basis for understanding the biodata-criterion relationship.

These calls for a more conceptual framework for biodata do not, however, mean that work on empirical construction should be stopped. Instead, the issues should be examined within the conceptual framework as outlined by Mumford and Owens (1987). They called for methodological research on item selection and weighting techniques, and comparative studies investigating how these new scaling techniques perform in a variety of criterion settings.

Subgroup Differences. The fact that gender-based differences in biodata validity have occasionally appeared is troubling, especially now that the role of women in the military is expanding. Given that the 1991 Civil Rights Act makes it illegal to set up separate selection systems for subgroups, it is imperative that norms and cut scores be the same across subgroups. On a more positive note, the absence of adverse impact for women and minorities are advantages that suggest further research and application of biodata to military selection. This finding stands in stark contrast to the approximately one standard deviation difference found between blacks and whites on the ASVAB.

222

Other Validity Issues. Until now, the military's investigations of biodata have been limited in terms of criteria. Biodata may also have predictive validity for criteria that are relatively independent of cognitive attributes (e.g., leadership). Some consideration should be given as to what additional criteria might be predicted by biodata. Also, it remains to be seen whether the various Services can use a single biodata instrument. The different organizational missions and problems, types of jobs, and member characteristics may necessitate different scoring keys, if not different instruments.

Though this volume focuses on adaptability *screening* of military applicants there are other ways to combat attrition. Among them is classification which can be considered *selection* into jobs. Because of biodata's properties (e.g., item heterogeneity and factor independence), classification rather than selection for military entry might be a preferable *modus operandum* or at least an option worth pursuing. Attrition varies considerably across jobs. Using biodata among already-accepted applicants to improve the person-job match could reduce attrition while minimizing compromise problems.

Some Technical Conclusions Regarding Biodata and Temperament

Like most social science research, there is no guarantee that future biodata research will result in significant gains. The inability of cognitive measures to account for additional variance, however, speaks to the need to examine alternate assessment strategies. Also, the need to predict non-cognitive criteria (e.g., dysfunctional attrition) suggests that such alternate strategies are needed. Biodata may be one means for filling these voids that currently exist. At minimum, a research program to determine how biodata works in an operational setting is needed, particularly for military personnel selection. The limited attempts to evaluate the usefulness of biodata in a non-operational mode have left many questions unanswered regarding faking, temporal stability, and validity. The Services, understandably, are not ready to adopt biodata alone in lieu of the current, efficient and effective, attrition screens. Yet, abandoning biodata, as an aid to adaptability screening, at this time seems premature based on the findings from the civilian and military literature.

Practical Issues: Screening Based on Compensatory Screening Models (CSMs)

As biodata and temperament measures were being seriously considered for implementation, last-minute concerns over their shortcomings led to a reformulation of adaptability screening alternatives. In Chapter 5, McBride described the development and statistical evaluation of CSMs that would allow the Services to estimate, for each applicant individually, the probability of completing a given term of enlistment. Joint-Service and separate-Service CSMs were developed using existing accession data. All but one of the 10 models included ASAP biodata scores as a component; other statistically useful components included age at enlistment, aptitude test scores, and education credential attainment. Evaluation of the CSMs revealed that all 10 models had significant relationships to enlistment completion. The DoD-wide CSM had an estimated validity coefficient on the order of .30. Use of that model for personnel selection might improve the rate of service completion 2 to 5 percent. The largest improvement would be expected for the Army and Navy--the Services with the highest attrition rates. The lion's share of the validity was attributable to the biodata instrument, the ASAP. The CSM having the weakest association with service completion (a validity of .20) was the one that excluded ASAP, but even that model offered a slight improvement over the *status quo* in terms of attrition rates.

Despite the statistical success of the CSMs, other issues have clouded the picture. One issue is the possibility for response distortion with the biodata component. That is, score inflation in an operational mode could adversely affect the overall usefulness of the CSM.

Another issue is whether to use a single Joint-Service equation or separate equations for each Service. The value of a joint CSM or separate CSMs varies according to the organizational goal being maximized. Separate CSMs might improve accuracy but result in a greater administrative burden. From the perspective of entrance processing, a single model for all Services would be preferable. The estimated probability of completing a term of service would be the same regardless of which Service the applicant was considering. Thus, there would not be a need to recompute the probability of attrition should the applicant also seek entrance into another branch of the military. Conversely, separate Service-specific CSMs may be preferable because there are differences among the Services, both in attrition rates and in the statistical relationship between applicant data and service completion. Therefore, the probability that a given applicant will complete a term of Army service may be several points different from the probability of completing an enlistment in the Navy, Marine Corps, or Air Force.

The third issue is technical. Logistic regression CSMs developed solely by retrospective analysis of accession data may be statistically biased to the extent that the resulting estimates of individual attrition risk are inaccurate and misleading. Each attrition-risk CSM is predicted by an equation containing age, aptitude, ASAP score, marital/dependent status, and education credential. To the extent that one of these equations is in error, the probability estimates for attrition would contain systematic errors (i.e., bias). Subsequent to the development of the equations reviewed in Chapter 5, two sources of potential bias have been noted. One source is the manner in which the data from the 1985 and 1988 data bases were statistically combined. These technical concerns will not be reviewed again (because they are in Chapter 5). The Defer   ittee on Military Personnel Testing (1991) identified the se equations were developed by analysis of were intended for use with a broader popu

Cognizant of these technical concerns t Navy decided to implement this appro Recognizing the uncertainties associated v the Navy put these predictors aside and u (nongraduates and alternative credential As a result, high quality applicants who now given a chance. Though largely ur compromise between the old "sure" sy screening containing biodata and temp also produced a side benefit. The increasing the "market" and granting

Future Adaptability Screenin

Where should the Armed Serv adaptability screening on the basis c and accepted within the military, p selection criterion will probably c affected groups are accommodated

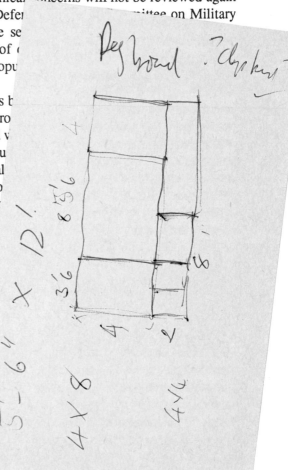

Armed Services should have an alternative in the offing. At this time, neither biodata nor temperament inventories seem ready for this role. Too many risks remain; and despite volumes of studies and many optimistic reviews, many questions are still unanswered. With regard to selection and the control of attrition, the CSM approach has definite merit despite being more cumbersome than simple education credential screens. However, two extremely important questions regarding CSMs remain: First, should biodata (and temperament measures) be a part of the operational CSM? Secondly, should there be a single Joint-Service CSM or a separate CSM for each Armed Service?

At times, technical professionals and policymakers perseverate over the advantages and disadvantages of new procedures. Military selection research cannot take place in a tightly controlled laboratory. Waiting until every technical issue is resolved to the satisfaction of all parties may mean prolonging implementation indefinitely. For even as the research matures, samples become dated and evaluators, coordinators, and proponents go on to new assignments. By the time new players are sufficiently "read in," momentum is too often lost. The standardized collection of self-reported life history and attitudinal information has held the hope, intermittently, of solving the credential dilemma and subduing attrition. Such noncognitive measures have been developed, administered experimentally (and in some cases operationally), analyzed, praised, damned, embraced, and eschewed. In that biodata are a point of contention, it is perhaps more promising for the near term to develop a CSM without such a predictor. Should that CSM perform well, then greater consideration can be given to adding a biodata component. Also, the additional time required for this evaluation can be used to determine answers to many of the questions that still plague biodata and temperament measures.

The Navy has already taken limited steps along these lines. The empirical foundation that results from that effort will be crucial to assessing the future of adaptability screening with CSMs and biodata. Upcoming CSM results should lead to revisions, additional variables, extensions across the Services, and applications to other enlistment groups.

References

Defense Advisory Committee on Military Personnel Testing. (1991). Chairman's letter summary of the May 1991 meeting.

Fleishman, E. A. (1988). Some new frontiers in personnel selection research. *Personnel Psychology, 41,* 679-701.

Hanson, M. A., Paullin, C., & Borman, W. C. (1990, June). *Development and pilot test of a biodata/temperament inventory to predict performance and attrition in the Naval Reserve Officer Training Corps (NROTC) scholarship program* (Institute Report No. 191). Minneapolis, MN: Personnel Decisions Research Institute.

Hough, L. M. (Ed.). (1987, June). *Utility of temperament, biodata, and interest assessment for predicting job performance: A review and integration of the literature* (ARI Research Note RN 88-02). Alexandria, VA: U. S. Army Research Institute for the Behavioral and Social Sciences.

Hough, L. M., Eaton, N. K., Dunnette, M. D., Kamp, J. D., & McCloy, R. A. (1990). Criterion-related validities of personality constructs and the effect of response distortion on those validities. *Journal of Applied Psychology, 75,* 581-595.

Mael, F. A. (1991). A conceptual rationale for the domain and attributes of biodata items. *Personnel Psychology, 44,* 763-792.

Mumford, M. D., & Owens, W. A. (1987). Methodology review: Principles, procedures, and findings in the application of background data measures. *Applied Psychological Measurement, 11,* 1-31.

Rothstein, H. R., Schmidt, F. L., Erwin, F. W., Owens, W. A., & Sparks, C. P. (1990). Biographical data in employment selection: Can validities be made generalizable. *Journal of Applied Psychology, 75,* 175-184.

Russell, T. H., Reynolds, D. H., & Campbell, J. P. (1992). *Building a joint-service classification research roadmap: Individual differences measurement* (Interim Draft Report). Alexandria, VA: Human Resources Research Organization.

Sparks, C. P. (1989, August). *Discussant's comments on symposium: Noncognitive predictors of military effectiveness and attrition using biographical data.* Presented at the 97th annual convention of the American Psychological Association, New Orleans, LA.

Steinhaus, S. D., & Waters, B. K. (1991). Biodata and the application of a psychometric perspective. *Military Psychology, 3*, 1-23.

Glossary

A

ABLE - Assessment of Background and Life Experiences

ABLE T - ABLE total scores based on the unit-weighted combination of achievement, dependability, and emotional stability scales

Accession - Personnel acquisition; person who enters the military force

ACE - American Council on Education

ACH - Alternative Credential Holder

AFQT - Armed Forces Qualification Test

Alphanumeric - A system which uses both alphabetical and numerical characters

Alternative Credential - Non-traditional diploma, certificate, or credential

AMCOS - Army Manpower Cost Model

Article 15 - A non-judiciary punishment in the Military Services

Attrition - Failure to complete obligated period of service

ASG - Adaptability Screening Group

ASP - Adaptability Screening Profile

ASVAB - Armed Services Vocational Aptitude Battery

B

Base Rate - Frequency with which an event occurs in the population

BIB - Biographical Information Blank

Biodata - Biographical Data

Bivariate - Consisting of two variables

C

Chi-square - A statistic that tests for differences between samples based on differences between observations and expectations

CHSPE - California High School Proficiency Exam

Cluster Analysis - The identification of groups of cases that are relatively homogeneous based on specified attributes

Coaching - Guidance that increases the likelihood of a desirable score

Cognition - Mental activities related to thinking, knowing, and judging

Cohort - A group of individuals with a specific relationship in common (e.g., accessions by fiscal year)

Compensatory Model - A statistical model which enables high values in one attribute to compensate for low values in another

Composite - A score created by combining scores from a number of tests or subtests

Confidence Interval - A range or interval of sample data for which there is a specified probability that it will contain the value of the population parameter

Construct - A psychological concept that is used to explain observable behavior and is assumed to vary across individuals (e.g., mathematical ability)

Corrected Score - A mathematical adjustment of an observed score to counter the effect of error due to chance or other factors such as sampling bias

Correlation Coefficient - A statistical index of the relationship between variables that can take on values between -1 and +1

Criterion - An evaluative standard that can be used to measure a person's performance, attitude, motivation, aptitude, etc.

Criterion Group - A group of individuals whose test scores may assist in evaluating the test scores of other individuals or groups

Criterion-Referenced Scale - A scale which uses a specific standard rather than relative comparison

Cross-Validation - Application of optimal weights calculated on one sample to data from another sample to estimate the strength of the predictor-criterion relationship without sampling error

CSM - Compensatory Screening Model

Cumulative Percentage - The percentage of cases in the comparison group that score equal to or lower than the case in question

Cut Score - A specified score below which examinees are not accepted

CV - Concurrent Validation

D

DAC - Defense Advisory Committee on Military Personnel Testing

DEP - Delayed Entry Program

Descriptive Analysis - Procedures using descriptive statistics (e.g., mean, standard deviation)

Dichotomous Variable - A response variable with only two values possible (e.g., present/absent)

Differential Prediction - The presence of significant differences in standard errors of estimate, slopes, or intercepts in subgroup regression lines

Differential Validity - The degree to which one or more predictors show different relationships with a criterion across groups, jobs, etc., or different criteria for a given group, job, etc.

DMDC - Defense Manpower Data Center
DoD - Department of Defense
Dollar metric - Use of dollars as the dependent measure

E

EBIS - Educational and Biographical Information Survey
Education Differential - The use of education criteria in conjunction with aptitude test scores to screen individuals for enlistment into the military
Empiricism - Reliance on observation to answer questions (e.g., data collection)
Empirical-Keying - The scoring of an assessment instrument's items based solely upon their relationship to some external criterion in a reference population
Equating Procedure - The process used to convert the measurement units derived from different tests so that they will be directly equivalent after conversion. Equating enables the comparison of different individuals who have taken different tests or versions of a test

F

Factor Analysis - A statistical procedure to analyze correlational relationships and arrange them into groupings or clusters
Faking - Subjects attempt to score differently than his/her true abilities to affect chances of selection
First-term enlistment - The initial specified period that an enlistee is obligated to serve
Flag Action - A disciplinary action used in the Army
FY - Fiscal year

G

GAO - General Accounting Office
GED - General Educational Development; high school equivalency

H

Hands-On Test - A performance test with a high degree of fidelity to the actual job tasks. The examinee is required to perform a sample of actual job tasks in a standardized setting
HASC - House Committee on Armed Services
HOI - History Opinion Inventory
Horizontal Percent Method - The simplest and most commonly applied scoring technique used in biodata which yields the proportion of high criterion respondents for each item option

HSDG - High school diploma graduate
HSG - High school graduate

I

IAR - Individual Achievement Record
Incremental Validity - The correlation increase provided when an additional predictor is added to the data set
Intercept - The point at which the regression line crosses the ordinate. For a set of standardized variables, the intercept is the origin

J

Johnson-Neyman Significance Boundaries - Ranges of values for the predictor or predictor composite where two regression lines are significantly different from one another

L

Linear Equipercentile Equating - A method of relating scores across testing instruments so that their scores are comparable
Linear Model - A model which evaluates various alternatives based upon weighted values
Linear Regression - A procedure for relating values of a predictor variable to the values of a criterion variable by a function denoting a straight line ($y = a + bx$)
Logistic Regression - A variation of multiple regression applying a logistic functional form to relate a predictor to a bounded criterion variable (e.g., a dichotomous variable)
Longitudinal - Research which follows subjects over time
LV - Longitudinal Validation

M

MAP - Military Applicant Profile; also Military Aptitude Profile
MAP - Manpower Accession Policy Steering Committee
MAPWG - Manpower Accession Policy Working Group
MAST - Military Adaptability Screening Test
MC - Marginal Cost
Mean Standard Error - Estimate of the dispersion of the distribution of the differences between actual and predicted values
MEPRS - Military Entrance Processing Reporting System
MEPS - Military Entrance Processing Station
Metric - Measurement that is associated with interval or ratio scales

232

METS - Mobile Examining Team Site

Moderator Variable - A variable that affects the relationship between other variables in some way

MOSAA - Army Job Specific Aptitude Test

MSE - Mean Square Error

MSG - Marine Security Guards

Multivariate - Dealing with many variables

N

NCO - Non-commissioned officers

Nested Design - A design in which a level of one factor (e.g., a method of instruction) appears only within a particular level of a second factor (e.g., schools), hence confounding the effects of each other factor. Such a design may preclude the calculation of interaction terms for the nested factors

NHSG - Non high school diploma graduate

NPRDC - Navy Personnel Research and Development Center

O

OFE - Odds for Effectiveness

Operational Setting - Administered in real-life setting; applied and not experimental

OPM - Office of Personnel Management

P

P Value - The probability of an event or outcome occurring by chance

Parameter - A numeric value describing a population

Path-Analysis - An analytic procedure rooted in regression that provides estimates of the causal relationships between a set of variables. The total causal effects are broken into direct and indirect effects

Percentage Difference Weighting - A method for weighing biodata scale items based on the difference in endorsement rates for groups scoring high and low on the criterion of interest

Percentage Weights - A method for weighting biodata items where the weight is the percentage of individuals who scored high or low on the criterion of interest, and who endorsed the items. If the members scoring high (low) on the criterion endorsed the item more often, the weight is positive (negative)

Point-Biserial Validity Coefficient - A variation of the linear Pearson product-moment correlation coefficient used in cases where one variable is continuous and one variable is truly dichotomous

Pooled Variance - An estimate of the population variance obtained by taking the weighted (by sample size) average of the variance estimates obtained from several independent samples

Predictive Power - The ability of a test to differentiate between persons at the high end and low end of the criterion

Predictive Validity - The extent to which a test predicts behaviors that it is supposed to predict

Predictor Variable - Any variable whose scores are used to forecast scores on one or more other variables, as in a regression equation

Probit Analysis - A variation of regression applying a normal functional form to relate a predictor to a bounded criterion variable (e.g., dichotomous variable)

Project A - A long-term personnel research project sponsored by the U.S. Army to provide a basis for the selection, classification, and job assignment of Army enlisted personnel

Psychometric - Pertaining to mental measurements and their statistical evaluation

R

R^2 - The squared multiple correlation coefficient estimating the amount of criterion variance accounted for by the predictor

Range Restriction - The reduction in observed variance on a variable due to the selection on one or more other variables

Rational Keying - In contrast to empirical-keying, test items are written to cover constructs relevant to the criterion and items are scored a priori

Raw Score - A numerical value representing a measured dimension

RBC - Recruiting Background Questionnaire

Regression Analysis - A statistical procedure for determining a mathematical expression for the relationship between a variable to be predicted (the criterion) and one or more other variables believed to be related to it (predictors). The expression can be linear or non-linear

Regression Line - A line that best fits the relationship between variables

Relative Frequency - See cumulative percentage

Reliability - The stability of a test; the ability of a test to yield equivalent results for individuals across time or comparable individuals within an administration

Residuals - Individual errors of estimate

Response Set - The tendency to select responses based on previously held biases

S

Scaling Factor - A function that transforms scores on one metric to scores on another metric. The scaling factor may be linear (e.g., an additive and/or multiplicative constant) or non-linear (e.g., exponential)

Scree Plot - A method of factor extraction where values are plotted to determine the number of factors to describe the data

SCREEN - Success Chances for Recruits Entering the Navy

Slope - The steepness of a line; the ratio of how much a line rises on the vertical axis to the amount of increase along the horizontal axis

Social Desirability - Subjects respond so as to portray themselves favorably

Standard Deviation - A measure of variability; the square root of the average squared deviation of scores from the mean

Standard Error - Index of the magnitude of the difference between predicted and observed values; the standard deviation of the error distribution

Standardization - Defining meaningful scores by comparison to representative group

Standardized Weights - Weights that have been stripped of their raw metric by multiplying them by the ratio of the predictor standard deviation to the criterion standard deviation

Statistical Bias -   A condition in which the generalizability of findings are limited

T

Test-Retest - A method whereby a test is administered more than once to the same sample to determine test reliability

TRADOC - U.S. Army Training and Doctrine Command

U

Unit Weighting - In the case of biographical data, a method of reweighting items with values of 0 or 1 according to their relative predictive or discriminating power

Univariate - Consisting of one variable

USMEPCOM - U.S. Military Entrance Processing Command

V

Validity - The ability of a test to measure what it purports to measure (e.g., SAT and success in college.) The basis for prediction of expected performance

Validity Scale - Items embedded within a test to detect the influence of a response set upon the subject's answers

Variance - A measure of the dispersion of scores

Varimax Rotation - A method used in factor analysis that reduces the number of variables with high loadings on a factor to increase factor interpretability

Vertical Percent Method - A scoring technique used with biodata whereby the percentage of respondents choosing each response option are calculated within the high and low criterion groups and the references between these percentages serve as the weights

W

WAB - Weighted Application Blank